POSTWAR BRITISH FICTION

POSTWAR
BRITISH FICTION

New

Accents

AND

Attitudes   BY James Gindin

GREENWOOD PRESS, PUBLISHERS
WESTPORT, CONNECTICUT

Library of Congress Cataloging in Publication Data

Gindin, James Jack, 1926-
   Postwar British fiction.

   Reprint of the ed. published by the University of
California Press, Berkeley.
   1. English fiction--20th century--History and
criticism. 2. English drama--20th century--History and
criticism. I. Title.
[PR881.G5 1976]   823'.9'1409   76-6558
ISBN 0-8371-8800-8

Originally published in 1963 by University of California Press,
Berkeley

Reprinted with the permission of University of California Press

Reprinted in 1976 by Greenwood Press,
a division of Williamhouse-Regency Inc.

Library of Congress Catalog Card Number 76-6558

ISBN 0-8371-8800-8

Printed in the United States of America

To Joan

Acknowledgments

I SHOULD LIKE TO THANK THE UNIVERSITY OF TEXAS *Studies in Literature and Language* for permission to reprint the chapter called "Alan Sillitoe's Jungle" and a substantial part of "Images of Illusion in the Work of Iris Murdoch," which appeared first as articles in that periodical. I should also like to thank *Modern Fiction Studies* for permission to reprint a very slightly altered version of " 'Gimmick' and Metaphor in the Novels of William Golding."

I should like to thank the following publishers and authors for permission to use quotations:

Alfred A. Knopf, Inc., for permission to quote from Alan Sillitoe's *Saturday Night and Sunday Morning,* Copyright © 1958 by Alan Sillitoe.

Mr. Alan Sillitoe for permission to quote from *The General,* Copyright © 1960 by Alan Sillitoe, and *The Loneliness of the Long-Distance Runner,* Copyright © 1959 by Alan Sillitoe.

Victor Gollancz, Ltd., for permission to quote from the novels of Kingsley Amis: *Lucky Jim, That Uncertain Feeling, I Like It Here,* and *Take a Girl Like You.*

Penguin Books, Ltd., for permission to quote from Doris

Lessing's *Each His Own Wilderness* and Bernard Kops's *The Hamlet of Stepney Green.*

Simon and Schuster, Inc., for permission covering U.S. rights to quote from *In Pursuit of the English,* Copyright © 1960 by Doris Lessing, and *My Friend Judas,* Copyright © 1959 by Andrew Sinclair.

MacGibbon and Kee, Ltd., for permission covering British rights to quote from *In Pursuit of the English* by Doris Lessing.

Faber and Faber, Ltd., for permission covering British rights to quote from *My Friend Judas* by Andrew Sinclair; *After the Rain* and *The Centre of the Green* by John Bowen; *Lord of the Flies, Pincher Martin,* and *Free Fall* by William Golding; and *Look Back in Anger* by John Osborne. Acknowledgments are also due Faber and Faber, Ltd., for permission covering all rights to quote from *Storyboard* by John Bowen and *The Inheritors* by William Golding.

Ivan Obolensky, Inc., for permission covering American rights to quote from *The Centre of the Green,* Copyright © 1959 by John Bowen.

W. W. Norton & Company, Inc., for permission to quote from *Billy Liar* by Keith Waterhouse.

Martin Secker & Warburg, Ltd., for permission covering British rights to quote from *Hurry On Down* and *Living in the Present* by John Wain, and from *Hemlock and After, Anglo-Saxon Attitudes, The Middle Age of Mrs. Eliot,* and *The Old Men at the Zoo* by Angus Wilson.

The Viking Press, Inc., American publishers, for permission to use quotations from the following novels by Iris Murdoch: *The Flight from the Enchanter,* Copyright 1956 by Iris Murdoch; *Under the Net,* Copyright 1954 by Iris Murdoch; *The Bell,* Copyright 1958 by Iris Murdoch; *A Severed Head,* Copyright 1961 by Iris Murdoch.

Chatto and Windus, Ltd., for permission covering British rights to quote from *The Flight from the Enchanter, Under the Net, The Bell,* and *A Severed Head* by Iris Murdoch.

I should also like to thank the following: Doubleday, Inc.,

American publishers of the novels of Kingsley Amis; Oxford
University Press, publishers of *The Writer's Dilemma*; Signet
Books, Inc., American publishers of Anthony Glyn's *I Can Take
It All*; W. H. Allen, Ltd., British publishers of Alan Sillitoe's
novels; Alfred A. Knopf, Inc., American publishers of *The
General* and *The Loneliness of the Long-Distance Runner* by
Alan Sillitoe, and of *Born in Captivity* by John Wain; Jonathan
Cape, Ltd., publishers of Arnold Wesker's *I'm Talking about
Jerusalem*; Criterion Books, Inc., American publishers of John
Osborne's *Look Back in Anger* and *The Entertainer*; Michael
Joseph, Ltd., British publishers of *Retreat to Innocence, Old
Chief's Country, The Grass Is Singing, A Proper Marriage,
Martha Quest*, and *Going Home* by Doris Lessing; Penguin
Books, Ltd., publishers of *Five* by Doris Lessing; Longmans,
Green & Co., Ltd., publishers of David Storey's *This Sporting
Life*; Chatto & Windus, Ltd., publishers of *The Truth Will Not
Help Us* by John Bowen and *The Uses of Literacy* by Richard
Hoggart; Macmillan, Ltd., London, British publishers of *The
Contenders, A Travelling Woman*, and *Nuncle* by John Wain;
The Viking Press, Inc., American publishers of *Hemlock and
After, Anglo-Saxon Attitudes, The Middle Age of Mrs. Eliot*,
and *The Old Men at the Zoo* by Angus Wilson; Faber & Faber,
Ltd., publishers of *The Breaking of Bumbo* by Andrew Sinclair,
A High-pitched Buzz by Roger Longrigg, and *Justine, Balthazar,
Mountolive*, and *Clea* by Lawrence Durrell; Harcourt, Brace,
Inc., American publishers of *Lord of the Flies* by William
Golding; Charles Scribner's Sons, Inc., American publishers of
Homecomings by C. P. Snow; Victor Gollancz, Ltd., publishers
of *Ritual in the Dark* by Colin Wilson; The American Heritage
Publishing Co. publishers of *Horizon* magazine; and the pub-
lishers of *The New Yorker* magazine.

I am indebted to the staff of the University of California
Press, particularly to Geoffrey Ashton and Mrs. Grace Stimson.
For comments and suggestions, some of which they may not have
realized they were making, I wish to thank Hazard Adams,
Marvin Felheim, and Geoffrey Hill. My debt to Donald Hall is

much greater. He carefully read the entire manuscript and made a large number of pertinent, detailed, and sympathetic comments. Finally, I wish to acknowledge my enormous gratitude to my wife, Joan Gindin. Not only did she encourage me consistently and type most of the manuscript, but she constantly offered lucid and intelligent argument in order to help me discover what I wanted to say.

J. G.

Ann Arbor, Michigan
March 4, 1962

Contents

1

THE FIRST STEPS 1

2

ALAN SILLITOE'S JUNGLE 14

3

KINGSLEY AMIS' FUNNY NOVELS 34

4

ANGER AS AFFIRMATION 51

5

DORIS LESSING'S INTENSE COMMITMENT 65

6

EDUCATION AND THE CONTEMPORARY CLASS
STRUCTURE 87

7
CREEPING AMERICANISM 109

8
THE MORAL CENTER OF JOHN WAIN'S FICTION .. 128

9
ANGUS WILSON'S QUALIFIED NATIONALISM 145

10
COMEDY AND UNDERSTATEMENT 165

11
IMAGES OF ILLUSION IN THE WORK OF IRIS
MURDOCH 178

12
"GIMMICK" AND METAPHOR IN THE NOVELS OF
WILLIAM GOLDING 196

13
SOME CURRENT FADS 207

14
IDENTITY AND THE EXISTENTIAL 226

NOTES ON THE AUTHORS 239

1

The First Steps

IN 1946 PHILIP LARKIN, THE POET, PUBLISHED A NOVEL called *Jill*. In the novel a young man from the Lancashire working class, John Kemp, comes down to Oxford on the train. He is so apprehensive about the etiquette of eating in railway carriages that he rushes into the lavatory and bolts the door in order to eat the sandwiches his mother has carefully prepared for him. At Oxford, John is self-conscious, ill at ease, far too deferential toward his roommate (Christopher Warner, a suave, elegant, and callous young man from London). John often feels like the stableboy invited, as a consciously democratic gesture, to tea at the manor house. The sons of the working class may come to Oxford (as Whitbread does in the novel) to study hard, isolate themselves in their rooms with books and bad coffee, prepare themselves assiduously for careers in Workers' Education. But John wants more: the wit, the glamour, and the ease of Oxford life. In the novel, set in 1940, John finds the distance between his Lancashire background and the Oxford he wants impossible to bridge. Because he is rejected by Christopher Warner's set (they regard him as gauche and "stuffed") and, in turn, rejects Whitbread's Oxford of careful accumulation,

John can only retreat into an impossible fantasy that both intensifies his loneliness and dissipates the force of the novel.

Since the end of World War II, the issues have been much less clear. Although John Kemp is still self-conscious and class distinctions still exist, he is no longer quite so deferential toward his well-bred superiors, and the distance between Lancashire and Oxford is not quite so vast or so easily demonstrable. John Kemp is no longer a curiosity. He is both more complex and more central to British society. And, in the past ten years or so, as evident in the work of Kingsley Amis, John Wain, John Osborne, Iris Murdoch, and numerous others, he has become a principal character in British fiction and drama.

This kind of hero, the intelligent and irreverent young man from the lower or lower middle classes, educated by scholarship but let loose in a society still permeated by class distinction and respect for breeding, has been fixed by many journals and reviews as a contemporary phenomenon. Arguments, based on superficial labels like "angry young men," concerned with whether or not Jim Dixon's preference for beer will ultimately ruin Britain, neglect the issues of the novel in which Jim Dixon appears, but these arguments, by their very existence, do show that the novels bear some relevance to contemporary society. The heroes in novels by Amis, Wain, Keith Waterhouse, and others both reflect the postwar British society and demonstrate a good deal of similarity with one another. These heroes are all better educated than their fathers were, although they frequently retain an emotional allegiance to their fathers' habits and attitudes; they are all concerned with getting jobs and women in a competitive society; they care about how one behaves in pubs and at cocktail parties; they all berate the aristocracy's emotional vacuity, although they often, in varying degrees, envy the aristocracy's smooth composure; they all worry about how they can operate in a world in which they exert only very limited control. In other words, these are all novels of conduct and of class placed in contemporary, usually urban, society.

The novel of conduct and class is certainly not new in the

English tradition. Richardson and Fielding dealt extensively with class distinctions and struggles in eighteenth-century society and, a century later, Dickens, Trollope, and then Hardy frequently used the theme of the young man from the lower or lower middle classes attempting to enter a more urbane and cosmopolitan society. Class lines, throughout the eighteenth and nineteenth centuries, were not prescribed with absolute, immutable rigidity, although the problems and the stresses holding back the young man of energy were invariably greater than the opportunities before him. In the twentieth century, however, and particularly since the end of World War II, the young man finds moving from one class to another superficially easier. He may earn a grant to study at the university, and the marks of accent and appearance are less completely distinctive in contemporary Britain. Hardy's Jude the Obscure was, no matter what his ambition, indelibly categorized as a stonemason with a rustic background. Keith Waterhouse's Billy Liar, in contrast, is both less marked and less explained as a young man who, the son of a haulage contractor in a grimy Yorkshire town, half-heartedly works in a funeral office. But if, for Hardy's hero, the background from which he wished to escape was firmer and stronger, so also was his aspiration strong and definite. Christminster, no matter how impossible for Jude, was a fixed and unvarying aspiration, representing the truth, beauty, and dignity of scholarship. Billy Liar's aspirations are far more vague; he is, in ways, wiser than Jude, but he has less sense of where he wants to go. In the nineteenth-century novel of class, the alternatives were more apt to be fixed. Not that the hero had an easy time choosing between the alternatives, for easy choice would signify simplification in any century, but both the background and the aspiration or aim were apt to be thought of as more firm and definite entities, no matter how irreconcilable with each other. The contemporary novel of class, however, depicts a society of somewhat greater mobility in which the hero is apt to be a good deal less sure of from what or to what he is moving. The basic problem of the novel of class and conduct, the issue

of how the hero can come or not come to terms with himself
and his flexible world, is the same as it was during the eighteenth
and nineteenth centuries. But the terms themselves are vastly
different, and, in a society in which change seems to accelerate
geometrically, the tone also seems significantly different from
that apparent in earlier fiction.

Early in the twentieth century writers realized that values
and alternatives in society were becoming far less fixed and
secure. In part because of rapidly changing values of conduct
and class, novels frequently tended to center on personal and
metaphysical issues, to use social issues only as temporary decoration for the structure of permanent metaphysical and personal
concerns. Arnold Bennett, for example, despite all his precise
and acute social observation, was more interested in demonstrating a general theory about time than in dealing profoundly with
conduct and class. And when novels of this period did deal with
class, novels such as E. M. Forster's *Howards End* or Virginia
Woolf's *To The Lighthouse,* they tended to view class issues
from the perspective of the vanishing intellectual aristocracy.
Certainly the portraits of Leonard Bast and Charles Tansley are
given from a regretful and condescending point of view. Yet
neither novel can be judged by its portrait of the aspiring young
man from the lower classes, for Forster's novel depends on personal relationships among the equally cultivated and Mrs. Woolf's
is both a personal and a metaphysical vision. The novel of conduct and class (except, to some extent, in the work of D. H.
Lawrence) gave way to other, less traditional means of dealing
with the quickly altering values of the twentieth century. Since
the end of World War II, however, many young writers have
been attempting to return to a traditional nineteenth-century
theme, the theme of how a man works his way through society,
with a characteristic twentieth-century lack of assurance about
what the man or the society is really like.

In outlining a society full of class changes, judgments, and
distinctions, these contemporary writers often exhibit and express
sympathy for the lower classes, for those not granted the auto-

matic privilege of an inherited position within the Establishment. The search for a lower-class perspective is often deliberate; Doris Lessing, at the beginning of her documentary called *In Pursuit of the English,* states that when she arrived in England, having been brought up in Southern Rhodesia, she spent her time "in pursuit of the working-class" as material for her fiction. She did not find the rugged, sensitive, innately honest and perceptive proletariat she sought. John Kemp or Amis' Jim Dixon is also not the genuine representative of the working classes, for this is the son of the lower or lower middle class who is granted a university education. The education itself tangles the lines of class identification, and the novels of Amis, Wain, and Larkin do not, for all their concern with house painters and Welsh miners' sons, delineate any clear working-class attitude as such. John Kemp and Jim Dixon may suffer in the genteel university, may feel keenly their cultural dislocation, but their problems and their aims are put in terms quite different from those of Alan Sillitoe's capstan lathe operator in a Nottingham bicycle factory. Alan Sillitoe best demonstrates working-class attitudes, for John Braine's workers (in both *Room at the Top* and *The Vodi*) are so caught in endless repetitions of maudlin self-pity, so blurred by a lack of distance between author and hero, that they are left little room to express or observe any issues outside themselves. Sillitoe, in a recent collection of essays published as *The Writer's Dilemma* (ed. Stephen Spender, 1961), a collection culled from a *TLS* symposium originally called "Limits of Control," has directly stated the need for a working-class perspective in fiction:

> These working-class people who are not afraid to take a hard-cover book in their hands suffer from certain disadvantages compared to the middle-class reader. The latter, no matter what values he lives by, can take out a book and see in it either a mirror of himself, or someone he knows: he is fully represented in contemporary writing, while the man who works at the lathe is not. Working men and women who read do not have the privilege of seeing themselves honestly and realistically portrayed in novels. They are

familiar with wish-fulfilment images flashed at them in cliché
form on television or in the press, and the novels they read in
which they do figure are written by those novelists of the Right
who are quite prepared to pass on the old values and who, unable
to have any feeling for the individual, delineate only stock characters.   [P. 74.]

Sillitoe is, in this respect, not typical of most contemporary
British writers. While others, such as Wain and Amis, would
probably agree in castigating the "novelists of the Right" and
certainly demonstrate sympathy with the working classes, they
do not plead for a particular class perspective. Rather, they
recognize the influence of a class structure without acknowledging its worth. However strongly political and social leaders may
urge one to feel pride in whatever badges of social and economic
imposition he automatically wears (and, after all, the leaders
have little to lose because they wear the brightest badges), the representative hero, in much contemporary British fiction, resents the
public badge, the articulation of the system. He feels no class
unity, no public identification, and therefore works hard for the
direct and the tangible: the job that pays more or the more
attractive and exciting woman.

Most of these writers do not simply present social attitudes
as thinly disguised sociological reports. Usually, the social attitudes are filtered through individual emotions and reactions,
although some writers, like Doris Lessing, fill their novels with
long sections of sociological journalism. Similarly, these writers,
though seldom committed to a particular political cause or
doctrine, often show the influence of politics upon their characters. In *Under the Net* Iris Murdoch uses Lefty, a political
agitator, as one of the nets, the series of traps that capture un-
wary human beings; Angus Wilson describes the impact of
political engagement on scholars, writers, and television com-
mentators in both *Hemlock and After* and *Anglo-Saxon Attitudes;* William Golding traces his hero's temporary adherence
to communism in *Free Fall.* In their vital and consistent concern
with social and political problems, all these writers furnish

statements, both implicit and explicit, that the world is wider than the vicar's coming for tea or the hang-over of psychic guilt that characterized too many inferior British novels of past decades. Indeed, the vitality and the enlarged area of concern have been responsible for a good deal of the praise and the attention these contemporary novelists have received in the past decade.

For ten or fifteen years before these writers began to publish in the middle 'fifties, British writing seemed anemic and concerned with well-executed trivia. James Joyce and Virginia Woolf had been pioneers in creating a new kind of novel, developing complex and intricate devices to portray fully the patterns and the nuances of their worlds. In more recent years many of their followers, like Elizabeth Bowen, were refining, distilling, trying to get the gossip around the tea table more exactly and significantly shaded, or, like William Sansom, attenuating the complexities of the love affair almost to the point of irrelevance. And the genre lost energy. Similarly, the satirical novel was no longer the powerful weapon that Huxley and Waugh used to castigate their contemporaries, to depict the follies of a world grown increasingly callous and meaningless. Far more gently, people like Angela Thirkell delicately satirized a little world they wished to preserve, the world of teacups and the village parson. Satire became, in some instances, a defense to protect the narrow, shallow society, like that of Nancy Mitford, in which class and breeding really matter, after all. The social novel, without even an Arnold Bennett, became either a curious transfer of pre–World War I issues into contemporary terms (as in the work of L. P. Hartley) or the sober document outlining the problems our civilization faces (as in the work of C. P. Snow). Valid as these aims and attitudes were, they did not provide outstanding fiction.

The situation on the stage was even more moribund. The British theater was confined to magnificent revivals of great classics, insipid little comedies centering on Nanny's advice, and the sort of soap opera Terence Rattigan wrote for his Aunt

Edna who attended matinees in the second row of the dress circle. The popular novel was, at its best, a kind of well-constructed and well-decorated thriller, like the scientific and psychological thrillers of Nigel Balchin or the religious thrillers of Graham Greene. At the other end of the scale, the careful products of sensitive writers like the Sitwells, Henry Green, and Ivy Compton-Burnett seemed remote from the concerns of post–World War II Britain, a distance represented by the fact that *Horizon* folded in 1949.

The contemporary British writers are not concerned simply with depicting a wide segment of current British society. A number of them also occupy themselves with moral issues that are not specifically social or political, for John Wain, John Bowen, and Angus Wilson are all, in vastly different ways, firmly committed to moral points of view. Yet these writers do not compose a new branch of Moral Rearmament. They share no group moral position, as they share no specific political doctrine. And, in addition, they hold their various moralities with vastly different degrees of intensity. Doris Lessing's attack on the shallowness of the British colonial set in Africa is far more morally committed than, and has a very different pitch from, Kingsley Amis' attack on gentility at the provincial university.

Amis' pitch, however, is more generally characteristic of contemporary writers than is Doris Lessing's, for many of these novelists use a good deal of comedy. Amis, Wain, Iris Murdoch, William Golding, John Bowen, and Angus Wilson are frequently very funny, developing a concept of comedy that ranges from simple verbal jokes, farce, and comic images to complete projections of entirely bizarre and incongruous worlds. Each one views his material in an essentially comic perspective, aware of man's various and discordant experience, cognizant that a single view of man leads to pretentious oversimplification. This comic perspective, this multiple awareness, represents a world in which man faces many facts, many experiences, without any clear guide or formula around which to organize his experience.

Clearly the old guides and formulas have vanished. Two world wars, the threat of the hydrogen bomb, and disillusion with the Marxist version of world brotherhood have left these writers skeptical about the value of banners and causes. At the same time, they have seen enough during the days of the dole, the abdication, and the new Elizabethan coronation to doubt the ultimate value of Britain's clerical "pomp and circumstance." The target of many of their novels, the material for the comedy, is the public cause or the reverential generalization about an institution: Marxism, Welsh nationalism, the sanctity of the British Museum, the lay religious community that resembles the Boy Scouts.

This comic perspective would seem to lead to a relativism of both definition and value, and relativism is nothing new; the failure of old systems and definitions is no longer astounding. Relativism has become so deeply ingrained in twentieth-century culture that it permeates even the popular novel sold at the railway bookstall or the airline terminal. In one such novel, a conventionally heroic and banal love story called *I Can Take It All*, by Anthony Glyn, a novel distinguished only by some excellent descriptive accounts of contemporary Finland and the logging industry, the hero expresses this relativism of definition as one of his few profound perceptions:

> Everything is funny and serious both at once. If you get one without the other, then there's something wrong and you ought to start asking why. You oughtn't to go round saying, "Is this the funny bit or is this the serious bit?" It's like those masks you sometimes see outside theaters, you know, one grinning inanely and the other scowling and pulling his mouth down. Comedy and tragedy. There was a time when everything had to be one or the other. Either you ended up happily married to the king's daughter if it was a comedy or you died in the last scene. Nowadays it hasn't got to be either or. It's neither or both. And it's not so extreme either. You can marry the king's daughter if you like, but you probably won't be very happy and it won't last for long. And

you won't really be killed, you'll recover with penicillin. And both will be rather funny and rather serious at the same time. It's got to be both, that's the modern world.

[Signet edition, 1961, pp. 98–99.]

Glyn's hero may oversimplify the past, for tragicomedy is an old form, but his attitude toward the present is typical. The heroine, a mystic and a healthy Finn, feels that the hero is being cynical. He replies, "No, not cynical. If anything, humane." Glyn carries the point no further, but many of the more distinguished contemporary writers feel that some kind of commitment, some kind of choice, is possible even in the midst of a world of relative definitions and relative values. These writers, never having known that world of secure myth before 1914, have always lived without faith in any overriding public truth. They have always accepted uncertainty because they have never known anything else. Raw and sudden disillusion may shock a writer into complete relativism; never having had illusions, through two generations of uncertainty, may lead the writer to search for what he can, with modification and qualification, assert. Most contemporary writers go beyond the development of a comic multiplicity, assert a limited commitment, a kind of value, very carefully, sometimes hesitantly. The specific commitment varies a good deal. John Wain, in *The Contenders*, attacks the competitive instinct apparent in both the artistic and the business worlds, and advocates, in the character of his lumbering, awkward, yet understanding hero, a kind of pre–Industrial Revolution simplicity, William Golding's unique and striking metaphors both assert and qualify a commitment to orthodox Christianity. Iris Murdoch, through a vast structure of natural, philosophical, and contemporary images, insists on the value of the unstructured, spontaneous, creature side of man. Commitment may involve both engagement in contemporary life and assertion, in a limited sense, of a particular point of view toward that life.

Most of these writers, in an attempt to depict their engagement directly, have avoided the kind of technical innovation favored by an earlier generation of twentieth-century writers. It is not that these writers dismiss James Joyce; it is simply that they do not (and perhaps could not) compete. Their interest in man's exterior relationships leads to a less associative, internal style, to a style closer to the straightforward narrative of most of nineteenth-century fiction. They often deliberately try to reëstablish older and more conventional prose techniques. John Wain, for example, in *Hurry On Down*, his first novel, attempts to revive the picaresque, a tradition appropriate for his rootless hero leaving the university to survey the contemporary world. Kingsley Amis uses a good deal of farce in his first two novels, deliberately making his humor obvious and his incongruities ridiculous as a slap against a society in which humor is too delicate and genteel. And Angus Wilson, in *Anglo-Saxon Attitudes*, uses the large framework of the Victorian novel, the huge saga that portrays a society by cutting across numerous class and occupational lines. Like most new writers, these contemporary Britons are not entirely new. In addition to their formal conservatism and their attempts to revive older novelistic traditions, their insistence on man's limitations, their comic perspective, and their partial or hesitant commitment are all reminiscent of characteristics we tend to apply to eighteenth-century writers. They appreciate and echo the scale, if not always the assurance, of Pope, and two of them, Amis and Wain, have spoken of their debt to the comic placement of rootless man in the fictional world of Henry Fielding.

But in other ways these writers are uniquely part of the middle of the twentieth century. Although Anthony Glyn's hero may falsify the certainty of past definitions and values, man is, today, even less sure of what he is and where he is headed than he apparently was fifty or a hundred years ago. Almost all the contemporary novels are searches for identity, efforts on the part of the hero to understand and to define who or what he is. The hero accepts the fact *that* he is, but wonders what kind and degree of adjectival postulate he can build upon his existence.

These searches for identity vary from the comic roles and poses that Amis' heroes fabricate to the bewildering switches in personality and function in the bizarre world of Nigel Dennis' *Cards of Identity* to the character's constantly unsuccessful effort to define himself in the fiction of Iris Murdoch. The problem of identity indicates an existential attitude, a skepticism about ever knowing the essential nature of any person or thing. Man is a creature too limited, too unsure, to gain certainty of the essential nature of any of his various experiences, particularly when experience is received only through individual consciousness. At the same time, man must live and make choices, must act on partial knowledge without the assurance of abstract sanction, must come to some terms with his own existence and the existences around him. The limitations placed on man's knowledge and power, the puzzling search for identity and definition, and the necessity, in spite of all this, for some kind of human action or engagement, all contribute to the existential attitude common to most contemporary British writers. Each element of the existential attitude may surely be found in a prior time or place, but the combination of all of them and the degree to which the attitude permeates are unique, in British literature, to the middle of the twentieth century.

The existential attitude also has a public corollary in the constant iconoclasm directed against the established religious, political, and commercial order so evident in the work of Amis, Wain, Alan Sillitoe, and many others. Iconoclasm, to be sure, has a long intellectual history and is not simply the province of "angry young men," but an existential attitude gives this kind of iconoclasm particular support. The reigning society represents, for many of these contemporary writers, a pretentious and fallacious essence. In order to perpetuate itself, the reigning society strives to appear as if it were based on some hallowed principle of right or value, to refuse to acknowledge that it, like any other society, is really a partial choice of men with partial knowledge. The reigning society comes to believe that its values are essential. Therefore the writer with both awareness and an existential attitude tries to puncture the society's bloated self-estimation, to portray, with or without anger, the folly of human beings acting as if they were knowledgeable cosmic forces. Yet the destruction of the reigning society cannot be carried too far, cannot itself become a principle. Again, the existential man chooses, and some societies are better, less pretentious, less restrictive, than others.

This existential attitude, satirizing essences or fallacious abstractions, has provided fresh images for contemporary British fiction; it has also, in its refusal to outline essential truth, accurately represented the attitudes of many of the most sensitive and aware members of the generation who began to write after World War II. Certainly, contemporary writers have provided more forceful, more far-reaching, more relevant art than did many of those of the generation immediately preceding. But immediacy, energy, and temporal accuracy are not, in themselves, enough to justify these works. To praise the works on such grounds alone is to subscribe to the Peripatetic heresy, the fallacy that the greatest activity, the most vital energy, makes the best novel. Rather, the writers must be read and judged individually on artistic grounds. Each one considers himself an individual artist, not an interesting contemporary specimen, and the novels and plays need careful consideration as works of art.

2

Alan Sillitoe's Jungle

THE FIRST IMPRESSION ON ENTERING ALAN SILLITOE'S
fictional world is that the working class has "never had it so
good." Partly the result of a genuine change in the economic
structure of the country, partly a strongly felt pride and defiance,
the attitude of "I'm All Right, Jack" permeates a good deal of
Sillitoe's fiction. Alan Sillitoe has thus far published two novels,
Saturday Night and Sunday Morning (1958) and *The General*
(1960), and one volume of short stories, *The Loneliness of the
Long-Distance Runner* (1959). The satisfaction of a steady job
with a few pounds left over at the end of the week is evident in
Sillitoe's first novel, *Saturday Night and Sunday Morning*, in
which the young hero, Arthur Seaton, represents the working-
man quite content to spend his fourteen pounds a week (earned
on a capstan lathe at the local bicycle factory—he could earn
more, as he is paid by piece rate, but he doesn't see the point of
that) on clothes, women, and Saturday night binges at the local
pub. Yet Arthur is not so smug as all that. He recognizes that
even such limited satisfaction was impossible for the working-
man twenty or thirty years ago, and he is able to sympathize
with his father:

The old man was happy at last, anyway, and he deserved to be happy, after all the years before the war on the dole, five kids, and the big miserying that went with no money and no way of getting any. And now he had a sit-down job at the factory, all the Woodbines he could smoke, money for a pint if he wanted one, though he didn't as a rule drink, a holiday somewhere, a jaunt on the firm's trip to Blackpool, and a television-set to look into at home. The difference between before the war and after the war didn't bear thinking about. War was a marvellous thing in some ways, when you thought about how happy it had made so many people in England. [P. 22.]

The standards are entirely material; the only end is hedonistic.

But, among Sillitoe's characters, memories of empty bellies and inability to pay the rent are still sharp. Even in the postwar world poverty still exists, for not all members of the working class are so lucky as young Arthur Seaton. The young narrator of *The Loneliness of the Long-Distance Runner* (in Borstal for robbing a bakery) has seen his father die of cancer while the family lived on next to nothing. The father's death brought the temporary prosperity of five hundred pounds in insurance and benefits:

. . . so as soon as she got the money, mam took me and my five brothers and sisters out to town and got us dolled-up in new clothes. Then she ordered a twenty-one inch telly, a new carpet because the old one was covered with blood from dad's dying and wouldn't wash out, and took a taxi home with bags of grub and a new fur coat. . . . Night after night we sat in front of the telly with a ham sandwich in one hand, a bar of chocolate in the other, and a bottle of lemonade between our boots, while mam was with some fancy-man upstairs on the new bed she'd ordered, and I'd never known a family as happy as ours was in that couple of months when we'd got all the money we needed. [Pp. 20–21.]

Happiness, in large part, is dependent on money, money that supplies food, drink, sex, and the diversion of television in the working-class world.

Despite the more or less general prosperity of the working

class in the postwar world, Sillitoe does not romanticize the factory worker's life. The factory, steady pay packets and benefits notwithstanding, is still different from the plush board room or the book-lined study. Arthur, in *Saturday Night and Sunday Morning*, has been working in the bicycle factory since he was fifteen, save for two years in the army. Tough and realistic, he muses:

> . . . the factory smell of oil-suds, machinery, and shaved steel that surrounded you with an air in which pimples grew and prospered on your face and shoulders, that would have turned you into one big pimple if you did not spend half an hour over the scullery sink every night getting rid of the biggest bastards. What a life, he thought. Hard work and good wages, and a smell all day that turns your guts.   [P. 25.]

Arthur is often sick from the smell; at the age of twenty-two he suffers stomach trouble from constantly inhaling oil fumes. In addition, the factory system has perpetuated the struggle between workers and management. The workers in the bicycle factory are paid by the piece, but, should they work at full speed, management would lower the amount paid per piece. The workers, with nothing to gain by increased effort, fear that management will discover their elaborate stalling devices. Management, on the other hand, is vigilant, always ready to pounce on the worker slow enough or unlucky enough to be caught. Sillitoe's characters are constantly aware of the conflict of interest between workers and management, the cold struggle that keeps class antagonisms alive and allegiances firm. Each side may be dependent on the other, but it is a dependence that the past and the system allow them, only barely and grudgingly, to acknowledge. The worker's new paradise is only relative and comparative. As Arthur states, even when he has found a kind of value at the end of the novel:

> Born drunk and married blind, misbegotten into a strange and crazy world, dragged-up through the dole and into the war with a gas-mask on your clock, and the sirens rattling into you every

night while you rot with scabies in an air-raid shelter. Slung into khaki at eighteen, and when they let you out, you sweat again in a factory, grabbing for an extra pint, doing women at the weekend and getting to know whose husbands are on the night-shift, working with rotten guts and an aching spine, and nothing for it but money to drag you back there every Monday morning. [P. 239.]

The statement "I'm All Right, Jack" is not, in Sillitoe's world, the smug caption it sounds. The statement is partly comparative, a realization that the workingman is more "all right" than he was in the days of the dole. It is also partly his pose, his inherited and acquired defiance thrown up as a wall against a class with interests and values other than his own.

Sillitoe's working-class men still defy authority, still feel themselves the enemies of policemen, prelates, and the pillars of society. They care no more for religious or political authority than they do for the economic authority of the factory's management. Often, older characters recall past attitudes that linger. In *Saturday Night and Sunday Morning*, one of them says:

> I was on the dole eighteen months ago, same as yo', Harold. We all had a struggle to keep alive, and now they want to call us up. My mother had eleven to drag up, with Doddoe only at work now and again. Then one night I broke into the back door of a shop because we'd got nowt t'eat. When I got back that night—I shall never forget it, Harold—we had the best meal we'd ever had in our lives. I was fifteen at the time, and I broke into a shop every week for a couple of months, but one night the bastards got me. And do you know what I got for it? I know you do, Uncle Harold, but I'm just tellin' yer. Three years in Borstal. And then when I came out the war'd started and I got called up. Do yer think I'm going ter fight for them bastards, do yer? [P. 139.]

The speaker deserted from the British army during the war. Even young Arthur, far too young to fight, recalls that "Churchill spoke after the nine o'clock news and told you what you were fighting for, as if it mattered."

The defiance of authority, the attitudes of resentment, persist in the postwar world. The young narrator in *The Loneliness of the Long-Distance Runner* never mentions members of the governing classes, at whose instigation he has taken up cross-country running, without several pejorative adjectives such as "pig-faced" and "snotty-nosed." He divides all people into two classes, "In-law" and "Out-law," accepting the fact that, even though he is in Borstal for a first offense, his identification with the latter class is permanent. In Sillitoe's second novel, *The General*, the struggle between a wartime general and the orchestra he has inadvertently captured from the other side similarly carries overtones of the class struggle: the orchestra leader resents the general, regards him as an aristocratic agent anxious to devour the very "soul" of the plebeian orchestra.

Resentment of the governing classes is strong enough, in Sillitoe's world, to unify, at odd moments in particular situations, the workers and the put-upon. Arthur Seaton, having drunkenly fallen down a flight of stairs in a pub, can appreciate enough of the plight of the waiter sent to throw him out that the two strike up a relationship and begin to smoke together. Arthur recognizes the waiter's grim job and the waiter sympathizes with Arthur's gesture of defiance in getting drunk. But the relationship is quickly shattered when the publican, with "the slight cast of authority and teetotalness in his right eye," enters and enforces the separation between waiter and customer. The young cross-country runner, who bitterly hates all wardens and authorities, can trust his story to the boy who lives in his terrace. "He's my pal," the runner states at the very end of the story in the only statement that does not reinforce the runner's bitter resentment against everyone. In another story, "The Fishing-Boat Picture," an old postman holds no resentment against the wife who left him long ago but still returned to visit him, borrow money she could never repay, and pawn the picture he gave her as a sentimental gesture. She consistently took advantage of him, but when she is killed by a lorry the postman suddenly realizes that her little shoddy deceptions didn't matter. Both of them had to face the same poverty, the same class war, the same constant struggles against an unfriendly world, and he wishes he could have helped her more. The orchestra leader in *The General,* at first concerned only with his individual dignity, realizes, when the orchestra is captured and faces death, that the extinction of his orchestra, his group, his class, is a larger issue than is his own fate. The pressure of circumstances, the fact that man must constantly struggle in a hostile world, the power of established forces all push Sillitoe's characters into a kind of unity, of fellow feeling directed against the large and the powerful.

Yet this unity, this fellow feeling, springs from necessity rather than from belief. No Sillitoe characters talk of brotherhood or united action; they simply recognize that others are caught in the same way they are. In *Saturday Night and Sunday Morning,* tax collectors and Labour leaders are treated as the equivalent of big-business magnates or Tory politicians. Sillitoe's characters support no party or organization. At one point, when talking of what he would do if he won a football pool, Arthur says:

> I'd keep it all mysen, except for seeing my family right. I'd buy 'em a house and set 'em up for life, but anybody else could whistle for it. I've 'eard that blokes as win football pools get thousands o' beggin' letters, but yer know what I'd do if I got 'em? I'll tell yer what I'd do: I'd mek a bonfire on 'em. Because I don't believe in share and share alike, Jack. Tek them blokes as spout on boxes outside the factory sometimes. I like to hear 'em talk about Russia, about farms and power-stations they've got, because it's interestin', but when they say that when they get in government everybody's got to share and share alike, then that's another thing. I ain't a communist, I tell you. I like 'em though, because they're different from these big fat Tory bastards in parliament. And them Labour bleeders too. They rob our wage packets every week with insurance and income tax and try to tell us it's all for our own good. I know what I'd like to do with the government. I'd like ter go round every factory in England with books and books of little numbers and raffle off the 'Ouses o' Parliament. "Sixpence

> a time, lads," I'd say. "A nice big 'ouse for the winner"—and then
> when I'd made a big packet I'd settle down somewhere with fif-
> teen women and fifteen cars, that I would.
>
> But did I tell yer, Jack, I voted communist at the last election?
> I did it because I thought the poor bloke wouldn't get any votes.
> I allus like to 'elp the losin' side.   [P. 32.]

Not only political organizations are treated with derision,
for Sillitoe's characters level jeers and catcalls at any social
organization or anything smacking of noble purpose or ideal.
The runner mocks the pretense of his warden's attempts to help
him and to see that he becomes a useful member of society. Political organization is also satirized in the structure of *The General*,
for two vast sides are struggling over Europe, each with no
apparent end other than its own monolithic power. The sides
are referred to as "East" and "West," although efforts to trans-
late the mythical directions into current political terms are
futile, for Sillitoe deliberately throws clues in different directions.
The novel makes no distinctions in larger political and social
units. Abstractions, causes of any sort, seem out of place in this
world where power battles power. The leader of the orchestra,
humane and aware, leaps to his feet in anger when the general
asks him if he does not believe any freedom will be left in the
world. The orchestra leader cries out:

> Freedom! Why do you keep on using such a false and stupid
> word? Freedom, freedom, freedom! Listen to it. Doesn't it have
> a meaningless sound? It's been twisted, hammered, burned, and
> dragged inside-out. It's caused so much suffering in the world in
> these many disguises for tyranny that the sooner people forget
> that it ever existed the better.   [P. 68.]

The vast word, the generalization, deludes man and engages him
in something miserable and destructive. Only the direct and the
tangible—the good meal, the television set, the woman—offer
what they promise.

If Sillitoe's characters can be classified as supporters of any
kind of government, they are anarchists. Every now and then

Arthur, in *Saturday Night and Sunday Morning*, experiences fleeting desires to blow up Parliament or the War Ministry or the Palace. At one point, when walking along the street, he hears a window smash on the pavement. "Arthur was stirred by the sound of breaking glass: it synthesised all the anarchism within him, was the most perfect and suitable noise to accompany the end of the world and himself" (pp. 113–114). He follows the sound, and finds a woman in khaki holding the feeble culprit until the police arrive. He urges the culprit to break away and escape, but the culprit is afraid. Arthur has nothing but scorn for the police who would lock up this feeble little man just after his single expression of daring and defiance. The police, in fact, frequently are villains in Sillitoe's fiction. In "Uncle Ernest," the police prevent a lonely old man from innocently feeding and buying presents for two poor little girls. In "On Saturday Afternoon," the police try to prevent a man, out of work and deserted by his wife, from killing himself. When the man finally succeeds, the narrator comments: "In one way I was sorry he'd done it, but in another I was glad, because he'd proved to the coppers and everybody whether it was his life or not all right" (*Loneliness of the Long-Distance Runner*, p. 126). The police invariably stifle and restrict the working-man, bind him in laws that are cruel and irrelevant. The members of the orchestra in *The General* are anarchists, too, for they respect no government, least of all the one that inadvertently sent them to be captured.

To pose against the authority of policemen or governments, Sillitoe's characters generally have a strong sense of their own worth. The long-distance runner, although trained in Borstal to win the cross-country race, deliberately loses because he will not join the system that trained and ordered and jailed him. Although losing means six more months of carting dustbins and scrubbing floors instead of kindness from the governor, honor, and easy jobs, the runner feels too proud, too much a part of his own defiance, not to lose his race. He suffers for his pride, but not heavily or dramatically, for the world can do little to him that it has not done already. Similarly, Arthur Seaton feels that he's as good as any other man. His working-class environment and his own memories may have bred defiance, but they have not bred humility.

Sometimes Sillitoe's characters respect people other than themselves; sometimes they value the kind, the humane, the sympathetic. Arthur, for example, holds in great esteem his Aunt Ada, a large woman who feeds a dozen children and assorted guests. He is willing to confide in Ada, and he intends high praise when he says: "At fifty she still had the personality of a promiscuous barmaid, a kindness to listen to any man's tale and sob like a twin-soul into his beer, even to bring him home to bed if she thought it would make him feel better" (*Saturday Night and Sunday Morning*, p. 77). Arthur can even sympathize with others. His mistress (the wife of Jack, a worker at the same bicycle factory) becomes pregnant, and Arthur watches her try to lose the baby by taking a scalding bath while drinking a pint of gin. For a moment he understands her pain and her pride; he can really feel how much agony he's caused another person. Sillitoe is careful, however, not to dwell on the sentimental side of the revelation. After his moment of understanding and after the mistress has collapsed into a miserable insensibility, Arthur goes out to a pub, meets his mistress' sister, and ends the evening happily in another illicit bed. Sillitoe's characters can understand and sympathize, can react honestly and directly, yet they are never capable, except for brief moments, of heroic or even disinterested action. Born into a hard world, given little, pursued by the forces of an oppressive society, these characters take what they can and seldom revel in their emotions. Heroism is either folly or a game (as in *The Loneliness of the Long-Distance Runner*) calculated to delude the police and other governmental innocents who believe in such nonsense.

In addition, only some of Sillitoe's characters, like Ada, Arthur, or the long-distance runner, evince this honesty, this insight, this occasional burst of sympathy for others. Most of the characters in pubs and hovels and offices are cloddish and brutal. The malicious gossip at the end of the row and the brutal swaddies who beat Arthur up are part of the world of *Saturday Night and Sunday Morning*. The short stories are full of petty, brutal men who bully their wives, of domineering mothers who pretend to be superior to all other women of the same class, of feeble and frustrated men with the courage to attack only ten-year-old girls. In *The General*, Sillitoe frequently refers to the illiterate masses on both sides of the struggle. A gang of brutish soldiers nearly massacres the orchestra when it first arrives in enemy territory, and the general himself constantly speaks of his men as useless, stupid animals who live only in order to kill. Even Armgardson, one of the members of the orchestra (the men of art and insight), becomes so full of frustrated and barbaric energy that he strangles the cat that wanders about the barn in which the orchestra is imprisoned. Many men, in Sillitoe's world, are both vicious and stupid. Anxious to get whatever they can for themselves, they cheat, lie, steal, kill, seldom aware that the powers that curdle their energy into violence have also oppressed their victims. Sillitoe's world is a jungle. Governed by unjust and inhumane restrictions, confronted with the essential cruelty and stupidity of human nature, it resembles the jungle where creature fights creature without order or principle.

Frequently the novelist uses the image of the jungle directly. Toward the end of *Saturday Night and Sunday Morning*, after Arthur has suffered a severe beating for his sexual adventures with married women, he realizes what the world is like:

> He did not ask whether he was in such a knocked-out state because he had lost the rights of love over two women, or because the two swaddies represented the raw edge of fang-and-claw on which all laws were based, law and order against which he had been fighting all his life in such a thoughtless and unorganized way that he could not but lose. Such questions came later. The plain fact was that the two swaddies had got him at last—as he had known they would—and had bested him on the common battleground of the jungle. [P. 194.]

Despite welfare measures and more or less steady jobs, the workingman's life is still not safe or secure:

No place existed in all the world that could be called safe, and he knew for the first time in his life that there had never been any such thing as safety, and never would be, the difference being that now he knew it as a fact, whereas before it was a natural unconscious state. If you lived in a cave in the middle of a dark wood you weren't safe, not by a long way, he thought, and you had to sleep always with one eye open and a pile of sharp stones by your side, within easy reach of your fist.   [P. 197.]

Throughout *The General*, all the characters refer to man as a "primeval monster," living in a furious and barbaric slime that no rational means can order or make safe. Man himself has too much frustrated force, too much energy, to submit himself to any form of sane control. As Starnberg, the sage of the orchestra, reflects:

I used to think it would be a good world if all this energy spent in war was used for peaceful things, . . . but the energy necessary to make a happy and prosperous peace is too small. The only reason there'll always be wars is that man has too much energy, not that he has too little intelligence.   [Pp. 33–34.]

The general himself also talks of man's nature, man's excessive energy, as part of the reason man is unable to live in peace. Although the general's estimate of man's intelligence is different from Starnberg's estimate, the general expresses a somewhat similar view of what man is like:

Allow me to tell you that I've spent many years deciding what war is. It's the art of decimation. It is also nature's way of filling the empty sack-bag of men's ideals; it puts a machine-gun into their hands when a theory has been pushed to the limits of their intelligence.   [P. 64.]

Energetic, forceful, and irrational, Sillitoe's characters are surrounded by other energetic and forceful creatures. They can only pit their skill and power against the skill and power of others, as Arthur, without conscience, uses his charm and energy to win other men's wives and the long-distance runner pits his "cunning" in a direct struggle against the "cunning" of his governors and society.

Not all the jungles of Sillitoe's world are simple statements of man's nature. Some jungles are social or institutional, the codified and established representations of man's nature. The bicycle factory where Arthur works, an institution that regularizes man's struggle against his fellows, and pits foreman against manager, worker against foreman, workers against one another, is such a representation. The organized society becomes, in Sillitoe's world, the framework in which man's predatory instincts operate. Sillitoe calls his longest published poem "The Rats," and "rats" refers to all the agents of organized political, religious, and governmental society who prey upon and try to devour the individual. Twice (once in *Saturday Night and Sunday Morning* and again in a short story called "Noah's Ark"), Sillitoe uses a fairground amusement park as an image for the institutionalized jungle. The gaudy lights, the large wheels, the 'fast rides, the shoots, the fright, all form a structure that represents man's passion and furious energy. But, like the factory or the government, the amusement park structure, derived from man's nature, does not adequately satisfy the individual man's energetic aims. The fierce and predatory individual is invariably smacked down by his institutionalized image. Thus Arthur has to run from the amusement park to escape the swaddies, let loose by the whirling rides and lights. And young Colin, in "Noah's Ark," is maliciously pitched off the merry-go-round on which, excited by the sights and the sounds, he tried to ride free. Man's energy is constantly blocked by its own massive, corporate exaggeration, by the jungle.

Yet Sillitoe does not always use the jungle as the indication of evil. In contrast to the simple formulation, the rational or scientific means of controlling the human, the jungle (the very apotheosis of the human) is valuable. In one story, "The Decline and Fall of Frankie Buller," a narrator recalls his childhood gang, led by a feeble-minded young man of twenty. Years later the narrator returns and finds the feeble-minded man,

Frankie, running his own small wood business with a pony and a cart. Frankie has spent a year in a mental hospital, but, to the narrator, he does not seem changed:

> I realized that Frankie's world was after all untouchable, that the conscientious-scientific-methodical probers could no doubt reach it, could drive it into hiding, could kill the physical body that housed it, but had no power in the long run really to harm such minds. There is a part of the jungle that the scalpel can never reach.
>
> [*The Loneliness of the Long-Distance Runner*, pp. 174–175.]

The scalpel, man's rational and scientific instrument, cannot penetrate into all the darkness, the vigor, the complexity of the human jungle of feeling and desire. In Sillitoe's world part of man's nature remains beyond the reach of science, and if this part, this jungle, is often barbaric and destructive, it is also human and vital.

Sillitoe's jungle world is ultimately governed by pure chance. Events occur, far beyond the control or comprehension of individuals, which alter life through the whole world. In *Saturday Night and Sunday Morning*, Sillitoe frequently returns to the theme of World War II, the vast event that killed many in a cause they little understood, brought others out of the poverty and starvation they had come to accept as normal. Time, in the novel, is often a large wheel, a huge turning force that can crush or elevate man, but is not amenable to human principles or concerns. The wheel of the week blazes brightly on Saturday night, then slows to the weak stomach and cigarette aftertaste of Monday morning, while larger wheels, unchartable and unpredictable, raise man to the pleasures of good wages and women and drink, then lower him into the misery of war, bad health, and angry husbands. Arthur is aware that, given his time and place, he has been on the crest of the wheel most of his adult life. But he has no faith that he'll stay there. Even at the beginning of the novel, before any event has gone against him, he thinks:

No more short-time like before the war, or getting the sack if you stood ten minutes in the lavatory reading your *Football Post* —if the gaffer got on to you now you could always tell him where to put the job and go somewhere else. And no more running out at dinnertime for a penny bag of chips to eat with your bread. Now, and about time too, you got fair wages if you worked your backbone to a string of conkers on piece-work, and there was a big canteen where you could get a hot dinner for two-bob. With the wages you got you could save up for a motor-bike or even an old car, or you could go on a ten-day binge and get rid of all you'd saved. Because it was no use saving your money year after year. A mug's game, since the value of it got less and less and in any case you never knew when the Yanks were going to do something daft like dropping the H-bomb on Moscow. And if they did then you could say ta-ta to everybody, burn your football coupons and betting-slips, and ring-up Billy Graham. If you believe in God, which I don't, he said to himself.   [P. 23.]

The possibility of the H-bomb creates a good deal of the uncertainty in the background of Sillitoe's characters, yet they do not tremble when they speak of it or join committees to advocate a sane nuclear policy. On the contrary, Arthur rather enjoys telling his farmer uncle about the possible effects of radiation. The H-bomb is less an appalling horror than further evidence of life's essential uncertainty, another vast and unpredictable possibility that must be lived with.

Still, wages are good and no H-bomb has fallen yet. Thus Arthur is lucky and he recognizes it. In fact, he attributes his good job, his success with women, and his fine clothes to his good luck. In the midst of his affair with Jack's wife, he frequently thinks that Jack is just unlucky. Some men, Arthur feels, have a force of character that prevents their wives from being unfaithful. That Jack lacks this force of character is, to Arthur, just bad luck, just the way Jack happens to be. Similarly, Arthur does not give himself credit when he feels that no wife would be unfaithful to him; he's certain that he's just lucky with women. The "slow husband" (like Jack) and the henpecked one (like Mr. Bull, the husband of the gossip at the end of Arthur's street) might do more, Arthur thinks, to control their wives. Yet they are not the sort of people who exercise control and they have little responsibility for the sort of people they are. Arthur, like Sillitoe, neither pities them nor castigates them; people either are lucky or they're not. Similarly, in *The General,* Sillitoe makes it clear that man has little control over what happens to him. The imprisoned members of the orchestra recognize that they have no control over whether or not they will be permitted to live. They may hope or not hope, reason or not reason, as their own characters indicate, but their hopes or reasons have nothing to do with what occurs. As the leader of the orchestra says: "Hope has nothing to do with reason, because the impossible can always happen. If and when it does it nearly always turns out to be something nobody had thought of" (p. 114). Even the general, supposedly in control yet defeated and disgraced at the end of the novel, does not feel responsible for his own disaster. From an exterior point of view, he allowed his feeling for the captured orchestra, for music, to overrule his military judgment and obedience. Yet he was unable to cut off his attraction to music, unable to stop the appeal of art:

> But, he told himself, we've no power to alter the circumstances that are unknowingly shaping our lives. We can only wait, in our happy oblivion, or hopeful suffering, for the results of these unknown movements to affect us.   [P. 187.]

Man, the creature of the jungle, is determined by forces stronger than he.

Although the jungle is constant and man's nature is determined, Sillitoe's characters search for ways out of the jungle. In *Saturday Night and Sunday Morning,* Arthur recognizes what the factory world is like and that he cannot really exist outside that world. At the same time he longs for "peace," longs for an escape from the revolving Ferris wheel of his job and his relationships. When he gets the chance he goes fishing, out away from the factory and the pub and the town. Midway through the novel, Arthur says: "The only peace you got was when you

were away from it all, sitting on the osier-lined banks of a canal
waiting for fish to bite, or lying in bed with a woman you loved"
(p. 140). Although his excursions into bed sometimes become
more complicated, and reflect the jungle itself, his fishing remains a means of finding temporary peace and comfort. And,
late in the novel, Arthur meets Doreen, the simple girl who
understands, the girl he finally decides to marry. Doreen, like
fishing, is a refuge, and at the end of the novel Arthur finally
takes her fishing with him. Doreen and the fish cannot blot out
the factory jungle, but Arthur can recognize his "peace" and
keep it with him. In other words, the sentimental pastoral quality
of the end of the novel is only partial; Arthur still needs to face
his job and himself. And Doreen is not just a fish. She is also
a woman, a creature who forces issues and who makes demands
on Arthur.

At one point Sillitoe projects the pastoral vision into the past,
shifts the perspective so that the jungle becomes not a permanent
part of man's nature but an outgrowth of the Industrial Revolution:

> Arthur was happy in the country. He remembered his grand-
> father who had been a blacksmith, and had a house and forge at
> Wollaton village. Fred had often taken him there, and its memory
> was a fixed picture in Arthur's mind. The building—you had
> drawn your own water from a well, dug your own potatoes out
> of the garden, taken eggs from the chicken run to fry with bacon
> off your own side of pig hanging salted from a hook in the pantry
> —had long ago been destroyed to make room for advancing armies
> of new pink houses, flowing over the fields like red ink on green
> blotting-paper.   [Pp. 223–224.]

Yet Sillitoe does not allow Arthur to indulge in such revery for
very long. If the jungle is specifically a twentieth-century
phenomenon, Arthur is a twentieth-century man, part of the
jungle and fully aware of the issues it forces man to face.

The fish, for Arthur, is a symbol of peace and contentment
in more ways than one. Sometimes, when he cannot get off to
the country, Arthur likes to spend the evening carving a fish

for his float, shaping it carefully as a means of capturing some of the pleasure of fishing. He paints these carvings in intricate designs and gaudy colors, duplicating the passion and the energy associated with the amusement park in his image of contentment —and, for the moment, the world he lives in seems to vanish. Then, too, he recognizes his own identity in the fish:

> Mostly you were like a fish: you swam about with freedom, thinking how good it was to be left alone, doing anything you wanted to do and caring about no one, when suddenly: SPLUTCH!— the big hook clapped itself into your mouth and you were caught.
> [P. 236.]

The fish, too, is part of the jungle, that part of man which craves peace and contentment, yet is caught by the world as a whole. Arthur comes to recognize that the same jungle holds both fish and predatory, clawing creatures, that both kinds of vitality exist within man. On the last fishing excursion of the novel he is able to feel his identity with the fish strongly enough to throw his catch back into the stream. The fish, the representation of escape from the jungle, is really part of the jungle after all. Man has no genuine alternatives, only limited and temporary choices, and Arthur can, at least once, choose to throw a fish back into the stream.

Man's possible ways out of the jungle in *The General* are more abstract. (Although this novel avoids any sentimental or pastoral note, it loses some of the immediate power of *Saturday Night and Sunday Morning*.) In *The General*, man's possibilities revolve around a conflict between maps and music as two abstractions capable of lifting him from the primeval slime of his own nature. Early in the novel Starnberg, the most articulate member of the orchestra, talks of his boyhood desire to be a surveyor. Maps fascinated him, but he finally decided to study music instead. The principal conflict between maps and music, the more precise and the more humane abstraction, takes place, however, within the general, the central figure in the novel. At the beginning he is preoccupied with maps:

He closed the door, and the presence of surrounding maps filled him with a sense of poetic veneration. Walking from one wall to another he was shrewdly entranced by the beauty of their design, calculatingly fascinated by the black curving railways and the differing geometrical shapes of plain and forest land. Nothing could mar the beauty of topographical maps, he said to himself; they were faultless representations of the earth's surface, with all the numerous marks of man's and nature's accomplishments set plainly upon them.   [P. 49.]

At this point the general is victorious, at the summit of his wheel. His maps represent his intellectual achievement, his means of applying his reason and his power to experience in order to bring it under his conrtol. So far, like his maps, he has been faultless. But when his troops capture the orchestra, the general decides to talk to the orchestra leader rather than, in obedience to orders, kill all the captives immediately. The orchestra leader does not understand maps, and the general begins to realize the possibility of other forms of abstraction, other arts. The general hesitates, and finally asks the orchestra to give a concert for him in return for two additional days of life. During the concert he realizes that music is a more complete, more inclusive, form of art than the map; music manages to capture more relevant and intrinsic forms of human experience:

> The final music caught the General dwelling on one of the mass surprise attacks for which he had become famous; it dragged him like a gust of cannon fire from the pedestal on which he had set himself, and the barbarous loud rhythms flayed his mind and mocked him, showed the wake of an offensive: conventional signs of blooded tree stumps and mounds of rubble, horizontal levels of burning ground, spot heights covered by the representative fractions of dismembered bodies, streams red with blood an hour after sunrise, lanes of fire and roads of smoke, scorched hachuring to mark the heightened elevation of his searching guns. . . . The music illuminated his vision, and its final symphonic beats synchronized his resignation to the slow steps of advancing fate.
> [Pp. 126–127.]

Maps no longer work for the general. He permits the orchestra members to live, and he begins to make tactical and military mistakes. Finally he formulates a plan for the orchestra's escape, an escape that triggers the counterattack that defeats the general. The more comprehensive, the more humane, art form has no place in the jungle world of military achievement, but the general neither regrets nor applauds his choice. The development was inevitable. Once he apprehended the greater relevance of music, he had to abandon maps, even though the less coherent form provided a successful chart through the jungle. Man's highest achievements, the most comprehensive abstractions of human experience, are, ironically, of little use within the terms of experience itself.

"The Loneliness of the Long-Distance Runner" makes explicit still another possibility for man in his attempt to fight his way out of his jungle. The young runner, born and bred in poverty, sent to Borstal at the age of fifteen, has little chance to win in the world of the jungle. But he can be honest; he can recognize the facts of jungle life, the inevitable warfare between those who jail and those who are jailed. As he runs his deliberately losing race, the runner ponders the question of honesty. He feels that the governor, who has urged him to run and has promised him lenient treatment if he wins, is essentially dishonest, for the governor is, on the surface, working against his own class, using kind words and bland promises to cover his basic opposition to the young runner. The governor is refusing to admit the constant antagonism between the two warring sides in the jungle. The runner has far more respect for the policeman who captured him: at least the policeman, though vicious, was honestly antagonistic. The runner finally decides to lose:

> I say, I won't budge, I won't go for that last hundred yards if I have to sit down cross-legged on the grass and have the governor and his chinless wonders pick me up and carry me there, which is against their rules so you can bet they'd never do it because they're not clever enough to break the rules—like I would be in their place—even though they are their own. No, I'll show him

what honesty means if it's the last thing I do, though I'm sure he'll never understand because if he and all them like him did it'd mean they'd be on my side which is impossible. By God I'll stick this out like my dad stuck out his pain and kicked them doctors down the stairs.   [*Loneliness of the Long-Distance Runner*, p. 51.]

In his defiance the young runner asserts his only means of transcending the jungle. He isn't able to escape or to create art; he can simply and honestly stick to his own class and his own values, no matter what the consequences may be. His recognition of his jungle and his refusal to barter for a better position in a scheme he never made are the only ways he has of exercising his force and imagination.

Nothing really changes Sillitoe's jungle world. A man may win or lose, depending on the wheel of chance, but he cannot control the wheel or change his position. Often, too, the wheel is rigged, for the same numbers keep coming up as privilege and power keep reinforcing themselves. But not all of man is controlled by the wheel. Man can invent escapes, create art, focus defiantly on the wheel's essential structure. And the escape, the art, and the honesty, unable to alter the world, are themselves a part of man's nature, an illusory route out of the jungle which stems from the fertile and vibrant jungle itself. The wheel, the exterior fortune, is rigid and inflexible; the jungle, the interior, is dark and rich and alive.

3

Kingsley Amis'
Funny Novels

KINGSLEY AMIS HAS WRITTEN FOUR FUNNY NOVELS:
Lucky Jim (1954), *That Uncertain Feeling* (1955), *I Like It
Here* (1958), and *Take a Girl Like You* (1960). Each of the
novels is distinguished by a thick verbal texture that is essentially
comic. The novels are full of word play and verbal jokes. Any
chance observation is likely to bring forth a list of vaguely associated comic improbabilities. This verbal texture is often made
up of lists of specific and contemporary references, strung together in a comic manner. One character in *That Uncertain
Feeling* need only mention the growing Welsh industrial area
for another to expand immediately: ". . . like the mounted toy
soldier factory near Fforestfawr, they're making denture boxes
just on the other side of Llantwrch, and then there's the bicycle
saddles starting up next month at Cwmpant" (p. 183). In
addition to the comedy of specific reference, Amis also phonet-
ically reproduces various forms of speech for comic effect. All
Amis' heroes are mimics: Jim Dixon parodies the accent of Professor Welch, his phony and genteel professor, in *Lucky Jim*;
Patrick Standish, in *Take a Girl Like You*, deliberately echoes
the Hollywood version of the Southern Negro's accent. John

Lewis, the hero of *That Uncertain Feeling*, also mimics accents and satirically characterizes other people by the words and phrases they use. He supports his objection to Probert's pseudo-Welsh play by enumerating its misty abstractions, and he tears apart Probert's use of diction:

> Words like "death" and "life" and "love" and "man" cropped up every few lines, but were never attached to anything concrete or specific. "Death," for example, wasn't my death or your death or his death or her death or our death or their death or my Aunt Fanny's death, but just death, and in the same way "love" wasn't my, etc., love and wasn't love of one person for another or love of God or love of blackcurrant purée either, but just love. There were also bits from the Bible turned back to front ("In the word was the beginning" and so on), and bits of daring jargon ("No hawkers, circulars or saints," "Dai Christ"). Dear, dear, the thing was symbolical all right.   [P. 109.]

Garnet Bowen, the protagonist of *I Like It Here*, makes fun of the way his foreign students mispronounce English, as they refer to authors like "Grim-Grin," "Ifflen-Voff," "Zumzit-Mum," and "Shem-Shoice," and are fascinated by the popular novel "Sickies of sickingdom" by "Edge-Crown." Aided by garbled telephone calls and telegrams, this phonetic humor helps to establish the rich, comic texture of Amis' writing.

Amis also frequently uses an incongruous comic image drawn from contemporary life. Often such an image serves as an introduction to a character. Early in *That Uncertain Feeling*, John Lewis spots Elizabeth, his future mistress, at a party: "She was wearing an orange-reddish dress which gave her an air of ignorant wildness and freedom, like the drunken daughter of some man of learning" (p. 35). Patrick Standish, in *Take a Girl Like You*, first meets the expensive woman with whom, as arranged by a friend, he will spend the night: "She looked like a brilliantly catty novelist and reviewer with a Ph.D. on Wittgenstein" (p. 220). Frequently the comic image intrudes at some supposedly serious or vital moment, as, for example, when Patrick makes his first attempt to seduce young Jenny Bunn:

> Before long Patrick slipped his left hand under her dress in the
> non-important places: back, shoulders, upper arms. It was rather
> like one of the kids at school getting out of his seat to borrow
> a pencil-sharpener or pick up a writing-book when you knew that
> what he really wanted to do was run round the room yelling.
> [P. 58.]

Later in the novel, when Jenny, upset, drinks too much at a
party, she "ran into the bathroom and was sick, hurling herself
forward like a rugger-player on TV scoring a try" (p. 308).
Sometimes the comic image is repeated and becomes a tag that
identifies the fact throughout the novel. In *Take a Girl Like You*,
the cooking at the Thompsons' boardinghouse, where Jenny
lives, is described in terms of the haddock that tasted as if it
came from the "lionhouse" at the zoo, the beef that tasted of
"damp tea-towel," the "rusty-knives steak pie," the "cardboard
chicken" and the "dirty-dog mince." These images go through
the novel like a refrain, appearing whenever the Thompsons'
cooking is mentioned.

Amis seems to erect a whole comic world through the fabric
of his writing. The same kinds of lists, of images, of comic specific
references figure in each of the novels. Occasionally comic references are carried over from one novel to another, reinforcing
the notion of a complete comic world. For example, one of the
characters in *That Uncertain Feeling* is the dentist's mistress.
She appears at every party in the novel and seems to be available
to almost any man, yet she does not play an important part in
the action, is never individualized, and is always referred to as
"the dentist's mistress." Then, at one point in *I Like It Here*,
Bowen muses about his wife's interest in riding: "You never
knew the sort of people you might meet in connection with
horses: auctioneers' wives, solicitors' daughters, dentists' mistresses, on a bad day even—he supposed dimly—aristocrats with
titles" (p. 178). An apparently more deliberate example of the
same kind of link between two different novels occurs in the
character of Dr. L. S. Caton. Caton is a somewhat shoddy editor
in *Lucky Jim* who refuses to say when he will publish an article

on medieval shipbuilding which Jim has written, even though he has presumably accepted it for publication. Near the end of the novel Jim learns indirectly that Caton has run off to accept an appointment in Argentina. In *Take a Girl Like You,* which takes place four or five years after *Lucky Jim,* Patrick's headmaster shows him a letter in which the writer, recently returned from Argentina, offers to give a talk to students on Argentine educational institutions. The writer, sounding as slimy as ever, is L. S. Caton.

Within Amis' world the comic image or comparison is so important that it frequently interrupts a crucial scene or relationship. Digression and irrelevance are continually played against presumably important action or revelation. In *Lucky Jim,* for example, Jim is speaking to Christine, the London girl who becomes his final reward. At this point in the novel Christine is still connected with Bertrand Welch, the professor's son and a pseudo artist. Christine and Jim are first beginning to recognize and acknowledge their feeling for each other when the following dialogue takes place:

> "Yes, that's right. You talk as if it's the only thing that is. If you can tell me whether you like greengages or not, you can tell me whether you're in love with Bertrand or not, if you want to tell me, that is."
>
> "You're still making it much too simple. All I can really say is that I'm pretty sure I was in love with Bertrand a little while ago, and now I'm rather less sure. That up-and-down business doesn't happen with greengages; that's the difference."
>
> "Not with greengages, agreed. But what about rhubarb, eh? What about rhubarb? Ever since my mother stopped forcing me to eat it, rhubarb and I have been conducting a relationship that can swing between love and hatred every time we meet."
>
> [P. 147.]

Love takes second place to greengages and rhubarb. In *That Uncertain Feeling,* John Lewis' immediate memory of his evening on the beach with Elizabeth is far more concerned with the meaning and the magnitude of his three mosquito bites than with their initial love-making or the serious argument that followed. And Garnet Bowen is kept from infidelity with a lovely Portuguese girl only by the untimely sting of a wasp. In fact, sexual crises are more apt than any others to be interrupted by a comic image or an extraneous fact. All kisses are comically compared or discussed at some length; all sex, particularly in *Take a Girl Like You,* is made a matter of semicomic maneuver or is interrupted by an irrelevant thought or incident. The fabric of the novels, the quick verbal incongruities and the comic incidents, takes precedence over supposedly significant action.

As the action in the novels is frequently interrupted for a comic image or a joke, so the apparent moral issues of the novels do not follow a clear or consistent line. All Amis' heroes talk a great deal about honesty and integrity, make fun of others who indulge in pretense or self-delusion, and regard themselves as simple, direct, and honest. To some extent this version of themselves is accurate, for they all share a respect for the work they do. Jim Dixon may have taken up medieval history because it was the easiest subject at his university, but he recognizes and respects good teaching and good scholarship. Part of his lack of ease stems from his difficulty in substituting the trivia of academic life for genuine knowledge and relevance. Similarly, John Lewis is a competent librarian; Jenny Bunn is well able to deal with the little mongrels in her I*a* class; and Patrick Standish, despite his love for drink and women, is a skillful, perceptive, and popular teacher.

Yet occupational integrity, for Amis, is only a small part of a much larger issue. The social and the sexual consume far more time and speculation in all Amis' novels, and here the characters are less easy, confident, and honest. Jim Dixon refuses to be caught by academic or arty pretense and needs to convince himself that the neurotic Margaret's hold on him is deceitful before he can happily abandon her for his prize, Christine. Yet Jim does leave Margaret, deceit notwithstanding, just when she needs him most, and his values have always been those of the

opportunist: the prettiest girl, the easiest job. Although he
spends a good share of the novel in a kind of earthy opposition
to the genteel hypocrisy at the provincial university, he ends
by receiving the opportunist's reward. He is offered a new and
better job in London from the fairy godfather, Gore-Urquhart,
who explains: "It's not that you've got the qualifications, for
this or any other work, but there are plenty who have. You
haven't got the disqualifications, though, and that's much rarer"
(p. 238). But Jim's victory is accomplished only by a shift into
the realm of fantasy. He has lost his job, has been beaten by the
world of sham, when he suddenly receives the prizes of the girl
and the new job in a fairy-tale ending. The ending is a gesture,
a representation in fantasy of all that Jim wants, not the logical
outcome of the moral issues demonstrated in the novel.

John Lewis constantly debates and worries about moral issues.
Each time Elizabeth carries him off for the evening, he suffers
pangs of guilt for deserting his wife, for consorting with the
"Anglicized Upper Classes." Yet he is never honest with Elizabeth. At one point he even intends to project his guilt by phon-
ing her and telling her off, but after a long diatribe he notices
that he's forgotten to press Button A; she hasn't heard a word
he said. Clearly this guilt is part posture, for John is singularly
dense about moral issues. He does not understand Elizabeth and
judges her by the rigid nonconformist code of his home village.
When he maintains that he will give up the better job he gained
through his affair with Elizabeth, he is unable to understand his
wife's moral position: as he had already violated their marriage,
he might just as well reap the benefits of the violation. John, in
the complex world of Aberdarcy, can neither understand and
follow a moral line of conduct, nor live with the consequences
of his own immorality. He is, therefore, unable to operate successfully in society. At the end he can only recognize his own
cowardice and retreat to the mining town he came from.

Heroes in the later Amis novels are able to handle themselves
and their worlds more successfully, although integrity is still
more a matter for debate and comic speculation than an under-

lying guide for action. In *I Like It Here*, Garnet Bowen is a free-lance writer. He takes a holiday in Portugal, but he is also there, at the request of a publisher's agent, to discover whether or not an old novelist is the genuine Wulfstan Strether. Garnet's wife keeps insisting that the snooping involved is immoral, and that Bowen must give up the project and assert his own convictions. Yet Bowen, morally ambivalent, without ever really resolving the issues his wife presents, persists and makes his discovery (the old man is genuine). For all the debate, morality and integrity are not the issues of the novel. The point is that Bowen, unlike John Lewis, has been able to cope successfully with the world about him. Morality is ultimately irrelevant. As Bowen muses when he visits Fielding's tomb in Lisbon:

> Perhaps it was worth dying in your forties if two hundred years later you were the only non-contemporary novelist who could be read with unaffected and whole-hearted interest, the only one who never had to be apologised for or excused on the grounds of changing taste. And how enviable to live in the world of his novels, where duty was plain, evil arose out of malevolence and a starving wayfarer could be invited indoors without hesitation and without fear. Did that make it a simplified world? Perhaps, but that hardly mattered beside the existence of a moral serious-ness that could be made apparent without the aid of evangelical puffing and blowing.   [P. 185.]

Morality and integrity, as simple and unpretentious issues, are now only echoes from a past world. And Amis is not the sort of novelist to spend many of his pages lamenting what is past and gone.

Similarly, in *Take a Girl Like You*, morality, specifically sexual here, is the subject of incessant debate but does not affect the outcome of the story. Jenny Bunn, a young girl from the more cloistered north, is determined to keep her virginity; Patrick is just as determined to take it from her. The argument, often handled in comic terms, runs throughout the book. Jenny loses her virginity, but not as a result of moral or immoral suasion;

Patrick tricks her into capitulation while she is drunk. Although moral issues make Jenny periodically resolve not to see Patrick again, such resolutions never hold, and at the end she is able to say, "Well, those old Bible-class ideas have certainly taken a knocking, haven't they?" Jenny has learned that, in order to keep Patrick and to operate successfully in the more sophisticated town she has moved to, she must abandon the moral principles she grew up with. Self-interest demands the abrogation of principle, and Jenny, living in a world different from her parents', is no fool. Again the relevance of morality is pushed back into another age, for, as Patrick explains during one of his earlier arguments with Jenny:

> There used to be a third sort, admitted. The sort that could, but didn't—not with the girl he was going to marry, anyway. You'd have liked him all right, though, and he wouldn't have given you any trouble trying to get you into bed before the day. The snag about him is he's dead. He died in 1914 or thereabouts. He isn't ever going to turn up, Jenny, that bloke with the manners and the respect and the honour and the bunches of flowers *and* the attraction. Or if he does he's going to turn out to have a wife in Birmingham or a boy friend in Chelsea or a psychiatrist in . . . wherever psychiatrists live.   [Pp. 159–160.]

These days, people either can or can't.

In Amis' contemporary fictional world, morality is simply material—conversational, controversial at times, but never the issue along which the novel is directed. The theme of the novels is ultimately adjustment, adjustment of the individual and his aims to the wider society in which he lives. The first two novels, by demonstrating that the adjustment is either in the realm of fantasy or altogether impossible, at least provide some commentary, some question, on the value of adjustment. But the two more recent novels neglect the commentary entirely; the individual must adjust to his world in order to make his way successfully through it. This attitude fits with the comic imagery, the interruption, the comic perspective in Amis' world. If man faces a world where experience is constantly fragmented and incongruous, where no single line of conduct is invulnerable from the ridicule of another point of view, his only possibility is to concentrate on his individual desires and make his way through the world as best he can. Amis' point of view is ultimately a comic acceptance of the contemporary world as it is, a recognition of multiple facts of experience without any commitment concerning the relative value of those facts. That the first two novels seem to provide some commentary, even if it requires extension into fantasy or limitation to a mining town, makes them more satisfactory novels. But the plethora of moral issues in the two more recent novels makes their abnegation in favor of adjustment seem not only an example of comic acceptance but an indication of the novelist's taking too easy a way out. The material itself demands a more committed resolution.

The difference in point of view between Amis' early novels and his more recent ones is also apparent in his use of different comic techniques. In the first two novels, for example, characters often explain the motives of others in a fairly straightforward way. John Lewis, at first, attributes Elizabeth's interest in him to her money and her desire to parade it. And Jim Dixon indulges in some frank, and damning, accounts of the Welches' motives. Yet this kind of speculation is absent or comically modified in the later books. In *Take a Girl Like You*, Patrick replaces the direct account of others' motives with generalized, pseudological categories. For example, when he fails to seduce Jenny, he reasons that

> he was now in a position to codify as an axiom the fact that willingness to be impressed was inversely correlated with willingness to be assaulted. Another such axiom, perhaps axiom 1, said that to have frank lechery inspired in oneself bore no correlation whatever to the lechery coefficient, frank or other, of the inspirer.
>
> [Pp. 79–80.]

Patrick frequently develops axioms, categories, coefficients, mock-logical devices in order to explain experience. Jenny also uses categories, for she divides the men she meets into stooges, duds, middles, tops, and smashers, in ascending order of approval. She is proud of her ability to spot a stooge instantaneously. The two early novels also demonstrate an involved comedy of incident which is, on the whole, absent from the two later books. Long, involved episodes, such as Jim's cigarette burning the bedclothes at the Welches' and his frantic efforts to hide his crime, or John Lewis' involved misadventures while masquerading as a plumber in Elizabeth's house, do not take place in the two later books. Amis' humor has become increasingly less farcical and more verbal and imagistic.

The disappearance of farce from Amis' world is connected with the gradual disappearance of Amis' comic trade-mark: the bumbling, self-conscious hero who stumbles against the established social and cultural world, making fun of both the world and himself in the process. Each successive hero is more competent, less afraid of petty officials, more able to drive a car or seduce a woman, more in control of the world around him. And, as the hero bumbles less, the opportunities for farce and comic incident decrease. In addition, less of each successive novel is filtered through the perception of the hero. *Take a Girl Like You* does not even have a single hero, for both Patrick and Jenny are equally central. As the heroes become less an essential perspective for the novel, as the comedy consequently becomes more direct, the novels themselves become flatter and more like a series of scattered comic images and verbal jokes. While Amis retains his ability to draw quick, scathing portraits of minor characters and his facility with comically incongruous specific references, he seems to have lost the essentially comic conception of the antihero bumbling through society. *Take a Girl Like You*, without the opportunity for farce and without the centrally comic conception of the antihero, is two dimensions less funny than *Lucky Jim*.

Yet, despite this diminution of comic dimension, much of Amis' comic world remains remarkably consistent. Almost every novel contains at least one long conversation between the hero and a child, a conversation full of improbability and *non sequitur*, as the one in which Garnet Bowen is plagued by his son who wants to know whether or not two tigers could effectively demolish a whale. More important, all the principal characters make faces. Jim Dixon keeps a battery of practiced faces ready for appropriate occasions: his Martian-invader face, his Eskimo face, his Edith Sitwell face, his lemon-sucking face, his sex-life-in-ancient-Rome face. John Lewis often copies faces from American films and he is proud of his ability to look calm and above-it-all or mature and distinguished or solid and responsible at any given moment. Jenny Bunn, in *Take a Girl Like You,* has a whole series of looks, sorted out and catalogued, to discourage the wolfish glances she gets from men in restaurants and on buses. Patrick Standish and Dick Thompson also make faces to represent the roles they would like to play. Patrick, when told off by one of his superiors, tries to look "like the kind of bus-company official who is kept in reserve to announce delays, changes of boarding-point and suspension of services."

Along with the faces, Amis' characters also deliberately play roles in a kind of comic masquerade. John Lewis parodies Elizabeth's manner and talks of his whole set of roles, ready at any given time. In *Take a Girl Like You,* Patrick exuberantly plays the role of an export-import man in order to impress his expensive woman in London:

> "No," he said, preparing to enjoy himself. "I'm to do with export and import. Chemical fertilisers. Disinfectants. Pest sprays. Sheep dip. Cattle dip. Goat dip. Horse dip. Pig dip. Donkey dip. Mule dip. Camel dip. Elephant dip. Llama dip. Buffalo dip."
>
> [Pp. 221–222.]

But the roles are more than material for parody. They illustrate the perspective, the view of man's position in the world, that runs through all Amis' novels. Jim Dixon, with his arm around Christine, is able to say:

> More than ever he felt secure: here he was, quite able to fulfil his role, and, as with other roles, the longer you played it the better

chance you had of playing it again. Doing what you wanted to
do was the only training, and the only preliminary, needed for
doing more of what you wanted to do.   [*Lucky Jim*, p. 149.]

As Jim's favorite role consists in doing what he wants to do, and
he is stumbling against the world he lives in, *Lucky Jim* ends
in fantasy, in an improbable justification of Jim's romanticized
wishes. But the other novels, if less romantic, are no less concerned with roles. In *That Uncertain Feeling*, John Lewis, at the
point where he thinks he can manage to keep Elizabeth and all
she represents, also plays his favorite role:

> I sat there in an easy posture, my arm along the back of the thing
> some inches from her shoulders, my head lolling comfortably. I
> was now being the man used to the company of attractive women,
> the man who accepts without dramatics whatever experience may
> come his way, but who never strives for anything beyond the
> bounds of expediency or of self-possession.   [P. 115.]

But John cannot sustain his role; he soon trembles and then
moves away. In *Take a Girl Like You*, Anna le Page has mas-
queraded as French throughout the novel as a means of explaining her all-consuming interest in sex, her objections to English
society, her worship of art. Finally revealed as English, Anna
explains: "Playing a part's the only thing left these days, it shows
you won't deal with society in the way it wants you to" (p.
302). And Anna, unable to deal with society at all outside her
role, must move somewhere else at the end of the novel. The role
is, on one hand, a comic game; at the same time, as a semicomic
fabrication, it is the only means through which the individual,
that ill-assorted mess of chaotic impulses, can represent himself,
deal with his world, and get the most he can from it.

In Amis' novels no individual is free from the incessant awareness of disparate and incongruous experience, as no experience
itself is free from verbal interruption or contradiction. In order
to try to simplify and manage the experience, man needs to
establish roles, to invent disguises. The roles are more or less
successful, depending upon how fully they can account for the

multiple facts of experience, how well they can aid the character in getting what he wants. The value of the role is judged pragmatically. But the role, by its very nature, by the incongruity between role and whatever chaotic individual that role is designed to represent, cannot become an abstraction or a truth in itself. Roles must change; they must continually be knocked down and set up again. Man, in his pragmatic alternation of roles, is existential, for the sane man does not allow any of his roles to become abstract manifestations of general truth or guides to conduct. Existence is the only necessary condition, and the opportunistic hero plays any role he can in any world he can (the fantastic, the limited, or the deceitful) in order to get what he simply happens to want. Amis does not fundamentally commit himself in his novels. He does not choose among roles, even on the limited and existential basis used by many of his contemporaries for partial choices. His failure to choose, his willingness to provide something close to equal stature for all the separate facts of incongruous contemporary experience, indicates both a central acceptance of the world around him and a purely comic perspective.

The central acceptance of the world and the purely comic perspective may also be demonstrated by Amis' treatment of social and political issues. Specific references to contemporary issues crowd all the novels and provide many of the comic and incongruous details. All the heroes, for example, support the Labour party and the Welfare State. Yet this support is less a consistent political or social allegiance than an instrument used to puncture the pretense and gentility of others or to conceal the hero's own social embarrassment. Jim Dixon, John Lewis, and Garnet Bowen equate their support of the Labour party with behaving badly, shocking others, and making nuisances of themselves at cocktail parties. John Lewis, surveying the room at a party, wonders:

> Should I break in in a renewed effort to be marked down as "impossible," bawl a defence of the Welfare State, start undressing myself or the dentist's mistress, give the dentist a lovely piggy-

back round the room, call for a toast to the North Korean Foreign
Minister or Comrade Malenkov?

[*That Uncertain Feeling*, p. 47.]

In the two most recent novels, adherence to the Labour party
gradually becomes more respectable. Patrick has no need either
to conceal or parade his Labour sympathies, but he does object
to the lack of urbanity and assurance in some of the "stooges,"
like Dick Thompson, who join him at the local Labour club.
The role of using Labour sympathies as a weapon against genteel
society changes as the pragmatic value of the role declines.

All Amis' heroes, however, are iconoclastic. As Jim Dixon
punctures the folly of recorder revivals and myths about "Merrie
England," so John Lewis is scathing about phony revivals of
Welsh poetry and about arty, self-conscious attempts to live in
another society. Garnet Bowen in *I Like It Here,* mocks the kind
of reviewer who demonstrates his cosmopolitan knowledge by
writing phrases like: "Mr. Shagbag has caught to perfection the
atmosphere of those precipitous little streets that run up from
the Rua Latrina to the Palazzo del . . . Allegro non Troppo"
(pp. 30–31). Patrick Standish derides the woman's magazine
side of Jenny: her domesticity, her interest in neat flower arrangements, her enthusiasm for interesting Yugoslav recipes.
Behind all these iconoclastic comments is the implicit and simple
statement that "Life isn't like that." Amis' heroes deride the
foreign, the complex, the pretentious, but not from any particular political or social point of view. Even the standard of the
simple man of common sense is never allowed to become an
articulate point of view. Garnet Bowen mocks the possibility
of this in *I Like It Here*: "It would be unendurable if they all
turned out to be full of instinctive wisdom and natural good
manners and unself-conscious grace and a deep, inarticulate
understanding of death" (pp. 61–62). This iconoclasm is evidence of the incongruities of the comic perspective, rather than
an instrument stemming from a particular social or political
theme.

Other social and political issues frequently appear in Amis' books. Often the satire against the arty and the foreign develops from a kind of English nationalism, not the nationalism of fifes and drums along the Irrawaddy in the Kipling tradition, but that of someone sticking to what he knows and feels comfortable about. On these grounds, John Lewis berates phony Welsh poets and Garnet Bowen is apprehensive about travel abroad. Bowen, even when he returns from Portugal, says:

> It's a very nice-looking place all round and if you exclude the Government and the upper classes the people are as decent as you'd find anywhere. It's just that the place is located abroad and the people are foreigners, which for the purposes of this discussion means that they and I belong to different nations, so we can't understand each other or get to know each other as well as chaps from the same nation can. I'm all for international co-operation and friendship and the rest of it, but let's be clear what we mean by it. [*I Like It Here*, pp. 205–206.]

And he later adds:

> London was looking full of good stuff. Admittedly it, together with most of the rest of the United Kingdom, was the land of Sorry-sir (sorry sir bar's closed sir, sorry sir no change sir, sorry sir too late for lunch sir, sorry sir residents only sir), but one couldn't expect to win all the time. [P. 207.]

Yet, despite all this modified veneration for England, Bowen does learn a good deal in Portugal. He realizes that trips abroad contain more than phony searches for atmosphere, and he greatly extends the range of the world he can control. John Lewis may berate the Welsh from a contemporary English point of view, but he also, and just as volubly, blasts the casual materialism in contemporary English society. Jim Dixon tries to puncture nationalistic myths wherever he finds them. And even simple, unpretentious nationalism becomes a silly and highly vulnerable provincialism in *Take a Girl Like You*, for Jenny Bunn is made to look ridiculous when she repeats her little English saws about the French, or foreigners in general, or the virtues of the English middle classes. Feelings about nationalism, one way or another, also provide material for Amis' comic debates.

The aristocrat, in Amis' world, is seldom deceitful, pretentious, or corrupt. Gore-Urquhart, the hyphenated fairy godfather of *Lucky Jim*; Wulfstan Strether, the craggy novelist in *I Like It Here*; and Lord and Lady Edgerstoune, the honest and admirable couple in *Take a Girl Like You*, are all representatives of a venerable aristocracy, above the niggling pettiness of the lives around them. They never need roles or subterfuge in order to operate successfully in their worlds. Luckier than most people, these characters also demonstrate a kind of respect for the aristocracy which helps to counterbalance the socialist and leveling attitudes often exhibited by Amis' heroes. The Labour party, as party, may be preferable to the Tory, but the social and political attitudes of Amis' characters are essentially conservative, essentially a comic and tolerant acceptance of the power structure of the contemporary world.

The comic acceptance of the contemporary scene, along with the verbal texture of incongruous image and reference, provides whatever unity exists in Amis' fiction. Social and moral references abound because man deals with social and moral facts continuously, but the facts, assiduously kept apart whenever too vast a generalization or abstraction threatens, remain separate and incongruous. Comedy well conveys the multiple facts, the lack of order or system, which confront contemporary man. Amis' novels reflect this condition, but too often they provide no comment on it. They thrust all possible comment, by the interruption of incongruous image, back into the mass of separate facts that form the comic perspective. In the two most recent novels, man simply makes his way as best he can; all comment or judgment is scrupulously avoided. The purest comedy, the complete insistence on the separate quality of all facts and experiences, is also irresponsibility. And this pure comedy, unshaped and uncommitted, simply reflects what is, a simple reflection that explains a certain flatness in *I Like It Here* and *Take a Girl Like You*. In *Lucky Jim* and *That Uncertain Feeling*, novels with some hint of a central force of comment about the world, the comedy is both more rich and less pure. The farce and the central concept add comic dimensions. Both novels center on a hero, not an embodiment of all value, but a protagonist whose perceptions and experience shape a meaningful kind of statement. Jim Dixon blunders against a world of pretense and cannot make his way through it. That the issues are resolved in a romantic fantasy falsifies the representation of the world but preserves the energy and the meaning of Jim's commentary. John Lewis is not so lucky as Jim. John tries to control experience in a world larger and more complex than the one he came from. He fails and retreats; he wanted success among the multiple levels of jobs and art and allegiances in Aberdarcy, but he can only operate within the rigid nonconformism of the mining town. Yet, despite his failure, he provides a prismatic comment on the world around him. This central comment, though vulnerable itself, provides a perspective against which all the incongruity of experience can be seen. And the ending of the novel, limited, constricted, adequately represents John's failure. *That Uncertain Feeling* is Amis' best, and least consoling, novel.

Yet Amis' enormous verbal facility marks all four novels. The comic image, the specific and irrelevant reference, the frequent iconoclastic interruption, and the verbal texture all give each of the novels a certain amount of distinction. In addition, the process of knocking down and setting up roles, of constantly showing the incongruity between the role and the vague and disparate reality it is supposed to represent, is surely funny. As Amis himself has so often claimed, his primary intention is to write funny books. But this is not really enough. Good comedy also requires the richness and the force that derive from some form of commitment or commentary. The flatness of the pure and uncommitted comedy, its satisfaction with simple reflection, may often become repetitious and dull.

4

Anger as Affirmation

THE ASSUMPTION THAT ONE CANNOT FULLY APPRECI-
ate the plays of Osborne, Wesker, and other contemporary
British dramatists unless he has been part of or has intimately
known the specific society they present has frequently appeared
in reviews, criticisms, and comments about the plays. Although
the work of Osborne and Wesker has been praised as an energetic
antidote to a theater long dominated by ingenious productions
of the classics or insipid little comedies assuming that manners
have really not changed since 1914, the praise has centered on
the notion that these new plays are sociological statements,
presentations of how a heretofore neglected part of British
society lives and thinks. Both Osborne and Wesker do set their
plays in contemporary societies unfamiliar to Mayfair, but the
plays are essentially emotional and dramatic statements that
apply far beyond the realm of a particular time and place. Osborne's first play to be produced, *Look Back in Anger* (1956;
this date, and all other dates given for plays in this chapter, are
those of the first production), is less a play about the rebellion
of the educated young man of the lower classes against current
society than a play about what it means to give and receive love.

Jimmy Porter does rant against bishops and "posh" Sunday papers, against any form of aristocratic gentility or pretense, but his invective is part of a plea for human honesty and vitality, for people to live emotionally as fully and as deeply as they can. He may berate his wife for the genteel background she cannot help; but he is really hurt by her emotional nullity when she ignores the illness of the old woman who established them in the sweet stall. When Helena, Jimmy's mistress, leaves him because his wife Alison has returned, Jimmy, in his frustration, voices what is both the play's major theme and its principal indictment of society:

> They all want to escape from the pain of being alive. And, most of all, from love. I always knew something like this would turn up—some problem, like an ill wife—and it would be too much for those delicate, hot-house feelings of yours. It's no good trying to fool yourself about love. You can't fall into it like a soft job, without dirtying up your hands. It takes muscle and guts. And if you can't bear the thought of messing up your nice, clean soul, you'd better give up the whole idea of life, and become a saint. Because you'll never make it as a human being. It's either this world or the next.   [Pp. 93–94.]

Both Helena and Alison understand what Jimmy is saying, and they are able to love him, not because they agree with his attacks on religion or other forms of hardened and genteel abstractions in society, but because they recognize and ultimately respond to his human energy. The game of squirrels and bears which Jimmy and Alison play seems, at first, a trivial evasion of the complexities found in any marriage. But at the end of the play the game becomes a statement of the nature of human love—the willingness to immerse oneself completely in creatureness, to share the pain and the pleasure of the limited animal.

Osborne's *The Entertainer* (1957) is also more a dramatic and emotional statement than an analysis of the decline of the English music-hall tradition. Archie Rice, the fading and shoddy music-hall comic, does, in a way, represent the decline of England by his shabby allegiance to and his cheapening of the old patriotic songs. His old father, a more genuine version of the tradition who never has had to sell himself to the daughters of the *nouveau riche* from Birmingham in order to get money for a new production, is now a greedy old man emotionally insulated from everyone around him. Archie's talented son has spent six months in jail as a conscientious objector; his untalented son, in the course of the play, dies a useless hero's death in the Suez campaign. Yet these indications of the passing of old England, important as they are, are not the central stuff of the play. Rather, the play's center emerges in scenes such as the one in which Archie's battered wife spends the last of her tiny savings to buy an ornate cake for her son's welcome home from Suez (she doesn't yet know that he's been killed). While the cake is in the kitchen, Archie's old father wanders in and, quite gratuitously and absent-mindedly, eats a large piece of it. Archie's wife explodes in frustrated rage, while the old father only dimly and uncertainly comprehends what he has done. The scene, apart from its sociological flavor, demonstrates how blind people are, even those living together in the same house for years, to what matters to others. No one is to blame, all the motives can be understood, but people just casually destroy one another day by day. The whole play is a fabric of similar emotional destructions: Archie and his wife, Archie and his father, the father and Archie's wife. Certainly, all these destructions are made more meaningful and more poignant within the terms of a dissolving sociological entity. But the emotional destructions themselves form the center of a play with ramifications far beyond the traditions of music-hall comedy or of old England.

Arnold Wesker, another young dramatist, has writen a trilogy (*Chicken Soup with Barley*, 1958; *Roots*, 1959; *I'm Talking about Jerusalem*, 1960) dealing with a family of Jewish-Communist intellectuals and tracing their occupations and attitudes from 1936 through 1959. The plays are, in part, sociological documents, and scenes frequently begin with references to some external historical fact relevant to the action: the 1936 marching of Mosley's Fascists, the Labour victory of 1945, Group Captain Townsend's dignified exile in 1955, the Conservative sweep of 1959. Yet the family itself, the Kahns, and their relationships are even more significant than are any of the social and political definitions. The whole trilogy is polarized by the opposing values of the mother and the father. The mother, strong, active, a militant leftist with a vital concern for others, keeps repeating, "You've got to care or you'll die." The father, on the other hand, weaker, more bookish, a supposed revolutionary who sneaks off to the movies or to his mother's for tea whenever any form of violence threatens, frequently says, "You can't alter people. You can only give them some love and hope they'll take it." This contrast between the militant activist and the more passively limited applies to human relationships as well as to politics. The children, a daughter Ada and a son Ronnie, neither as simply active or passive as their parents, shuttle from one pole to the other. Ada begins as a young admirer of the gallant anti-Fascist forces in Spain, but, after World War II, limits her socialism to a personal attempt, along with her husband, to make furniture in a farming community in Norfolk. Yet the attempt is not entirely personal. It carries a kind of William Morris attitude of social reform, and Ada often still feels the necessity to defend herself, to explain her position in terms of a larger world. Ronnie, less consistent than his sister, alternates more frequently between an attempt to convert others, to argue them into the realization of a significantly wider world, and an awareness that human beings have only little and limited impact on others. When Ada and her husband are finally defeated (modern commerce has made it impossible for them to continue making a living by turning out furniture by hand at the Norfolk farm, and, besides, they have made some serious mistakes), Ronnie is dejected. He feels that a vision of something important, something better, is lost. When Ada's husband bitterly replies that visions never work, Ronnie answers: "They *do* work! And even if they don't work then for God's sake let's try and behave as though they do— or else nothing will work" (*I'm Talking about Jerusalem*, p. 76).

Ronnie seems his mother's son. Yet, ironically, Ronnie, often jobless and disillusioned, experiences his only triumph, that of Beatie Bryant's discovering herself (a triumph that he never witnesses or knows about), when he follows his father's dictum, "You can only give them some love and hope they'll take it." Wesker never resolves the conflict between militant and limited human activity, as Doris Lessing never really resolves the conflict between the political attitudes of two different generations which underlies her play, *Each His Own Wilderness* (1958). The conflicts simply motivate the significant human action of the plays.

Roots, the middle play of Wesker's trilogy, does not deal directly with the Kahn family or with leftist politics at all. In this play Beatie Bryant, engaged to Ronnie, returns for a visit to her family of Norfolk farmers. She persistently quotes Ronnie, trying to engage her limited and complacent family in her new-found awareness of a wider world of politics, art, and sensitivity. Her efforts make little impression on her family, caught up in crops, losing jobs, family feuds, and bad digestion. In the last act, however, when Ronnie jilts Beatie by letter and does not arrive for his expected visit, the girl, in arguing with her family, suddenly discovers herself. In the midst of a tirade about why people like her family are an easy market for the third-rate and the commercial, Beatie suddenly realizes that she is no longer quoting Ronnie's convictions. She has become a person on her own, and yet Ronnie is, in part, responsible. As Beatie cares and fights and becomes more of a human being, the little bit of love has taken.

In Wesker's work, as in Osborne's, the social or the political, the Norfolk farm or the rally in Trafalgar Square, is the vehicle through which the emotionally and permanently human is effectively transmitted. Unlike the proletarian plays of the 'thirties, in which the individual dramatized illustrated some general social or political truth, these plays simply use political or social details to illustrate points about individuals. *I'm Talking about Jerusalem,* the last play in Wesker's trilogy, does not depict the failure of a social ideal. Rather, the play presents the failure of two individuals, of Ada and her husband, to shape their lives in terms of the William Morris kind of ideal. The abstract truth or falsity of the ideal is irrelevant. Social ideals are simply one of the ways through which people find or lose, discover or betray, themselves. And Ada and her husband, though apparently defeated, have discovered what they care about and what they can do. Even Jimmy Porter's famous statement about causes, in *Look Back in Anger*, is as personally revealing as it is politically pointed:

> I suppose people of our generation aren't able to die for good causes any longer. We had all that done for us, in the thirties and the forties, when we were still kids. There aren't any good, brave causes left. If the big bang does come, and we all get killed off, it won't be in aid of the old-fashioned, grand design. It'll just be for the Brave New-nothing-very-much-thank-you. About as pointless and inglorious as stepping in front of a bus. No, there's nothing left for it, me boy, but to let yourself be butchered by the women.   [Pp. 84–85.]

The statement expresses both political skepticism and personal frustration. It is both a comment on society and a way for Jimmy to express the anger churning within him, an anger that originates in his inability to communicate with others as fully and meaningfully as he feels. And, in addition, the last sentence of the passage defines the only realm, as the whole play illustrates, in which communication can be meaningful or important. In part, a vast and complex world has made specific and limited communication the only kind possible for man. But, in part also, Jimmy Porter is the kind of person who needs the specific anchor and the intensity that only a relationship with an individual can provide. Causes are, and always were, too abstract for people like Jimmy. And one need not know the Midlands or the history of the International Brigade in Spain to recognize that.

Another contemporary play that uses social terms in order to portray a more personal and universal theme is Shelagh Delaney's *A Taste of Honey* (1958). *A Taste of Honey* is set in a grimy Manchester flat with a shared bathroom and an excellent view of the gasworks. Jo, an adolescent girl, and her mother have just moved into the flat. Jo's mother, who has made a career out of the various men in her life, goes off to marry a brassy, drunken, loutish man, the only one she can get. Jo, left alone, falls in love with a colored sailor who is on leave, sleeps with him, becomes pregnant, and then is helped through her pregnancy by a young homosexual art student. The mother belatedly returns to help Jo, gets the art student to leave the flat, and is shocked to find that her grandchild may be black. The play contains elements of urban poverty, the color bar, the ease of moving in and out of bed among the lower classes. Yet all these are carefully understated; they are made to seem quite an ordinary part of human experience rather than a burning issue or a sociological observation. The play is really about love, about Jo's experience with several different kinds of love: the feeling, created primarily out of loneliness, for the colored boy she sleeps with; the comfortable domestic love and concern the art student gives her; the final awareness that, despite her mother's inconsistency and irresponsibility which have led to a thorough skepticism about the virtues of family life, Jo will now have a child whom she can genuinely care for. The play is almost entirely free from sentimentality; Jo's search for love and security is conveyed through a series of direct and simple observations of what goes on around her. The social environment provides the material for most of the observations, the terms through which Jo discovers something about people and about love. But any note of strident social consciousness, or any call for the amelioration of the social evils that form the background of the play, is completely absent from the theme and the texture of *A Taste of Honey*. Jo, like many others in entirely different situations, finds experience beset with difficult problems, and finally works things out with help from unlikely and unpredictable sources.

Contemporary British dramatists do not seem to be fashioning, either implicitly or explicitly, any cry for reform. Miss Delaney never protests, as such, against the conditions that have landed

Jo in the spot she is in. Even Jimmy Porter indulges in a few sentimental reveries about the sunshine of Edwardian England, knowing that it's gone and that it was partly phony, but strongly attracted to it nonetheless. Both Helena and Alison feel that he was born out of his time, that he belongs to an earlier and more heroic age. And Osborne himself creates a highly sympathetic portrait of Alison's father, the India army officer who was forced out of his function and his world when India became independent in 1947. He provides another version of Jimmy's problem, another man with feelings and attachments and loyalties who has trouble finding a place to fasten them. The retired India officer, human as well, deserves almost as much sympathy as does the displaced young man. Similarly, *The Entertainer,* far from advocating reform, expresses a good deal of sympathy for Archie Rice's shoddy and impotent Britannia. At the end of the play Archie and his family are offered a chance to make a new start in the hotel business in Canada. But Archie is too much a part of England ever to leave, a feeling he can only express in tired clichés or in deliberately trivial statements like "one can't get draught Bass in Canada." It is left to his daughter Jean, the clear-sighted commentator throughout the entire play, to make the final statement showing why England cannot desert itself:

> Here we are, we're alone in the universe, there's no God, it just seems that it all began by something as simple as sunlight striking on a piece of rock. And here we are. We've only got ourselves. Somehow, we've just got to make a go of it. *We've only ourselves.*
>
> [P. 85.]

Another Osborne play, *Epitaph for George Dillon* (1958; this play was written some years earlier in collaboration with Anthony Creighton), also displays a good deal of sympathy for the English life it satirizes. A young man, George Dillon, who wishes to write great plays, is taken in by a lower middle-class family. Ungrateful, George thinks of the family as a series of caricatures, a group of people who speak only in terms of accounts and fads and the latest programs on television. Yet, dull and commonplace as these people are, George takes advantage of them. He sponges money and food, seduces their silly daughter, plays upon the mother's feeling for their son who was killed in the war. Finally, having been unable to finish his great work of art, George sells out. He begins to write trash to formula for weekly repertory theaters and makes a good deal of money. The family, insensitive to his artistic betrayal, are delighted that all their notions of an artist and a gentleman have been so grandly reinforced. Yet George's success and the fact that the daughter of the house has become pregnant force George into marrying the girl and becoming a permanent part of the family. The artist, sullied by the material world, is locked together with the dull and the commonplace. Osborne's sympathy is about equally divided between the two. Respectable members of the lower middle class, people who have always paid their own way, are saddled with a dishonest parasite they can only dimly see through; the artist is squelched by the unimaginative life around him. So people work themselves into relationships that are essentially alien to what they feel.

In some contemporary drama, the relationships and the structures man builds for himself do not provide satisfactory sanctuary for human emotions and impulses. Archie Rice's music-hall England breaks down, leaving him a trivial and defeated man. And George Dillon, now part of the Elliot family of caricatures, has no longer any room to express the genuine artistic impulses he began with. Yet other contemporary plays leave a wider area for affirmative human communication. Bernard Kops, for example, has written two fantasies that affirm the importance and the value of human existence. His first, *The Hamlet of Stepney Green* (1958), applies the Hamlet legend to the family of Sam Levy, a pickled-herring seller who lives in Stepney Green. The Hamlet legend is reversed, for the ghost of Sam Levy, after his death, does not want his son to avenge his killing: "Oh, well— listen—even if I was killed, I don't want revenge for that, whether I was poisoned, gassed, burned, or struck by lightning. I want revenge for the way I lived—for the self-deception, the petty lies and silly quarrels" (p. 130). Levy/Hamlet's father's ghost rejoices in the marriage of Solly Segal/Claudius to Bessie /Gertrude, enjoys his ghostlike travels around the historical London that he never had the chance to see during his lifetime, and persuades his son to marry the local Ophelia. Although the play is incidentally full of topical satire directed against contemporary commerce, the reversal of the Hamlet legend carries the major theme. The ghost is finally liberated because his descendants have discovered how to enjoy and value life, an enjoyment that Sam Levy/Hamlet's father never recognized while he lived. Another play by Kops, *The Dream of Peter Mann* (1960), is also dependent on a fantastic structure. The play begins in a London market place, but Peter Mann's dream changes the market place into a shroud factory with a huge concrete shelter from atomic weapons, and the people in the dream become savages who would kill any outsider. The dream is the result of Peter's desire to escape the market place and make a great deal of money prospecting for uranium. But, when he awakens from this nightmare, he recognizes the value and the vitality of the market place itself. He also finds his true love (in the dream, he had thought he loved an unresponsive phantom of a girl). At the end Peter recognizes that one must both live and find pleasure and emotional meaning within his own environment. Kops does not, however, sentimentalize the people who run the market stalls, for even at the end most of them are still primarily concerned with chasing the phantoms of wealth and power, the phantoms that led Peter into his dream in the first place. This play, like *The Hamlet of Stepney Green*, is full of songs and chants, and embroiders the fantasy with touches of British musical comedy. And although both plays contain satirical comments on current society (many of the songs, for example, parody little materialistic clichés like "I've got to make a living" or "Money is time and time is money"), the fantasy that directs attention toward the value, no matter how limited, of life is the center of the play. These plays seem to show some influence of Ibsen's work, but it is the Ibsen of *Peer Gynt* rather than the Ibsen who carefully probed sociological problems current in his society. The fantasy is the dramatic vehicle, similar to other nonfantastic vehicles in the work of Wesker, Osborne, and Shelagh Delaney, by which the dramatist communicates his affirmations to his audience.

The theme of communication is directly relevant to the work of Harold Pinter. In *The Caretaker* (1960), an old tramp lives with two strange brothers in a broken-down room in an old London slum. The three characters rarely connect with one another, in a manner somewhat reminiscent of Beckett's *Waiting for Godot;* they hold conversations as disjointed and incoherent as are the various impediments, a gas stove that isn't connected, a toaster that doesn't work, odd blankets and shoes and wooden planks that clutter the room itself. Each of the three characters is locked in his own world, surrounded by his own impediments, and finds a great deal of difficulty in breaking through to any other. The old tramp must turn sycophant, play each brother off against the other, in order to try to keep a roof, however leaky, over his head. One brother had to have a lobotomy, a deliberate paring down of his mind and emotions, in order to be able to accept the fragmentary and incoherent world he found around him. He is now content to talk of working with his hands, of decorating, of building a shed, but he never completes any of the projects he so constantly talks about. The other brother, who owns the run-down house, keeps talking of his ambitious plans as an entrepreneur, but he never does anything either. All three are locked together in mutual frustration and impotence. Nothing they say is really meaningful or important, as even the Electrolux does not produce any order or coherence in the room. Yet something of the private world of each does get across to the others by the end of the play; a few little bits and pieces seem more meaningful than others in the midst of the fragmentation of the whole dramatic world. The old tramp finally asserts his desperate need for a place to stay.

In another play by Pinter, *The Dumb Waiter* (1960), two thugs are waiting in a basement, cut off from the rest of the world, for orders concerning the next killing they're to commit. In the boredom of waiting one repeats all the isolated facts in a newspaper he's reading, while the other reminisces about football games and happy crowds. No conversation ever really takes place between the two; in fact, at times they simply go through a verbal routine of question and answer without meaning. But characters in Pinter's work, unlike those in Beckett's, are never really completely isolated from the world around them. The basement contains a dumb-waiter leading up to an abandoned restaurant. After the thugs discover it, they receive requests for various dishes and send back the few cakes or chocolate bars they happen to have. Communication exists in a way, but it is misunderstanding, useless and impotent. The dumb-waiter shuttles back and forth on ropes that cannot accurately connect request and reply. In the same way, as the thugs wait for an order to beat up someone else, one of the thugs is himself beaten up. The lines that should connect things within the world are somehow crossed. In both plays the fragmentary details, the bits and pieces, are details from lower-class London life. Yet, as in the work of other contemporary playwrights, the kind of detail is far less significant than is the lack of communication the details illustrate.

Few contemporary British dramatists limit communication so thoroughly and severely as Pinter does. The impact of Ronnie on Beatie Bryant in *Roots,* the kind of emotional force in a relationship with a woman that Jimmy Porter is capable of, the relationship between the father's ghost and the son in *The Hamlet of Stepney Green,* all indicate forcefully that a limited amount of meaningful communication between human beings is possible. The time, the place, the sociological environment often help to define the limitation, but the communication, something genuinely human in all times and places, makes these plays active and significant theatrical experiences. Kenneth Tynan, the drama critic who has so frequently praised the work of Osborne, Wesker, Shelagh Delaney, and others, made the point in connec-

tion with a new French play, *Tchin-Tchin*, by François Billet-
doux:

> The curtain falls on a note of true, hard-earned optimism, which
> I prefer to the facile pessimism of so much Left Bank writing.
> . . . M. Billetdoux is in his early thirties, and has plenty of time
> to lure the younger French playwrights out of the blind alley
> into which the Messrs. Beckett and Ionesco have beguiled them.
> To assert that all communication between human beings is im-
> possible is rather like putting on a strait jacket and then complain-
> ing about the impossibility of shaking hands. If I understand him
> rightly, M. Billetdoux is saying that communication is desperate
> and rare, always difficult and seldom total; but possible, with
> whatever qualifications; possible, all the same.
>
> [*The New Yorker*, Aug. 1, 1959.]

This passage might serve, in varying degrees, for all contemporary British playwrights. Although communication in the
plays of Harold Pinter is far more rare and difficult that in the
plays of Arnold Wesker, it is still sometimes possible; and, fur-
thermore, individual and limited communication is the only
thing worth having.

The theme of communication—its limitations and its importance—is a constant human problem. But contemporary British
dramatists have given the problem new force and strength, new
terms. The use of Jewish culture in the work of Wesker and
Kops, Osborne's use of the English music-hall tradition, the
details spelling out the attitudes of the lower classes in the work
of Shelagh Delaney, Pinter, Osborne, and Wesker, are all new
terms for the British theater. The terms themselves do not form
the centers of the plays; these plays are not simply interesting
sociological reports. But the newness and the sharpness of the
terms do give the plays a sense of force and immediacy. In addition, the playwrights avoid the familiar terms of the recent
past in the British theater, the genteel reticence of the Mayfair
set, because the familiar terms, by their very familiarity, may
block the vital communication the playwright wants to achieve.

A storming Jimmy Porter or a politically and personally baffled Ronnie Kahn may, by his theatrical uniqueness, illustrate a human intensity which a more traditionally conceived character might fail to do. The play, an art form more immediate and more emotional than the novel, requires sharply incisive illustrative terms. The play also has less time than the novel to define issues cautiously, to shade qualifications, to deliver discursive essays. Given the limitation of time and the necessity for immediate emotional contact with an audience, the play needs the energy and the excitement of new terms, terms not saddled with the vague preconceptions that accrue with constant repetition. But the presentation of the terms, fascinating as they are, cannot be regarded as the playwright's final aim. Through the terms of the lower-class intellectual or the adolescent girl from Manchester or the London tramp, each of these writers is dealing with the perplexities of the human being, the creature not strong enough to stand alone and stronger than he needs to be to follow mindlessly whatever mass rampage he sees around him. The individual needs to find out what he is and where or how he can connect with what is going on about him.

5

Doris Lessing's
Intense Commitment

AMONG YOUNG CONTEMPORARY ENGLISH WRITERS, Doris Lessing is the most intensely committed to active persuasion to reform society. In a series of loosely connected essays, entitled *Going Home* (1957), published after she had returned to her early home in British colonial Africa for a visit, Miss Lessing frequently advocates direct participation in political action. She talks of the "sense of duty" that makes her join organizations, defends (on biographical rather than ultimate grounds) her own support of communism, and ends her essays by unfurling a qualified banner:

> In this book I have made various statements about the possibility of Communism becoming democratic. Since writing it the Soviet intervention in Hungary has occurred. It is hard to make adequate political assessments on notes added hastily to galley proofs as a book goes to press. But it seems to me that during the last three years the great words liberty, freedom and truth have again become banners for men to fight under—in all the countries of the world. It seems to me wrong that so many people should be saddened and discouraged by this sudden violent crisis we are all living through: it is a crisis in the battle of truth against lies, of

honesty against corruption, of respect for the goodness of people
against cynicism.   [Pp. 252–253.]

Miss Lessing's interest in the battle permeates most of her short
stories and novels. Frequently the theme of the work is whether
or not, despite a hostile or indifferent society, strong commitment to a particular cause or political doctrine is justifiable.

The issue of commitment is most tersely stated in Miss Lessing's
play, *Each His Own Wilderness* (first presented in 1958). The
play presents a violent conflict between mother and son. The
son, Tony Bolton, just discharged from the army, returns to his
mother's London home while she is preparing for one of her
frequent rallies to champion worthy causes. Tony, whose first
memory is the bomb that killed his father in World War II, is
skeptical about causes and rallies, bitter that so much of his
mother's energy has been given to Spain and Hungary and other
world problems. In one argument he rails at his mother: "You're
so delightfully old-fashioned. Getting killed for something you
believe in is surely a bit of a luxury these days? Something your
generation enjoyed. Now one just—gets killed" (p. 15). His
contemporary, Rosemary, talks of six big men somewhere who
could blow up the world any time they wished, a concept that
renders all protest against the H-bomb useless. Tony is no closer
to his mother on the subject of domestic politics:

> Why are you sitting there looking so tortured? You've got what
> you wanted, haven't you? Well? You've spent your life fighting
> for socialism. There it is, socialism. You said you wanted material
> progress for the masses. God knows there is *material* progress.
> Hundreds of millions of people progressing in leaps and bounds
> towards a materially-progressive heaven. . . . Do you know what
> it is you've created, you and your lot? What a vision it is! A house
> for every family. Just imagine—two hundred million families—
> or is it four hundred million families? To every family a front
> door. Behind every front door, a family. A house full of clean,
> well-fed people, and not one of them ever understands one word
> anybody else says. Everybody a kind of wilderness surrounded by
> barbed wire shouting across the defences into the other wilder-

nesses and never getting an answer back. That's socialism. I suppose it's progress. Why not? To every man his wife and two children and a chicken in the pot on Sundays. A beautiful picture—I'd die for it. To every man his front door and his front door key. To each his own wilderness.   [Pp. 50–51.]

The conflict between generations is not only political, for Tony, a highly Oedipal young man of twenty-two, becomes furious whenever his liberated mother mentions one of her love affairs. He shrieks that she lives "like a pig," yet he would rather live in her house than find a flat on his own. Similarly, the mother finds Tony a bore, a stupid "insufferable prig," yet she is willing to sell all her possessions to provide him with an allowance for self-discovery. The final exchange of the play summarizes both the political and the personal conflict, focuses on the issue of the sort of commitment a person ought to make. Tony's mother speaks first:

I'm nearly 50—and it's true there's nothing much to show for it. Except that I've never been afraid to take chances and make mistakes. I've never wanted security and safety and the walls of respectability—you damned little petty-bourgeois. My God, the irony of it—that *we* should have given birth to a generation of little office boys and clerks and . . . little people who count their pensions before they're out of school . . . little petty bourgeois.
                                                                   [P. 94.]

After his mother leaves, Tony turns to Rosemary to deliver the final lines of the play:

Rosemary, listen—never in the whole history of the world have people made a battle-cry out of being ordinary. Never. Supposing we all said to the politicians—we refuse to be heroic. We refuse to be brave. We are bored with all the noble gestures—what then, Rosemary? . . . Leave us alone, we'll say. Leave us alone to live. Just leave us alone.   [P. 95.]

Even though Tony is given the last speech, his point of view is not that of the author. Tony is made too childish, too petulant, to represent anything more than a contemporary phenomenon.

Rather, the play simply states, without resolving, different attitudes toward political and social commitment.

Some of Miss Lessing's novels, however, develop these issues a good deal further. The series of novels that deals with Martha Quest's growing-up (a sequence, as yet unfinished, which includes *Martha Quest*, 1952; *A Proper Marriage*, 1954; and *A Ripple from the Storm*, 1958) demonstrates a strong endorsement of the heroine who is anxious to change society, to work actively for a more humane and just world. Martha, the heroine, encounters difficulty in attempting, within the severely restrictive society of colonial Africa, to define herself both personally and politically. The books by Havelock Ellis she has read as an adolescent do not square with the attitudes toward sex she finds around her; the books about socialism and economics have little to do with the problem of the color bar she sees every day. Martha's books, her associations, her kind of perception, have all helped to make her very different from her mother, the representative of conventional colonial society.

The conflict between mother and daughter begins early, and, like the conflict between mother and son in *Each His Own Wilderness*, covers both political and sexual issues. Martha is disgusted with her mother's combination of purity and calculation about sex, her mother's Victorian propriety and constant assumptions concerning the laziness and the dishonesty of all African natives. Her mother, on the other hand, finds Martha blasphemous and immoral. But the two, like Tony and his mother, cannot simply ignore each other. Mrs. Quest, though continually rebuffed, keeps returning to her daughter, trying to help Martha and give her unwanted advice, as if the bitter quarrels had never occurred. And Martha, when seriously ill, wonders why her mother has never really loved her. Her emotional attachment to her mother is deeper than that to either of the two husbands she marries in unsuccessful attempts to discover herself.

Martha, in her quest for values, joins the Communist party early in World War II, but finds the party, with all its interminable bickering and its anxiety to remain a force within a hostile society, unable to do anything about colonial Africa's principal problem, the division between white and black. Yet, despite her many mistakes, Martha never retreats into the indifferent complacency or the assumption of eternal rightness which she sees all around her in colonial society. Martha searches for herself and battles for what she believes.

Julia Barr, the young heroine in *Retreat to Innocence* (1956), represents a more complex treatment of Miss Lessing's kind of commitment. In ways, Julia, who frequents espresso coffeehouses and wears black sweaters, is like Tony Bolton. Both are products of the new generation, born in the mid-'thirties to liberal and aristocratic parents, handed educations their mothers had to fight for, wanting only to find some personal meaning to hang on to. Julia, too, fights the parents she cannot break from and bitterly opposes what she calls her parents' "messiness" about politics and sex. Her desire for stability and her wish to disassociate herself from political issues seem priggish and selfish to her concerned father: "A more self-centred, selfish, materialistic generation has never been born into this unfortunate old country. All you want is to cultivate your own gardens. You really don't give a damn for anyone but yourselves, do you?" (p. 195). Julia, who offers less childish defenses for her attitudes than Tony Bolton does, feels that her parents' political concerns have kept them from understanding and appreciating human beings. She recalls that on a trip through Spain with her mother, after a peasant had mended a puncture in their tire and they had spent several hours talking with the peasant's family, all her mother could speak of was the need for "a sensible English town Council and a birth control centre."

Julia, unlike Tony Bolton, develops as the novel progresses. She falls in love with a Communist refugee writer, Jan Brod, a man more than twice her age, long since defined by political forces Julia can barely comprehend. Julia, the product of a wholly different time and place, cannot share Jan's deep involvement in politics. But this involvement, this overwhelming concern, gives him an energy, a force, an attraction that Julia cannot find in any of the agreeable and socially acceptable young men she knows. Julia argues with Jan about politics, and makes him acknowledge his awareness of all the purges and iniquities the Communists have created. Yet she can also understand and feel the emotional force of Jan's ultimate defense of the Communists:

> But don't you see, when people formed themselves together in the Party, for the first time in history, without God, without excuses, relying on themselves, saying: We accept the responsibility for what we do, we accept all the good and the evil of the past, we reject nothing—then for the first time in history man became free; he became free because he rejected nothing.
>
> [Pp. 228–229.]

Jan's defense stands as the affirmative battle cry in the novel. Jan himself, however, cannot remain in England, for the established hypocrisy will not grant him citizenship. Julia is not sufficiently converted to follow him back to central Europe, for the affair with Jan is part of her means of self-discovery. But she is able to realize that her shelter and comfort have something hollow about them and that in losing Jan she has lost more than she has gained. Julia, being herself, has no genuine alternative. Still, Miss Lessing makes it clear that Julia and her generation are lesser beings than their predecessors because they lack the energy and the purpose of a Jan Brod.

Miss Lessing's commitment usually involves opposition to the reigning precepts of English or Anglo-colonial society. Both Julia and Martha Quest, despite their different political attitudes, are enormously attracted to an aristocrat, a representation of the society's model. Martha is fascinated by Mr. Maynard, the magistrate who, although reactionary, maintains a steady and biting wisdom about Africa. Julia is strongly drawn to her father, that liberal, tolerant, stable representative of the basic English virtue of fair play. Yet, in both instances, the aristocrat betrays the faith placed in him. Mr. Maynard runs a vigilant spy service directed against radicals which belies his pose of sardonic intelligence; more directly, he lies about Martha's close friend in order to cover up his failure to persuade her to lose by abortion the child fathered by Maynard's dissolute son. Julia, too, is betrayed by her father, the benevolent liberal and patron of the arts, living on the income earned in the family business now managed by a "competent commercial person from the Midlands." Julia asks her father to help secure British citizenship for Jan. Her father promises but, after making a casual inquiry, refuses to push the matter further and retreats into the shell of upper-class complacency, sure that the government must know what it's doing, confident of the judgment of the British Home Office. Julia's father's liberalism is hollow, despite the appearance he gives of genuine concern. Even Tony Bolton's mother, who had seemed fine and elegant and truly solicitous of others, stupidly wounds another person and betrays Tony by selling their house, his symbol of security and permanence. The liberals, the people who apparently manifest concern about social and political problems without objecting to the fundamental society itself, and the aristocrats, those sustained and honored by the society, stand revealed holding shoddy or dishonest poses.

Yet many of Miss Lessing's heroines, disillusioned by their own societies, can find themselves through an older person denigrated by most of society. Martha Quest, for example, has her first affair with a Jewish orchestra leader much older than herself, who is patronized with sneers by most of her colonial friends. His very difference, the fact that he cannot be defined in terms of the society, is part of his attraction for Martha. Similarly, the young actress in "The Habit of Loving" (a story in a volume of the same title, published in 1957) marries a much older actor who cannot understand the contemporary quality of her lost-gamin routine, who believes the theater should contain violent, bombastic gestures. The young actress requires definition outside the world by which she has been conditioned. Julia Barr, too, in loving Jan, has reached outside the society established for her, embraced the alien and the unexpected. Women define themselves through the sexual relationship, and Julia, Martha, and others all demonstrate their partial or essential rejection of their own societies by affairs with the ineligible and the unexpected. And conversely, in Miss Lessing's fiction, the aristocrats and the halfhearted liberals, those endorsed by the society, are apt to be worth little as men.

Doris Lessing has consciously sought the socially rejected. When she moved to England in 1949, her sense of social responsibility and her distrust of those who sanction and are sanctioned by the reigning society led her to search for her values and for her literary material among the working classes in London. As she herself explains in a recently published documentary (*In Pursuit of the English*, 1960):

> I propose to admit, and voluntarily at that, that I have been thinking for some time of writing a piece called: In Pursuit of the Working-Class. My life has been spent in pursuit. So has everyone's, of course. I chase love and fame all the time. I have chased, off and on, and with much greater deviousness of approach, the working-class and the English. The pursuit of the working-class is shared by everyone with the faintest tint of social responsibility: some of the most indefatigable pursuers are working-class people.   [Pp. 12–13.]

But the pursuit, as Miss Lessing describes it in her documentary, did not uncover any unanimity of repressed nobility among the London proletariat. Miss Lessing reports her difficulties in finding a place to live, her encounters with sharp operators and grasping landlords among the working classes. A poor clerk, Rose, finally helps her get settled, and the landlords, Dan and Flo, invite her to vast spaghetti suppers and round up the furniture she needs. Still, the same landlords are cruel to an old couple in the house, whom they want to evict, and neglect their own young daughter so badly that authorities threaten to take the child to a state home. Some of the people Miss Lessing encounters do reinforce conventional ideas of a concerned and humane working class:

Two houses down on the opposite side lived an old man on the old-age pension, who was reading for the first time in his life. He was educating himself on the *Thinker's Library*. He had been a bricklayer, his wife was dead and he was now half-crazed with loneliness and the necessity to communicate what he had so slowly and belatedly learned. He lingered on the pavement at the time people were coming home from work, made a few routine remarks about the weather, and then whispered confidentially: "There's no God. We aren't anything but apes. They don't tell the working-man in case we get out of hand."   [P. 138.]

But few of the Londoners described would provide so fertile material for a potential uprising among the proletariat. In fact, most of them become capitalists themselves whenever they get the opportunity. Dan, the head of the household, first began to acquire extra cash in the war when he was personal servant to a surgeon commander and received tips for squiring the commander's mistress in and out of quarters. Right after the war he stripped washbasins and baths from bombed houses and sold them. With these two sources of income, he was able to buy and furnish the house he now owns. An enterprising capitalist, Dan has solid hopes of increasing his holdings and becoming a fairly wealthy landlord. Though able with his hands and skillful at remodeling furniture, Dan has no thought whatever of emulating William Morris.

Miss Lessing also shows the insularity of these people. They often hate the French and hate the Jews, and are aware of little outside their own corners of London:

Flo's London did not even include the West End, since she had left the restaurant in Holborn. It was the basement she lived in; the shops she was registered at; and the cinema five minutes' walk away. She had never been inside a picture gallery, a theatre or a concert hall. Flo would say: "Let's go to the River one fine afternoon and take Oar." She had not seen the Thames, she said, since before the war. Rose had never been on the other side of the river. Once, when I took my son on a trip by river bus, Rose played with the idea of coming too for a whole week. Finally she said:

"I don't think I'd like those parts, not really. I like what I'm used to. But you go and tell me about it after."

[*In Pursuit of the English*, p. 104.]

These people have little respect for British institutions and the justice of the law courts. In one of the funniest episodes in the book, the family goes to court to evict the old tenants from their house. In the antechamber their lawyer coaches them to lie consistently, to make a coherent case out of a long history of mutual grudges, cruelty, and complaints about dirty bathrooms. They win the case only because the old couple are even more incoherent and gratuitously foul-mouthed than they. But the point of the scene is that all the parties—the family, the old couple, the lawyer, even the judge himself—make the whole notion of the supposed fair play of British courts seem ludicrous. The people from the working class are simply less verbally skillful, less proficient in handling the forms, less sophisticated versions of their counterparts who compose the Establishment. No one is adequate to carry the banner for the revolution.

In portraying the working class, Miss Lessing often uses women to present the argument in favor of restricting one's activity to the comfortable, the sheltered, the safe. In the short novel called "The Other Woman" (one of a series of short novels published as *Five* in 1953), a young working-class girl chooses to break her engagement when her mother is killed by a lorry just before World War II. She decides to stay with her father in the basement they have always known, rejecting any outside influence. She chides her father for wasting his time at political meetings where nothing is ever accomplished, berates Parliament periodically, and lumps Hitler, Churchill, Attlee, Stalin, and Roosevelt together as people who make her sick. Her small security is blown up when her father is killed in a bombing in the war. She clings to the demolished basement as long as she can, until a kind young man almost carries her out by force. Once out of the basement, she can live with the man quite easily, clinging to that which is most readily available. She discovers that her young man has been married before, and his attentions soon begin to wander toward a third woman. The girl and the young man's first wife, accepting the male's infidelity without scenes or recriminations, finally agree to start a cakeshop in another basement and leave the young man to his newest mistress. The heroine does not search for romance or for passion; she simply accepts conditions around her and tries to work things out as safely and securely as she possibly can.

Rose, one of the central figures in *In Pursuit of the English*, is much the same kind of person. A hard life has taught her to fend for herself, to value her daily round, her drop of tea, her security. She, too, is skeptical about and indifferent to political parties or slogans. Her view of political personalities has little to do with the policies or the programs the personalities supposedly represent:

> Rose would listen to Churchill talk with a look of devotion I entirely misunderstood. She would emerge at the end of half an hour's fiery peroration with a dreamy and reminiscent smile, and say: "He makes me laugh. He's just a jealous fat man, I don't take any notice of him. Just like a girl he is, saying to a friend: No dear, you don't look nice in that dress, and the next thing is, he's wearing it himself."
>
> "Then why do you listen to him?"
>
> "Why should I care? He makes me remember the war, for one thing. I don't care what he says about Labour. I don't care who gets in, I'll get a smack in the eye either way. When they come in saying Vote for Me, Vote for Me, I just laugh. But I like to hear Churchill speak, with his dirty V-Sign and everything, he enjoys himself, say what you like."   [P. 121.]

Rose also objects to the false film versions of the Cockney and to any kind of slogan concerning brotherhood. Yet she sentimentally misses the warmth and the comradeship of the war when the usual class barriers were down and people all felt closer to one another. Rose's attitude toward politics, like that of the heroine in "The Other Woman," is handled somewhat sympathetically because she's had a hard life, she's a woman, and she's a member of the working class. Because of these, Miss Lessing can make Rose's insistence on her own narrow world and her rejection of all political questions both faintly comic and sympathetic.

People without Rose's warrant who still hold the same attitudes receive much more biting treatment. The younger generation has had a much easier time, and their choice in favor of limiting experience to the secure is made much more selfish and materialistic. In *Retreat to Innocence*, Julia is frequently labeled as selfish, and the young Cockney lad who tends the coffee bar is made to say:

> My old man, he was a proper old Bolshie he was. I don't hold it against him, mind. They had it tough when he was young. And he was on to me when I was a nipper, giving me the *Herald* and all that. I've been raised on William Morris and Keir Hardie and all that lot. And I wouldn't say a word against them—grand old boys they were. But I says to my dad, I says, what's in it for me?
>
> [P. 111.]

Yet Miss Lessing treats the middle-class woman of limited and nonpolitical interests with even more sharpness. Working-class people have, at least, the excuse of a certain amount of economic and educational deprivation. But the middle classes often receive no sympathy whatsoever. A middle-class couple spending a holiday abroad appear in "Pleasure" (another story in the volume called *The Habit of Loving*). The young couple are interested only in spear fishing, in impressing their neighbors with the fact that they've been abroad, in justifying everything English to themselves and to anyone else they happen to meet. Not a shred of sympathy enters the one-dimensional characterization of the empty couple in "Pleasure," and the woman seems singled out to bear the brunt of Miss Lessing's disapproval. This commonplace middle-class woman is treated with a fierce contempt, an attitude far more shrill than any leveled against stupid, materialistic Cockneys or patronizing and deceptive aristocrats or those nasty, bigoted, lonely colonial women on farming out-posts in Africa.

Miss Lessing's commitment to a sense of social responsibility and to a pursuit of those oppressed by society also infuses her fiction about colonial Africa, where she spent most of her first thirty years. In Africa the pursuit centers on the color bar, and, in all Miss Lessing's fiction dealing with Africa—her first novel, *The Grass Is Singing* (1950); the three novels dealing with Martha Quest; a volume of short stories called *This Was the Old Chief's Country* (1951); and four of the short novels collected as *Five*—the division between white and black is central. Often, in Miss Lessing's fiction, the white man is an inter-loper, attempting to wrest independence or security from the African soil or asserting himself in a colonial office established to govern the alien country. The white man carries his European culture and attitudes with him, preserves his religion and his heavy oak Victorian furniture, and brings up his children as he would in England. The child, from whose point of view the story "The Old Chief Mshlanga" is told, is living in British Africa:

> This child could not see a msasa tree, or the thorn, for what they were. Her books held tales of alien fairies, her rivers ran slow and peaceful, and she knew the shape of the leaves of an ash or an oak, the names of the little creatures that lived in English streams, when the words "the veld" meant strangeness, though she could remember nothing else.
>
> Because of this, for many years, it was the veld that seemed unreal; the sun was a foreign sun, and the wind spoke a strange language.   [*This Was the Old Chief's Country*, p. 8.]

In many of the stories the white settler's assertion of his inherited culture is, in this new land, his means of establishing his differ-ence from the black men all around him. Some of the white settlers, like Dick Turner in *The Grass Is Singing*, have been failures in English society and have come to Africa in order to reëstablish themselves; others, like the old farmer in "The De

Wets Come to Kloof Grange," are motivated by an urge to bring new land into cultivation.

Most of Miss Lessing's alien white settlers, and their more shrill and insistent wives, regard themselves as sensitive, aware, and reponsible, and look at the blacks as happy, amoral, and irresponsible. In one story in *This Was the Old Chief's Country*, a black woman is missing and the clues surrounding her disappearance point toward possible suicide. But the whites hesitate to endorse this supposition: "Later, we talked about the thing, saying how odd it was that natives should commit suicide; it seemed almost like an impertinence, as if they were claiming to have the same delicate feelings as ours" (p. 73). Farmers and businessmen grumble about the useless and ignorant blacks as regularly as they discuss the crops, the weather, or the prospects of business; the women complain that the household blacks are lazy, dishonest, fully deserving of the cuffs they get, and then wonder why the blacks are not more grateful for their civilized servants' jobs. In *The Grass Is Singing*, a successful neighboring farmer helps Dick Turner, for whom he has little love and less respect: "He was obeying the dictate of the first law of white South Africa, which is: 'Thou shalt not let your fellow whites sink lower than a certain point; because if you do, the nigger will see he is as good as you are'" (p. 221). Any kind of human relationship between white and black, within the strictures of this environment, is impossible.

The Grass Is Singing traces the horror that can result from a subterranean relationship between white and black within colonial African society. Mary, a thirtyish office worker in an African town, marries as her last chance Dick Turner, the inept and inefficient farmer. Gradually Mary shrivels in the midst of their futile battle to achieve security from the land. Only the Negro houseboy has the energy and the skill to force Mary's attraction, yet she, having always lived in Africa, is also repelled by the sight of him. She cannot bear to look him in the eye, fears even talking to him, while she unconsciously reveres his competence, strength, and grace. Mary would like to preserve her sanity by discharging the boy, but she has been unable to handle servants before and her husband insists that she keep this one. The conflict within Mary, the alternating love and hate toward the Negro, the frightening awareness that she possesses the one emotion her society most violently condemns, leads to her murder. She is destroyed by her inability to reconcile a human emotion with her own deep commitment to the rigid line her society maintains between white and black.

Like Mary Turner, many of the colonials feel a deep fear, a constant emotional apprehension about living in Africa. They are aware that they are interlopers, white aliens in a black world. The little girl in "The Old Chief Mshlanga" fears the isolation of her whiteness as she walks through the brush to the native village. Her wealthy father can force the natives to move, but he cannot control the mounds of mud, the rotting thatch, the tangled growth of pumpkins, and the hordes of white ants which the natives leave behind them. And the girl is frightened. Most often it is the woman, like the poor farmer's wife in "The Second Hut," or the wealthy farmer's wife in "The De Wets Come to Kloof Grange," who feels this fear, this inability of the white man to control the black, lush growth around him, yet men, too, sometimes have these moments of perception. The able farmer in "'Leopard' George," a man who has never married because he thought himself in perfect control over his native mistresses, is surprised when a young, hitherto discreet mistress embarrasses him in front of white guests:

> In that moment, while he stood following the direction of his servant's eyes with his own, a change took place in him; he was gazing at a towering tumbling heap of boulders that stood sharp and black against a high fresh blue, the young blue of an African morning, and it was as if that familiar and loved shaped moved back from him, reared menacingly like an animal and admitted danger—a sharp danger, capable of striking from a dark place that was a place of fear. Fear moved in George; it was something he had not before known.
>
> [*This Was the Old Chief's Country*, p. 209.]

The apprehension that the sensitive white feels in Africa is the mark of his failure to impose himself and his standards completely on the dark, fertile continent he inhabits. The fear is also, simultaneously, the sign of his own awareness in contrast to his denser, more complacent fellow colonials. Martha Quest, the perceptive heroine of *A Proper Marriage*, who has made a bad, hasty first marriage with a young colonial, uses the black of the native as the image of her own awareness:

> There were moments that she felt she was strenuously held together by nothing more than an act of will. She was beginning to feel that this view of herself was an offence against what was deepest and most real in her. And again she thought of the simple women of the country, who might be women in peace, according to their instincts, without being made to think and disintegrate themselves into fragments. During those first few weeks of her marriage Martha was always accompanied by that other black woman, like an invisible sister, simpler and wiser than herself; for no matter how much she reminded herself of statistics and progress, she envied her from the bottom of her heart.   [P. 85.]

For Miss Lessing, the recognition of the black's simplicity and value is the admission of the white settler's failure to civilize Africa.

Not all the white settlers are identical in Miss Lessing's fiction. As in her work dealing with the English, her fiction about Africa frequently relies on a conflict of attitudes between different generations. In *Going Home*, Miss Lessing praises the motives of the older generation of white colonials:

> It seems to me that this story of the man who preferred to die alone rather than return to the cities of his own people expresses what is best in the older type of white men who have come to Africa. He did not come to take what he could get from the country. This man loved Africa for its own sake, and for what is best in it: its emptiness, its promise. It is still uncreated.
>
> [Pp. 14-15.]

Newer settlers, in contrast, are likely to be more dedicated to hard cash or to redeeming previous failures. The comparison between generations is not, however, always so one-sided. In "The De Wets Come to Kloof Grange," the older generation may have established a more comfortable and peaceful settlement, but the younger generation is more willing to try to meet Africa on its own grounds, to swim in its streams and talk to its natives. In another story, "Old John's Place," the newer generation is rootless, an example of those who use Africa to find a security they have been unable to find in Europe. Yet in this story the older community, dogmatic, sure of itself and its moral standards, can find neither room nor sympathy for the new, more morally flexible immigration. In a few isolated instances the new generation can even, personally and temporarily, break down the color bar. In "The Antheap," one of the short novels in *Five*, a white boy and a black boy, born on the same farm, manage to remain close friends despite the older generation's constant attempts to remind each that he owes allegiance only to his own color. The two boys finally win and go off to the university together. Martha Quest herself, brought up in Africa, tries to break through the color bar, an aim that appalls her parents. But Martha does not represent the majority of her generation. Her contemporaries rebel against their parents, but in a very different way. They build a club,

> and inside it, nothing could happen, nothing threatened, for some tacit law made it impossible to discuss politics here, and Europe was a long way off. In fact, it might be said that this club had come into existence, simply as a protest against everything Europe stood for. There were no divisions here, no barriers, or at least none that could be put into words; the most junior clerk from the railways, the youngest typist, were on Christian-name terms with their bosses, and mingled easily with the sons of Cabinet ministers; the harshest adjective in use was "toffee-nosed," which meant snobbish, or exclusive; and even the black waiters who served them were likely to find themselves clapped across the

shoulders by an intoxicated wolf at the end of the dance: "Good old Tickey," or "There's a good chap, Shilling," and perhaps even their impassive, sardonic faces might relax in an unwilling smile, under pressure from this irresistible flood of universal goodwill.

[*Martha Quest*, pp. 183–184.]

But clapping the waiters on the back is only part of the story. At a later party some of these drunken colonials try to force a Negro waiter to perform a "war dance," making rather malicious sport of him. Their parents engage in a different sort of cruelty, a more tight-lipped and morally defended white superiority. The younger generation never bothers to defend white superiority; the young club members simply, and casually, assume it.

Miss Lessing's African fiction, like her other fiction, often shows her scorn for the halfhearted liberal, the aristocratic do-gooder who does not really commit himself to the downtrodden. The newly arrived colonial woman in "A Home for the Highland Cattle" (one of the short novels in *Five*) is anxious to treat her native houseboy with justice and humanity. She is even willing to steal her landlady's huge picture of prize highland cattle so that the houseboy can legitimize his mistress by buying her as a wife. The white woman tries to understand the way black society operates, and the boy genuinely appreciates her efforts, but still, at the end of the story, the white woman, now no longer living in the rented flat, fails to recognize her former houseboy as she watches the police marching him off to jail. She is too busy buying a table for her new house, although her gifts have led to his prison sentence. In "Little Tembi," a white woman's special fondness for a black boy whose life she once saved turns the boy into a wheedling thief. The boy is unable to accept his position in the black society and yet he is not, despite the special favors, allowed full equality with the whites. His ambivalent position destroys him, while the kindhearted white woman sits by wondering what has happened. Both these women ultimately betray those they tried to help. But Miss Lessing strongly endorses those more systematically committed to working for the socially oppressed. In "Hunger" (another of the short novels in *Five*), a young Negro leaves his native village for the jobs and the lights of the large city. He is sent to some Communist whites who try to help him. But he neglects their advice; he lies, steals, falls in with prostitutes and professional thieves, and is finally carted off to jail for trying to rob the Communists' home. Yet the Communists stick with him and send him a letter, telling him so. From prison, the Negro returns the following message:

> Tell him I have read it with all my understanding, and that I thank him and will do what he says and he may trust me. Tell him I am no longer a child, but a man, and that his judgement is just, and it is right I should be punished.   [P. 364.]

The attempts of the person fully committed are apt to have impact and meaning.

Not all Miss Lessing's Communists are similarly effective. In *A Ripple from the Storm,* the third novel in the series dealing with Martha Quest, Martha's Communists, whose interminable debates take up about half the novel, are severely split over whether to follow their sympathies and fight the color bar or attempt to gain acceptance among the white population. What should be the crucial question for African reformers is abandoned as the party attempts to work its way into colonial society. The Communists' failure here is an example of the way history operates: the forces of time and place prevented the Communists from reconciling their beliefs with their possibilities. The same doctrine, carrying for Miss Lessing the same intrinsic worth, might well have succeeded somewhere else, at some other time, under different circumstances.

Miss Lessing maintains a consistent interest in time and place. Both the use of the social class as a significant part of the identity of the individual, and the fact that conflicts are so frequently depicted as conflicts between generations, between the products of one time and another, indicate Miss Lessing's addiction to historical categories. Frequent parenthetical historical references fill all the fiction. An attitude stemming from the 'twenties or from World War I is accurately pinned down and labeled. Martha Quest is characterized in terms of details relevant to her time and place; she categorizes herself, and is categorized by others, as a socialist and an atheist, labels that stick with her throughout the novels. Early in the first novel, *Martha Quest*, Miss Lessing fixes Martha:

> She was adolescent, and therefore bound to be unhappy; British, and therefore uneasy and defensive; in the fourth decade of the twentieth century, and therefore inescapably beset with problems of race and class; female, and obliged to repudiate the shackled women of the past.   [P. 20.]

Similarly, early in *Retreat to Innocence*, Julia is fixed as a young London girl of 1955 in terms of black sweaters, frequent attendance at espresso coffee bars, and constant objection to the "phony." Minor characters are also defined by time and place, often in an introductory biography that leaves little for the character to do or say once he appears on the scene. Willi, the haunted revolutionary in *Retreat to Innocence*, is fully explained as soon as he momentarily appears. The case history of Miss Privet's career as a prostitute is documented in *In Pursuit of the English* to an extent hardly merited by a minor character. This extensive detailing of character detracts from Miss Lessing's effectiveness in two ways: it sometimes breaks the fiction into a series of journalistic essays or case histories, and it limits the author to the view that all people are almost completely conditioned by time and place, by historical environment.

The historically conditioned character sometimes suggests the cause of an aesthetic shortcoming in Miss Lessing's novels. (The short stories, on the other hand, emphasizing a single relationship, a single conditioning, or the impact of a particular commitment, are often much more effective.) For example, *The Grass Is Singing*, the novel concerning Mary Turner's destruction, begins and ends with an account of Tony Marston, a young Englishman with the usual progressive ideas who has just come to Africa and finds his first job on the Turner farm. Tony serves a valid

function in the plot, for he stumbles on a scene in which the
Negro is dressing a strangely transfixed and hypnotized Mary.
Mary cannot bear the white discovery of her fascination with
the Negro, and this incident precipitates her destruction. Yet
Tony himself reacts exactly as a young Englishman with vaguely
progressive ideas, the product of his place and generation, might
be expected to react: he falls right in with all the usual white
clichés, sanctioned by the wisdom of experience, about main-
taining the color bar. What might have been a device to extend
the point of view, to provide additional insight toward the
events of the novel, turns instead, because of the interest in
fixing Tony, into the dullness of another case history. Historical
accuracy, in this novel, cuts off a possible dimension of human
perception.

Frequently, Miss Lessing's journalistic essays do not deal with
specific characters but rather furnish sociological descriptions
of what it was like to be in a specific place at a specific time.
The Martha Quest series is full of such descriptions: the African
legal office in the 'thirties; the change in the colonials' club at
the beginning of World War II; the coming of British airmen to
African bases, and the difference this creates in the town; the
Communists' trying to sell their paper in the native quarter; the
predictable seediness and irrelevance of the Left Book Club's
meeting. A few of the short stories are entirely dependent upon
this kind of sociological description. "The Eye of God in Paradise" (a story in *The Habit of Loving*) is an illustration, seen
from the point of view of a pair of British doctors, of the
various forms and echoes of Nazism still evident in Germany in
1951. Some of the sociological essays in *Going Home*, like the one
defending the character of the Afrikander or the one pointing
out that the Union of South Africa is no more discriminatory
and at least more honest than is the British government of
Southern Rhodesia, are both intelligent and unconventional. But
essays are one thing and fiction is another. Too often Miss Lessing's fiction is dissolved in a long sociological or journalistic
insertion, like the accounts of communistic tactics and wrangles
in *A Ripple from the Storm* or the long, dull, clinical study of

discovering that one is pregnant which takes up about seventy pages of *A Proper Marriage*. Her politics are one-sided, her characters are limited in conception, and her world revolves in a simple pattern.

The same flaw is evident in the first novel of another young author. Margot Heinemann, in *The Adventurers* (1960), carefully documents a good deal of history concerning the Welsh miners after World War II. Much of the sociological description carries enormous interest, but the character become simply sociological representations: the young miner's son who rises as a journalist and betrays his old tribal loyalties; the young miner, for whom force of character takes the place of education, who remains loyal to his fellows; the upper-class sympathizers who stick to a Communist ideal that is no longer relevant to conditions among the working class. All these characters are completely determined by the forces that have molded them, completely predictable once the background has been established. Then, the course set, the novel simply reports, with journalistic accuracy, what the conference or the strike or the industrial campaign was like. Miss Heinemann's novel, like some of Miss Lessing's, is not only rooted in the social scene but becomes, completely and merely, the reflection of that scene.

Doris Lessing's intense feeling of political and social responsibility is carefully worked into specific historical situations. But the positive convictions can become heavy-handed, and the specific situations journalistic, while the strict allegiance to time and place can limit the range of perception about human beings. Miss Lessing's kind of intensity is simultaneously her greatest distinction and her principal defect. She produces an enormously lucid sociological journalism, honest and committed, but in much of her work she lacks a multiple awareness, a sense of comedy, a perception that parts of human experience cannot be categorized or precisely located, a human and intellectual depth. Intense commitment can cut off a whole dimension of human experience.

6

Education and the
Contemporary Class Structure

THE IDEA OF CLASS, THE DIVISIONS INTO WHICH MAN carves his society by means of background, geography, occupation, and money, has always received a great deal of attention in the English novel. Henry Fielding, in *Tom Jones,* established his hero as the natural man, the foundling, and confronted him with the rural worker, the country squire, the beginnings of an urban proletariat, and the London sophisticate. And, in the nineteenth century, novelists such as Dickens, George Eliot, and Trollope frequently dealt with class divisions and with the problems of attempting to move from one class to another. All these writers, in defining society in terms of class, worked on the assumption that man's social environment, to a large extent, conditions his attitudes and his responses to the world. They did not, however, rule out the possibility of the unique and individual hero, the man of insight or virtue that was not dependent upon time or place. At the same time, the terms of the social novel demanded that, for the majority of the people involved, time, place, family, and occupation both molded and explained the individual. Frequently, in nineteenth-century fiction, as in the work of Dickens, the hero, unique and individual, was set against a society in which all other forces were explained and categorized as rigid class forms. The hero represented virtue; the others represented vice or sterility or benevolent mindlessness. Yet class became, through the development of the novel, a convenient way of explaining the frequency with which social environment defines the individual.

If novels provide an accurate social history of the past two hundred years, the class structure in England has not been completely rigid. Individuals of energy and talent have always been able to consider moving from one social designation to another. The process of moving has not been either easy or always successful and the price of moving has, in one form or another, been high, but the possibility has existed. The serious writer, the intellectual, often emphasizes this possibility because he is interested in examining the society at its most complicated and ambivalent points. He tends to neglect the mass of men for whom class has usually been an accepted designation, even a support, in favor of the unique man for whom class is a problem or a perplexing issue. Thus the novelist has slightly falsified social history in exaggerating a fluidity about and a concern with a class structure that many people never consider.

In the twentieth century the class structure has become markedly more fluid and individuals have moved from one designation to another with somewhat greater ease and rapidity. A far larger literate public and a far greater opportunity for education have permitted many people to acquire both the necessary skill and the necessary interest to consider changing class identities. The radio, and more recently television, have publicized accents, once the distinct marks of class, so widely that the accent has become, for many people, the means of playful and dramatic pose rather than a single identifying mark. In addition, the overwhelming problems of British society, particularly since World War II, are not class problems, for the horrors of mass bombing and the common apprehension about nuclear warfare are not attitudes that can be organized or explained along conventional class lines. Man is, in the twentieth century, less sure that he can survive at all. And the social designation, in his voice or on his lapel, becomes a less meaningful definition for him. At the same time that the changing culture and the problems of a shrinking world have tended to make the class structure both less rigid and less relevant, other social and intellectual forces have made class issues an even more notable component of fiction. First of all, man, in the twentieth century, has less faith in himself and in the political or metaphysical systems he creates than he did during the eighteenth and nineteenth centuries. He is less sure of progress, virtue, God, and the independent uniqueness of his own soul. He is far more willing to acknowledge his own limitations, to recognize how little of himself is not dependent upon his parents, his social environment, his education, and his class. The nineteenth-century intellectual frequently asserted a heroic quality that was innate, though sometimes ineffable, as a primary human value and regarded society and class as restrictive barriers; the twentieth-century intellectual, on the other hand, often feels that the heroic and the unique are myths, while he regards society and class as forces that have had a great deal to do with what he has become. Class then becomes, for the contemporary writer, something to be treated, analyzed, dissected, worked with, rather than an image of the barrier the individual faces. Class is also, for the contemporary, more discussable, more controllable, than are statements about saving the world or the destiny of mankind. As we live in an age without world-wide political or metaphysical assurances, the intellectual frequently limits the range of his discussion, talks of the specific social problem because he can make more sense out of it than he can out of the problems of nuclear warfare or the existence of God. Class, for the contemporary intellectual, often serves as a limited and sensible substitute for far greater and more overwhelming issues, a limited topic through which he can express some perception and some control. In addition, the increasing fluidity of the class structure, and the increasing numbers of people changing or ignoring designations, have brought the problems of class more sharply under focus. As more sons of the working class leave the university, more of the stresses between origin and destination become apparent, significant, and material for the social novel or play.

The hero in a large part of contemporary literature illustrates these changing attitudes toward class. In the work of Amis, Wain, Philip Larkin, and others, the hero is frequently depicted at a point between two classes, between the lower or lower middle class of his origin and the higher class to which his education and his ability have brought him. These writers are not themselves children of the lower classes, but the contemporary writer, significantly, often places his hero in a social position lower than his own. This position creates the central problem of a man, conditioned by one environment, attempting to operate within the terms of another: Jimmy Porter, with his education and his elegant wife, running a sweet stall in a Midlands town; Jim Dixon, with his preference for beer and vulgar practical jokes, confronting the genteel university. Products of an age in which people can move between classes more easily, these heroes demonstrate both the comparative ease and the more intense strains of a rapidly changing society. The problem is not simply that of the Dickensian hero struggling to find himself within a higher society. The contemporary hero, like Jim Dixon, has had to struggle less and is considerably less the hero. No innate virtue or exceptional energy has fired him to make the unique attempt to break through social categories, nor is he nearly so willing as his nineteenth-century counterpart was to trade one class identity for another. Rather, the contemporary hero, the John Kemp or the Charles Lumley, is still in some ways part of the class he comes from, and is unwilling and unable to abandon all the attitudes of that class, particularly when he is not at all certain what he is abandoning them for.

Unlike the heroes in the work of Dickens or Fielding, the contemporary hero is not the rare spirit who is inexplicable in terms that account for the mundane majority, linked to the rest of us only as an image of what we would like to represent. The contemporary hero is rather himself the illustration of one of the central issues of the changing society. In earlier ages, when social values seemed more fixed, the writer could dwell on the energy and the exceptional quality of the hero, characterizing the society, in a somewhat peripheral manner, by the fixed alternatives the hero faced. But, in the middle of the twentieth century, the fixed alternatives seem far less fixed and the hero, neither exceptional nor exceptionally virtuous, is himself both a product and a problem of the society. Certainly the unheroic hero is not entirely a creation of the last decade, for earlier in the twentieth century writers like Arnold Bennett characterized a social world without heroism or any principle of virtue. Yet, in Britain, since the end of World War II, the unheroic figure has become the standard fictional representation of the age. Without a rigid class structure enabling him to display his virtue by romantic opposition, without even any publicly fixed definition of virtue at all, the would-be exceptional and heroic figure has become the fool, the man living in terms of an outmoded ideal or a hollow pretense.

Because, in contemporary fiction and drama, men are to a great extent products of the time and the place in which they were born and educated, writers spend a good deal of time outlining, describing, and accounting for time and place. In the work of Amis, Wain, Doris Lessing, and others, changing attitudes toward class and society are frequently illustrated by a conflict between generations. Parents are often used as examples of older and more rigid attitudes, firmer allegiances, in contrast to the more flexible social attitudes of the children. David Storey, another young novelist for whom class issues are centrally significant and whose work illustrates a fairly typical approach to the problems of class, also uses parents to demonstrate older social attitudes that no longer fit the facts of experience. In Storey's first novel, *This Sporting Life* (1960), the hero, Arthur Machin, a poor boy from the lower middle classes, attempts to work his way to money and dignity by playing professional Rugby in a northern city. As he plays Rugby, he acquires money, a mistress, flashy suits, and a high-powered Jaguar. His parents are quietly dismayed, for, although they had always taught him that money was a necessary means to all things worthwhile, they retain a class-bred distaste for any form of ostentatious living. As members of a certain class, they advocate an uneasy synthesis of materialism and gentility, a synthesis that Arthur, as he actually begins to earn money, finds impossible to work out. They do not see that they have helped to create this problem for Arthur; as good, poor, genteel, religious people, they are convinced that whatever happens to an individual is entirely his own responsibility. Storey's second novel, *Flight into Camden* (1960), deals more extensively with the problems of the older generation. The heroine, Margaret Thorpe, is the educated child of a hard-working miner. Although the miner has struggled to educate his children and firmly believes in education as the entree to a life better than the pits, he is upset when his children follow codes different from his own: his educated son, now a lecturer at a red-brick university, does not want to marry in church and argues against the importance of the family; his daughter Margaret moves to London to live with a married man. The father, physically ill because of Margaret's affair, blames it all on education, and fiercely regrets that he had ever educated his children. Ideally, he would have granted them an education on condition that, though it kept them away from the pits, the process would not have changed any of their social or moral attitudes. He wishes, over and over again, that his children had stuck with their class and had never learned the attitudes appropriate to other segments of society. Storey's depictions of parents serve as good examples, for there is nothing malicious or ill-intentioned about the parents in either novel. They simply preach vague values like "money" or "education" to their children, never realizing that the acquisition of real money or real education will lead to the means and the power to get away from the firmly held values of the lower middle class. John Kemp's parents, in Philip Larkin's *Jill*, are similarly unaware that education will ever produce a fundamental change in John's attitudes. They encourage John to try for a scholarship to Oxford, but, to them, working hard for a scholarship is exactly like working one's way up in a shop or a factory. Education is a magic word that will assure John's future.

Storey and Larkin are objecting, not to education itself, but to the aura of value which accrues about the term for people who have never experienced the fact. They are objecting, as other contemporary writers object, to vague ideals, vague aspirations, notions of something higher or finer that vaguely cling to certain terms for the older generation. The parents, in the works of both novelists, believe in slogans, remnants of another era in which the vague appeal might have had a stronger connection to the facts of experience than it does today. The younger generation, on the other hand, sees through the slogans and the vague ideals, attempts to deal with experience as directly and as individually as it possibly can. Education, in fact, acts to break down the vague ideal, to demonstrate the multiple facts of individual and social experience which cannot easily or accurately be summarized by a slogan or an ideal. To a great extent, education has helped to underline the conflict between the generations.

A recurring hero in contemporary fiction and drama is the young man whose education has helped to make him something different from his father. Recipients of university grants, the heroes in Amis, Wain, Osborne, Larkin, and others, have moved from their lower- or lower middle-class origins, through the university, and out into a society in which they have no clear function or class designation. Education has become both the instrument for helping to break down the class structure and the focal point of conflict between the old allegiances and the new skepticism. Dealing with the hero at the most difficult and bewildering point, many contemporary novels and plays focus on the student in the university or during the first few years after he leaves. Kingsley Amis' first two novels concern recent university graduates facing a society they could have known only dimly had they not studied on university grants; Philip Larkin's *Jill* takes place almost entirely at Oxford; John Wain's *Hurry On Down* is a statement of the possibilities open to a young graduate committed to nothing but a rejection of the society he knew before he entered the university. For all the central characters education is the instrument of the original separation from parents and from the attitudes parents represent, the necessary means for attempting to face society without preconception. Although the hero eventually finds that he is less free than he thought he was, his education has at least given him an illusion of freedom sufficient to initiate the action of the novel. In addition to this illusion of freedom, education provides learning, ease, and a pleasant holiday from the most rigid social and class commitments. But in most contemporary works it provides no convictions or attitudes that can be carried out into society. Rather, the university, by the very nature of the intellectual and critical examination it represents, works against the formation of simplified social convictions or vague and happy ideals.

Not only the boy with origins in the lower or lower middle classes finds that his attitudes change at the university. Peter Nicholas, the hero of Thomas Hinde's first novel, *Mr. Nicholas* (1952), is a fifth-generation Oxford student at home during the long vacation. Throughout the novel Peter is in conflict with his demanding and domineering father. Part of this is a simple conflict of wills between the authority of the father and the power of the emerging young man. But the generations are also defined in social terms. Peter's father, representative of his generation, feels that the young man home from Oxford should organize cricket matches, show allegiance to the local Conservative party, and entertain the proper people for tennis matches and cocktails before lunch. Peter would rather stay in his room and read or draw. He resists all his father's efforts to engage him in the accepted pastimes of their supposed class. Despite all his assurance, however, Peter's father is inept in trying to extricate a younger son from an attraction to an older, rather unsavory man. Mr. Nicholas storms and blunders, repeats, to no avail, all the manly and forthright slogans of his generation. The more he blusters the more psychotic he becomes until, at the end of the novel, he breaks his own rigid code and is then completely unable to handle any problem or relationship. Peter, on the other hand, less a part of a rigidly defined attitude, can better understand the facts of the experience he faces. The university has not given him a formula for operating within society, but it has enabled him to reject the simple formulas that no longer fit experience. Similarly, another of Thomas Hinde's heroes, the young man in *For the Good of the Company* (1961), discovers that his simple dedication to working hard, pleasing people, and assuming a sophisticated air does not ensure success in the vast corporation he works for. But this young man, Martin Mason, is not the product of a university; he is attempting to redeem his father's clouded career in the same firm his father once worked for.

As education so often breaks down belief in the sanctity of class and the sanctity of the ideal, many of the university graduates in contemporary British fiction are willing to investigate all levels of society. Like Jimmy Porter or like Charles Lumley in *Hurry On Down,* they examine the attitudes and the reactions of the urbanized working classes. This is not a kind of sentimental Orwellian disguise and immersion in the working classes. Rather, for most contemporary writers, the working classes are worth examination for their responses, without ideals, to a world they have found as perplexing and chaotic as the world the university graduate finds. Some contemporary writers, like Doris Lessing, seek a kind of political unity with the working classes. But for most contemporaries, whatever their own origin, the interest in the working classes is not political. Writers as different from one another in both origin and point of view as Osborne, Wain, Shelagh Delaney, Storey, and Keith Waterhouse have all examined the traditional attitudes of the working classes, not from any allegiance to them as such, but in an attempt to work out, for their heroes, the sanest and most effective way to survive in contemporary society.

Historically, most of the urbanized British working classes have not aspired toward the vague ideal of education or the even vaguer one of gentility, ideals that both the university and the history of the past fifty years have helped to puncture. The working classes have, on the whole, found it sufficiently difficult to maintain themselves without the additional burden of aspiring toward some unreachable ideal. As Richard Hoggart points out in *The Uses of Literacy* (1957), the working classes generally guard their own attitudes and their own positions jealously, and have a deep suspicion of civil servants or officials or people of higher economic or social status, "Them," a group totally distinct from "Us." Generations of economic inequity, followed by nearly ten years on the dole before World War II, have given the working classes a constant antipathy toward the rulers or the established people in society, an antipathy still fundamental despite the economic prosperity general in Britain since World War II. Automatically, almost instinctively, many members of the working classes feel antagonistic toward the police, toward the leaders of society, or toward any expression of political or governmental authority. Opposed to a society that he cannot conquer or defeat, the working-class man must often settle for preserving himself, keeping himself from knuckling under to the power of officials and civil servants. He views the world as a chaotic jungle, working for the benefit of those who already have money and position, and feels that the best he can do is preserve himself in the midst of the jungle. Arthur Machin, in *This Sporting Life*, essentially working-class despite his parents' hopes, plays Rugby primarily to retain his own identity:

> I was still kneeling, absorbed in an odd resigned feeling. My back teeth chattered as I pulled myself up, my hands shook with cold, and I despised myself for not feeling hate for the man who'd torn my nostril. I was used to everything now. Ten years of this, ten years of the crowd—I could make one mistake, one slight mistake only, and the whole tragedy of living, of being alive, would come into the crowd's throat and roar its pain like a maimed animal. The cry, the rage of the crowd echoed over and filled the valley—a shape came towards me in the gloom.   [P. 255.]

Arthur must subordinate the luxury of personal emotion to the problem of keeping his head above the mud. Alan Sillitoe, in *Saturday Night and Sunday Morning,* also feels that the working-class man must keep himself alive within the jungle without hope of reform or transformation.

In attempting to defend his own position while accepting the fact that he cannot change the world about him, the working-class man is seldom a patriot or a booster. He does not tend to support systems or talk about allegiances beyond those on a very direct and personal level. He is skeptical about the possibility of change, about political causes, about the efficacy of general ideas. He has little faith in the future, and feels, particularly in these days of comparative peace and prosperity, that he had best get what he can for himself while it lasts. Arthur Machin and his Rugby mates keep referring to this uncertainty about the future, to the necessity of getting and spending now because next year they might be at war, victims of radiation, or working in labor camps in Siberia. The feeling that so little comes under their control makes the working classes eager to do what they can while they have the power and the energy. Richard Hoggart maintains that they have always been like this:

> There are many thrifty working-class people today, as there have always been. But in general the immediate and present nature of working-class life puts a premium on the taking of pleasures now, discourages planning for some future goal, or in the light of some ideal. "Life is no bed of roses," they assume; but "tomorrow will take care of itself": on this side the working-classes have been cheerful existentialists for ages.
>
> [*The Uses of Literacy*, Pelican ed., p. 105.]

And, because no system or allegiance can assure the future, the working classes are apt to attribute a good deal to luck. Like Alan Sillitoe's hero who works on the capstan lathe, men are prone to conclude that pure chance has the largest share in determining what happens to a man or to a society. The man who feels he has little control is not likely to ascribe good fortune to his own virtue or make bad fortune his own responsibility.

The working-class man's lack of faith in the future, his insistence on preserving his own identity, and his refusal to trust governments or ideals are all essentially defensive measures in the midst of a society in which he has never had the upper hand. His ethos is frequently the preservation of a rear-guard action, stolid, tight-lipped, refusing to give up a morsel of identity or position. Society has, for so long, left the working class so few alternatives that, even in the midst of a more liberal or tolerant society, it holds itself to itself with intensity.

David Storey presents this defensive intensity brilliantly in both of his novels. He uses the working-class woman, apparently cold and sardonic, unable to demonstrate the love she feels, as an indication of the defensive intensity that permeates the working classes. Arthur Machin falls in love with a young working-class widow at whose grubby house he has rented a room. As he gathers in large checks from the Rugby club, he buys her clothes and a television set, takes her out to dinner in his elegant Jaguar. She becomes his mistress, but she never really yields to him, insisting coldly and rigidly on retaining her own shabby identity. The experience of having grown up in a class that expected nothing, added to the sudden and accidental death of her husband, has created such a sardonic shell that she is unable to show love. At one point, Arthur, now successful, berates her with the middle-class charge of ingratitude. But the working classes cannot allow gratitude for morsels to dissolve their position, and the woman, Mrs. Hammond, only retreats further and further into her defense. Arthur himself, despite his success, is often defensive. He knows he must conceal his feelings in order to play Rugby well, and he deliberately ignores his perceptions in relation to others in order not to be drawn too closely to them. Even Margaret, the supposedly liberated miner's daughter in *Flight into Camden,* has difficulty breaking sufficiently from her class-bred feelings of convention and guilt to respond fully to her lover. She feels that it is degrading to show strong feeling, but she finally does abandon home and parents to join her lover in London. Her lover constantly calls her a puritan, though her defensive self-discipline is not part of an adherence to any abstract code or ideal. She is simply enough the product of her home and her class so that she cannot easily break out of a rigid, defensive order. That her classless lover leaves her at the end of the novel, that he is the one who is ultimately unable to sustain the adulterous relationship, indicates that, in Storey's terms, Margaret has good reason for her defensive hesitation. She has been badly hurt by going outside the realm of her protective home, although her break has taught her a great deal. She can never simply adhere to or simply rebel against home and class again.

John Kemp's defense takes a different form in Larkin's *Jill*. Rejected by his cosmopolitan roommate at Oxford and unable to feel at ease among the casual students who crowd the pubs, he retreats into fantasy. He invents, at first for his roommate's benefit, a charming and precocious sister named Jill. The invention grows as John becomes more unhappy at Oxford, for he supplies his sister with a full diary, a small but elegant public school, and holidays in Wales. He fictionally gives his sister the upper middle-class background he has never had. Eventually the fantasy breaks down: its compensations are inadequate for John and he makes another, even more disastrously unsuccessful attempt to join his roommate's sophisticated circle by pursuing an actual girl named Jill. Yet the fantasy, for a time so dominant, provides the only moments of ease and comfort for the Lancashire boy at Oxford.

Fantasy is, however, a sign of creativity, a response to unhappiness possible for the writer or the incipient intellectual. It is not the usual defense of the member of the working class. He, unlike John Kemp, has neither the interest nor the leisure for fantasy, and keeps to his protection of himself, his assertion of his person, as his primary defense. The defense is often physical as well as personal. As Clancy Sigal points out in his book *Weekend in Dinlock* (1960), an account of two weekends the American author spent in a small mining community in the north of England, the miner's greatest pride is his physical ability to stick to the difficult job he loathes. Weaker workers, who stay above ground, feel humble and uncertain. Physical violence, under circumstances that do not allow the man to be labeled as a bully, is the indication of a man of power and talent, asserting himself in one of the few ways his society leaves open to him. Sigal's miners also follow no cause or creed or church, expect little from the government or the National Coal Board; the physical, in one form or another, is the only means for the individual to record his presence and his impact upon others. Margaret Thorpe, in *Flight into Camden*, also talks about the miner's extreme physicality. Partially ambivalent about class because she has been educated, she sometimes loathes the fact that her father responds physically to every emotion, throws up his food when he is upset, lashes out when he violently disagrees. She feels that his physicality destroys his dignity, yet she also understands that the man has no other way, no quickly fashioned phrases or learned arguments, in which to express his fierce resentment. The intensely personal, or even the crudely physical, becomes the ordinary means of expression for the working class. Adherence to the strictures of gentility would deny them any outlet whatsoever.

The heroes and the heroines of novels such as those by Storey and Larkin are frequently young people attempting to get beyond the simple class designation into which they were born. They begin by refusing to be limited by class or background, hoping to find a world with fewer fetters, fewer distinguishing marks. As educated people in the middle of the twentieth century, they are willing to start by ignoring their parents' sound precepts and trying to look at experience without preconception. Yet all of them, to some extent, carry the attitudes of the class they come from. Margaret Thorpe cannot look at a group of men without wondering who is a workman and who is not; John Kemp automatically notices the clothes of every young man at Oxford and is able to tell, in his mother's terms, whether the young man is like himself or not. Class is, for those people, a constant and unconscious point of view, a framework, whether they explicitly object to it or not, underneath all their perceptions. They become particularly self-conscious and aware of class whenever they attempt to engage in the larger society. Margaret is most keenly aware of her own origins when her brother takes her to a faculty reception at the university. Margaret's brother, despite his status as lecturer, never loses the identifying marks: he uses his work to make personal claims, as any workman does, and, according to Margaret's classless lover, he is both "extremely sentimental" and "incorrigibly hard" toward any discussion of class. Success, even success by middle-class standards, does not alleviate the defense of making an issue of oneself, of resolving things in terms of the personal, as Margaret's brother does throughout the novel. John Kemp, despite all his efforts to become as casual and as sophisticated as his roommate, is also unable to throw off his background. He is proud of his china and his neat filing system, and he can never adopt the casual habit of helping himself to the beer or the tea in another's room. His friend Whitbread, another poor scholar from the north, is even more insistent about his origin than John is. A hard-working drudge, Whitbread makes his background a point of pride, constantly claiming that it has taught him the virtues of hard work, of the careful accumulation of knowledge, and of Spartan living. Sometimes the new environment, even the university, doesn't seem to change the class-bred being at all.

In some situations, in the work of both Storey and Larkin, the insistence on lower-class identity seems petty and churlish. Characters cannot always govern their outlets or their defenses as gracefully as they might wish to. John rudely asks his roommate to return some borrowed money in the middle of a tea party, just as he is trying hardest to impress his roommate's elegant friends. Arthur Machin goes into a tirade at women smoking in the street, and one of his Rugby-playing friends, a man who has married into the middle classes, writhes whenever his wife mentions "mummy and daddy." Margaret's brother, the university lecturer, in a moment of anger, even asks Margaret to be careful of whom she is seen with because of his position at the university. On one hand, this behavior often seems trivial and boorish. Yet, on the other hand, in all these novels, the young person from the lower classes is often inexplicably rejected, made uncomfortable simply because of his background. John Kemp really is mistreated at Oxford, simultaneously snubbed and taken advantage of by his roommate and his roommate's friends. And when John, drunk, finally gets the courage to kiss the actual Jill (the cosmopolitan group has egged him on), he is cruelly thrown into the college fountain on a cold December night. Similarly, the wealthy people who own the football team that Arthur Machin plays for seem to toy with Arthur. They invite him to parties, lead him on, then withdraw their favor and their interest just when he has come to expect it. Triviality may sometimes become the only plausible defense for the young man operating in a new and insecure sphere.

In the work of David Storey, as in the work of numerous other contemporaries, the identification with class, trivial and difficult as it often is, emerges as a solid value. The heroes and the heroines do not completely return to the ways of their parents, for they have seen the modern world more clearly, but they do recognize that they cannot abandon what they've been born and brought up with. Arthur Machin recognizes the false glamour of the Rugby prestige and the Rugby pay check, and realizes that only Mrs. Hammond, thwarted, sardonic, bitterly a member of the lower classes, has really engaged his emotions. He can reject his parents' homely maxims and their theoretical praise of aspiration, but at the end he does revere his parents for having been able to formulate their lives with room for their personal emotional expressions. He has, in a roundabout way, subscribed to an old working-class value: the insistence on the importance of the personal emotion. Similarly, Margaret Thorpe, despite her puritanism and her various hesitations, remains faithful to her lover. The lover, on the other hand, an art teacher, always described as classless and rootless, is weak and undependable. He leaves Margaret, aware that he is not strong enough to create a life out of a personal allegiance. Storey suggests that his classlessness is his lack of strength. He has no defenses, no personal identity, so that he is forced to follow the simplest maxim of middle-class convention and return, without hope or meaning, to his wife. Like Storey, writers such as Alan Sillitoe and John

Wain assert values in terms that have been traditionally associated with the values of the working classes.

In the middle of the twentieth century, British writers have come increasingly to recognize the applicability of traditional working-class attitudes. The skepticism about authority and leadership, the sense that man controls so little of his destiny, and the realization that what man can achieve is limited and personal have all been strongly reinforced by the history of the last fifty years. The sensitive and concerned man has turned toward values that are simultaneously defenses, attitudes that allow man to live without pretense or falsification in the midst of a chaotic world. The individual, particularly the British individual, who is in conflict with the reigning society around him can no longer dash off to conquer a new empire without heavy space suits, carefully controlled oxygen intake valves, and constant electronic communication with the master government back home. The individual must simply try to survive as best he can in the uncertain and unsatisfactory place where he began, as the working-class man has always had to do. At one point in *This Sporting Life*, Arthur Machin is thoroughly depressed with his Rugby, his mistress, and his new, elegant friends. He thinks of an American novel in which the hero, a detective called Stulton, similarly fed up, just gets into his car and drives across vast American miles and out of his problems. Arthur admires him:

> That touched me. I thought if only I could break things up like this Stulton, and get on to the next place and leave all these wrecks behind. I even tried driving out of town fast. But the roads were crammed. They twisted and ducked about. And I'd only go a couple of miles, hardly leaving town behind, before I was in the next bloody place. One town started where the other left off. There was no place to feel free. I was on a chain, and wherever I went I had to come back the same way.   [P. 192.]

The man from the working class has never had a car or the room to drive, and he has never had many alternatives; and now he has come to represent a much wider segment of society. At the same time, as class lines loosen, many more people of working-class origin have become literate and articulate, retaining many of the attitudes of their class. History, by shrinking the world, by destroying the efficacy of past virtues and moralities, and by making change from one class to another more easily possible, has helped to make working-class attitudes—the insistence on the personal and the physical, the skepticism about an established truth, the belief that survival is mostly a matter of luck—applicable to a much wider range of British society.

This process, this effect of time, education, and history, is detailed in Philip Larkin's second novel, *A Girl in Winter* (1947). Katherine Lind, presumably a German refugee in England during World War II, serves as the central point of view through which all the events are seen. She contrasts the idyllic summer of her prewar visit to England with the cold, grubby reality of her present stay. She now files books in a library in a grimy Midlands town. The contrast is pointed even more sharply in the character of Robin, the young son of the family that entertained her at their house in Oxfordshire. During the prewar visit Robin was polite and self-contained, carefully efficient, constantly organized, and thoroughly considerate. Even at sixteen or seventeen he seemed sure of his career in the Foreign Office and of the sequence of steps necessary to arrive there. He was the model boy of his class and generation, and Katherine often regretted not being able to get through his perfect ease and containment. When she meets him again in wartime, he has changed completely. Now in the army, he is no longer in control of his future and himself. That his career has been interrupted or destroyed is of secondary importance; more important is that all his assurance, his whole manner of meeting all problems with methodical efficiency, has been beaten down by historical forces far stronger than he. He reverts, defensively, to the individual and the immediate. He now wants only to sleep with Katherine for the night because only the simple and personal act means anything. And Katherine, who had fabricated uneasy and elaborate fantasies about her reunion with Robin, accepts his proposition. After her first disillusion with him, she, too, realizes that only the simple and temporary relationship between two people holds any meaning within the small, shrunken, chaotic world. World War II acts as the single catalytic force in *A Girl in Winter,* and it is, for many contemporary writers, the most significant event in causing the shift from assured attitudes to the uncertain values represented by a single night in bed. Yet the history of the past sixteen or seventeen years, dominated by the threat of nuclear warfare and mass genocide, has done nothing to reverse the attitudes represented by World War II.

The contemporary writer turns to the traditional values of the working class not to find a proletarian utopia nor to endorse some vague notions about improving conditions or the equality of all men. Primarily, the writer values the working class for its traditional responses within a society it cannot control, for learning to live within a limited compass. The problems of the working class have, in one sense, become the problems of many of the thoughtful men in the whole society: how to assert and defend oneself in the midst of chaos and indifference. The fool, in contemporary society, is the man who does not realize the limited extent of his power or control, the pretentious man who talks or acts as if the assurances from another time or another class were still intact. Often the man of pretense is made ridiculous, as Philip Larkin satirizes Anstey, the head librarian in *A Girl in Winter,* who gives constant unwanted advice on how to succeed in business by careful attention to routine details. Anstey, a sententious fool whose clichés are punctuated by bits of self-congratulation and smoke from the pipe he cannot keep lighted, is a forerunner of Amis' Professor Welch. Similarly, in *Jill,* Larkin makes fun of Whitbread, the poor and pompous scholar who keeps repeating his little maxims about study and hard work as the means of assuring a comfortable future. At the end of the novel John Kemp is so fed up with Whitbread's homilies that he sneaks into Whitbread's room one night to smear butter and jam all over his clothes. The men of pretense, the fools, cannot see that the world will not allow them the extended assurances they prate about, cannot acknowledge that they are carrying outmoded maxims into a newer, less certain world. And in a world in which genuine or malicious evil is vast, vague, beyond the boundary of individual hate or control, the repetition of sententious and inapplicable statements becomes the greatest crime. The foolish man, the man who doesn't realize that his inherited maxims about the rewards of virtue or the necessity of prudence no longer fit experience, is the frequent butt of contemporary novels.

In one way the contemporary writer is more limited than many of his predecessors have been, for often his experience leaves him little room for cosmic visions or grand moral syntheses. The contemporary English writer, like the member of the working classes, is apt to be suspicious of anything that sounds like an abstract ideal, an intangible or distant goal toward which the human being strives. The workingman's lack of faith in vast purposes or vague promises leads him to respect the practical rather than the abstract ideal. Clancy Sigal's miners in *Weekend in Dinlock* laugh scornfully at the miner who would leave the temporary security of the pits (even though they hate the pits themselves) to try to become a painter. Man's job, they feel, is to stick to what he knows, his pick, his town, his woman, instead of following some vague nonsense like art. Contemporary novelists, too, satirize those who glamorize art as some divine goddess; Amis, Wain, and Angus Wilson frequently attack the man who worships at the shrine of his allegiance to art as well as the man who worships his morality or his politics. Yet most contemporary writers would not restrict the practical or the sensible to the narrow definition the miners in Dinlock give it. Wain, Amis, and Wilson are neither anti-intellectual nor scornful of art. Rather, they demand that art deal with the tangible, that art shape, control, and direct the multiplicity of contemporary experience instead of chasing phantoms of trite visions from the past. They try to distinguish the genuine artist from the phony, and the genuine artist is the man who, exploring important contemporary attitudes and perceptions, gives direction and meaning to his work. For many writers a genuine representation of contemporary Britain requires the examination and inclusion of perspectives traditionally held by the working classes. This is not because working-class perspectives are necessarily accurate, for the Dinlock miners are more limited than any writer would choose to be; nor is it to glorify the working classes as innately more noble or finer than other classes. Rather, working-class perspectives need examination because they have, in the course of history, come to represent the reponses of a segment far larger than merely those who work with their shoulders and their backs.

As the rigid distinction between classes weakens and as more young men become better educated, the British intellectual is, in a significant way, more free to choose his attitudes from any class he likes. He feels that he need not follow his parents, his school, or the dictates of his occupation. Although he carries a good deal of his environment with him, his very acknowledgment that it is his own environment, rather than the truth, helps to make his choice and his commitments both more free and more responsible. Yet at the very time that class leaves him most room, history and geography have enormously reduced his possible range of concern in comparison with the ranges of earlier writers. Cosmic speculation seems closed, world politics are precarious and accidental, heroic virtue is a figment of the illusory past. The history of the last fifty years has helped to give the British intellectual many of his working-class attitudes: his defensive insistence on the immediate and the personal, his scorn of the pretentious and idealistic formula for human conduct. The working classes have not, in Britain, taken over the ruling power of society, nor have they actively proselytized for converts to their points of view (the very nature of the points of view would work against any such activity). And intellectuals are probably still in the minority numerically, even in British society. Yet British intellectuals, in the face of somewhat similar obstacles, have adopted something of the limited intransigence that has, in industrial society, long been the workingman's only defense.

7

Creeping Americanism

THE CONTEMPORARY BRITISH SCENE, AS PRESENTED BY recent novelists, contains a great deal of American culture. Kingsley Amis' characters, for example, devising their faces and their roles, rely heavily on grade-C Hollywood westerns, detective stories, and often ape the dialogue of Humphrey Bogart. John Wain's work, too, is permeated by references to the infusions of American popular culture into British life. In presenting a series of cultural references that are less conventionally those of British fiction, these writers portray a world that is also less traditionally and uniquely British, that contains elements of Hollywood, rock and roll, and the teen-age consumer. This American influence is nowhere more evident than in an enormously funny novel called *Billy Liar* (1959) by Keith Waterhouse.

Billy Liar takes place in Stradhoughton, a small Yorkshire city. But the city is no longer full of the "sturdy buildings of honest native stone," the independent country charm, the "cobbled streets" that Man o' the Dales, the popular columnist in the local paper, wishes to preserve. The Man o' the Dales, with his talk of Yorkshire "piquancy" and the salutary effects of "brackish air," is romanticizing a Yorkshire that no longer exists. The town itself is portrayed by Billy, the young narrator:

> The brackish air I was no authority on, except to say that when the wind was in a certain direction it smelled of burning paint. As for the honest native stone, our main street, Moorgate, was—despite the lying reminiscences of old men like Councillor Duxbury who remembered sheep-troughs where the X-L Disc Bar now stands—exactly like any other High Street in Great Britain. Woolworth's looked like Woolworth's, the Odeon looked like the Odeon, and the *Stradhoughton Echo*'s own office, which Man o' the Dales must have seen, looked like a public lavatory in honest native white tile. I had a fairly passionate set piece all worked out on the subject of rugged Yorkshire towns, with their rugged neon signs and their rugged plate-glass and plastic shop-fronts, but so far nobody had given me the opportunity to start up on the theme. . . . Along Market Street, where the new glass-fronted shops spilled out their sagging lengths of plywood and linoleum . . .   [Pp. 20–21.]

American decoration is also apparent in the office of Shadrack, the progressive young funeral director for whom Billy works, who keeps his large executive, metal desk free from everything except a black ebony ruler. Shadrack looks forward to the day when all coffins will be made of Fiberglas. But Billy himself does not deliver ringing protests against the insidious Americanization of Stradhoughton. Throughout all Billy's vivid fantasies (and, as an incessant liar, Billy has a great many fantasies), influences from American books and films are evident. Billy is fascinated by a cemetery that reminds him of the neat campus in an American college musical. He has imbibed the romanticism of the American wanderer: "I can always get a job of some kind, maybe washing-up. I began to imagine myself in the tradition of American writers, driving lorries, sweeping up, South American revolution, soda jerk, newspaper boy" (p. 149).

Stradhoughton has not absorbed the many foreign influences of the postwar world very gracefully. The espresso coffee bar exists, but the new glass plates are already tacky and the walls still show the picture of Dick Whittington and his cat that characterized the old native milk bar. The formica-topped tables look odd in the old local pub. And the contemporary elegance of the Disc Bar, the new record shop, has faded quickly:

> The cone-shaped ashtray stands, their bright yellow smudged with black, were already tilted, broken and abandoned. The showcases, which were supposed to hang in mid-air on steel wires, sagged and lurched so dangerously that they had to be propped up on old packing cases. One of them was broken, a great jagged crack going along one corner. There were scuff marks all along the orange walls.   [P. 90.]

Perhaps the "brackish air" of Stradhoughton is too thick to allow all the infusions of image and décor from the world outside Yorkshire.

Keenly aware of the ludicrous mixture of the old, rugged Yorkshire tradition with the new coffee bars and record shops, Billy, the adolescent, makes fun of the clashes of experience he sees around him. The clichés of his straight-laced Yorkshire parents evoke from Billy the literal reply of the sharp-minded, as in the following dialogue with his father:

> "Well you can bloody well and start coming in of a night-time. I'm not having *you* gallivanting round at all hours, not at your bloody age."
>
> "Who *are* you having gallivanting round, then?" I asked, the wit rising for the day like a pale and watery sun.   [P. 9.]

Billy and Arthur spend their time at work (they are both clerks in the funeral office) designing comic routines that mix the native Yorkshire cliché with the plywood and the Fiberglas, and Billy's great desire is to write scripts for a popular television comic. Arthur spends weekends crooning American popular songs in the Roxy Dance Hall. In a way reminiscent of Kingsley Amis' heroes, both Billy and Arthur are mimics. They parody the broad Yorkshire accent of Councillor Duxbury, the "Gimme two cawfees" tone of the American serviceman stationed in England, the pompous and stereotyped advice they get from

their elders. Billy can seldom resist parodying the voice of anyone
he happens to be talking to at the moment. Waterhouse's comedy
is also Amis-like in the use of the quick contemporary portrait,
full of sharp and biting incongruities:

> He was, for a start, only about twenty-five years old, although
> grown old with quick experience, like forced rhubarb. His general
> approach and demeanour was that of the second-hand car sales-
> man, and he had in fact at one time been one in the south. He was
> in the undertaking business because his old man was in it before
> him and old Shadrack had been, so to speak, young Shadrack's
> first account. After that he rarely attended funerals and would
> indeed have found it difficult in view of the R.A.F. blazer and the
> canary-coloured pullover which, sported being the word, he
> sported. But he was useful to the firm in that, besides having
> inherited half of it, he could get round old ladies. He was a
> member of most churches in Stradhoughton and to my certain
> knowledge was a card-carrying Unitarian, a Baptist, a Methodist,
> and both High and Low Church.   [P. 33.]

A great deal of the comedy, however, stems from the plot. Billy
works himself into impossible situations: he is simultaneously
engaged to two girls, with a single ring that alternates, though
he's in love with a third; he constantly tells stories about a sister
or a dog or a job that he doesn't have; he has hidden more
than two hundred commercial calendars he was to have sent out
for the funeral firm, and he has never mailed the letter his
mother wrote to "Housewives' Choice." The single day on which
the novel takes place is the day of reckoning. All Billy's deceptions, one after the other, are discovered (many have been known
for a long time, but Billy wasn't sure that they were) and unraveled. And the tremendous number of complications—the two
engaged girls confronting each other, the director's revealing his
knowledge of the calendars (and Billy's attempts to get rid of
the evidence), the discovery that he has no sister or dog—form
the framework that carries the comedy along. Billy began lying
to avoid the drab contradictions of Stradhoughton life, but, as

his lies trap him more and more, he retreats into his private
fantasies: one fantasy centers on a set of sophisticated London
parents who regard truth a dreadful bore and tolerantly mock
his adolescent excesses; the other fantasy takes him to Ambrosia,
a mythical country in which he is war hero, prime minister,
famous comedian at the Ambrosia State Opera, and challenging
companion of Bertrand Russell.

In Stradhoughton Billy's lies never work. The net of discovery
by parents, bosses, and girl friends tightens more and more
closely around him. Yet Billy retains a respect for those who can
understand his lying and, without pomp or preaching, confront
him with it. For one moment he respects Old Councillor Duxbury, whom Billy had often made fun of and thought incapable
of noticing anything, because the councillor knows about the
calendars and refrains from a pompous lecture on the subject.
Billy can also respect Liz, the only one of his three girls who
both knows about and is permitted in Ambrosia. Liz never moral-
izes about Billy's lying. Unlike Barbara, the fiancée who is whole-
some, eats oranges, and wants a cottage with wall-to-wall carpets,
or Rita, the fiancée who won the Miss Stradhoughton contest,
works in the espresso bar, and always talks in clichés ("whole
sentences ready-packed in a disposable tinfoil wrapper"), Liz
can appreciate what Billy is: "We began chattering, eagerly
interrupting, laughing, grinning at each other as though we knew
the whole joke about the world and understood it" (p. 94).
Billy, talking with his mother just after his grandmother has
died, can also recognize the person who rests behind the structure
of pat expressions and parental homilies.

Aware that the funeral office is no career and trapped by his
lies in Stradhoughton society, Billy considers leaving for London.
He has had a letter from the television comic giving a vague hint
of possible partial employment, which Billy has of course elaborated into a certain promise of a job. For a moment Liz is even
ready to go with him. Yet both Liz and Billy realize that he is
not yet ready to define himself in London, as Liz goes off to

Doncaster and Billy returns home. It's not that Billy needs to face the consequences of his sin as a sort of moral purification. Rather, Billy is still the adolescent, still unable to work out the complexities of experience. Different from his parents, yet unable to assimilate the American movies he's seen or the novels he's read, Billy needs time to grow up and discover the limitations of his fantasy. No public school code has formed him (as it might have, still, had he been born into a different social or economic class), no unanimous sense of native honesty among the working classes protects him. To find himself in the midst of contemporary multiplicity, Billy will need all his wit, along with numerous trips to Ambrosia and back. Like the rootless and wandering hero in a good deal of American fiction, Billy is a dislocated adolescent. Keith Waterhouse's novel illustrates, both referentially and thematically, an American influence operating in contemporary Britain. But both Mr. Waterhouse and his hero retain a sense of humor about it, for Billy offers no declamatory pronouncements or dedications. He simply keeps his awareness, his wit, his recognition of the multiplicity of contemporary British life.

Another contemporary British novelist whose work shows a strong American influence is John Bowen. Bowen's first novel, *The Truth Will Not Help Us* (1956), tells the story of the unjust execution on a charge of "piracy" of three English seamen in a Scottish port in 1705. The story of the seamen, their growing unpopularity in an alien port, the ludicrous trial they undergo, is made parallel to the story of victims of the illogical investigations conducted by the late Senator McCarthy. The kind of accusation by rumor and ignorance which McCarthyism represents is made, by Bowen, a social monstrosity that can exist in many times and places. But the specific locus, the constant reference for this process of undermining human dignity, is in American terms. Bowen pokes fun at the defense of all injustice under the appeal to the idea of the "free country." When the people in the Scottish town begin to suspect the sailors, Bowen parodies their reasoning:

It was time for the authorities to do something, to act, to investigate, to bring the whole suspicious business out into daylight.
No honest man need fear investigation; it was a free country.
   It was a free country, people said; why were these sailors not
arrested? It was a free country; they should be on trial, in prison,
put out of the way. For piracy was a menace to freedom, which
could not exist until all the pirates were locked up.   [Pp. 70–71.]

At the trial of the sailors other characteristics of committees on
un-American activities are lampooned. The chairman of the
investigation insists that the lawyer for the defense cannot speak
because the process is simply an investigation, but at the same
time he maintains that the guilty must be punished. The chairman also states: "Whether the sailors were on board or not, it
cannot be denied that they have since associated with their comrades, and it is already a matter proven in these Investigations
that association is the same as guilt" (p. 131). The characters
all speak as if they were American; the falsifications of the investigation in the local press are put in American lingo. Recent
American history is the constant point of reference for Bowen's
universal theme.

   John Bowen's other novels also make frequent use of American
references and American themes. The world-wide flood that
provides the setting for the futuristic *After the Rain* (1958)
begins with an attempt to seed clouds in order to provide rain
artificially during a long drought in Texas. And the people who
survive the flood exist on Glub ("the Ideal Breakfast Food: You
Need No Other"), a product of the International Unitarian
Breakfast Food Company. An advertising conference in Bowen's
third novel, *The Centre of the Green* (1959), is full of jargon
that originated in America: "rethink," "motivewise," "If we
don't believe in Buttertoffs ourselves, we aren't likely to make
the consumers believe in them." In Bowen's most recent novel,
Storyboard (1960), the American influence is not just the lin-
guistic detail of the "finalized" concept or the quick reference
to whether or not the character wants to do his conventional
year on fellowship to the United States. The whole novel is, from

one point of view, a defense of advertising as a valid part of urban capitalist society, a part not necessarily more corrupt or more dishonest than any other. Bowen begins the novel with an essay explaining how the advertising agency works and pointing out its role in contemporary society. The institution of advertising and its carefully reasoned and connected defense may be new in Britain, but popular American fiction has long provided numerous examples of the same theme and the same treatment. The long introductory essay seems incredibly naïve to an American, just as, I suppose, a Briton would react if some American novelist proudly proclaimed that all people, whether they meant to or not, really made distinctions on the basis of economic or social class.

John Bowen is not, however, simply a British writer devoted to American references and themes. Like most of his British contemporaries, he makes contemporary references in order to make a comic point. *The Truth Will Not Help Us*, though set in 1705, is full of deliberate anachronisms, like references to television and photographs, that satirize the way in which society formulates its opinions. Sometimes the satire is strictly a contemporary slap with no application to the kind of inhumanity central to the novel:

> It was a kind of *New Statesman* friendship—a marriage of the professional and the working classes, in an atmosphere of highmindedness and classical music with no physical contact whatever, except that sometimes they would hold hands.   [P. 97.]

Bowen also excels in drawing the quick comic portrait of a minor character: the timid English consul in *The Truth Will Not Help Us*, who, when he should defend his countrymen unjustly accused, is concerned with his wife's profession as a *corsetière*, with not ruffling anyone's feelings or using harsh language, with the local bus routes. Mr. Monney, the father of a sixteen-year-old girl whom one of the principal characters in *The Centre of the Green* has seduced, is another example. He, a hard-working landlord, is deftly introduced:

He was not an educated man himself, but he knew the value of it. He liked a good play on the radio, but had taken against the idea of television. He read the *Daily Telegraph*, the *Sunday Times* and the *Reader's Digest* . . . , and he found the *Digest* particularly valuable, because it was not only a good read in itself, but gave you something to talk about. He would never have thought of subscribing to the *Digest* for himself, he said, but they had found out about him somehow, and had written to him specially suggesting it. He had always been struck with the thoughtfulness of this, although of course it was in their own interest as well. [P. 48.]

As in this instance, the humor often stems from the impingement of a detail from contemporary commercial society on an essentially older and more local culture. John Bowen also uses the comic list, the long series of associated details that reflect the incongruity of contemporary life, much in the manner of Kingsley Amis.

In *Storyboard,* a character is looking for a flat in London and picks up a paper:

Gloomily Ralph read the small advertisements on its back pages. A Socialist Guest House in Perranporth. A lady in Hampstead who wished to make a home for coloured students. A room and food in return for help with the children and instruction in Spanish. A large room in a Regency House overlooking the park, with a Study Circle that met on Fridays. Musical interests. Vegetarian interests. Cultural interests. Photographic interests. Theatre and Ballet. A gentleman with own car seeking another gentleman with whom to share a holiday in Andorra. [Pp. 87–88.]

In all his comedy Bowen sharply satirizes the hypocritical or the inconsistent. *Storyboard,* in particular, castigates the hypocrite: the academic who talks piously of integrity while accepting the first profitable journalistic offer he can find; the "progressive" young matron who uses grandiose psychological terms to try to manage her friends and marry them off. Hypocrisy is one of the elements Bowen satirizes in his treatment of *The Radical,* a leftist periodical:

> *The Radical* came out every week. It cost ninepence, and ran at
> a profit. Like the *New Statesman and Nation* and the *Spectator*,
> it gave its front half up to political matters, its back to literature.
> Like them it had benefited from the decision of the big corpora-
> tions and trade associations to advertise to what are called "opinion
> leaders," so that lucidly argued, passionately felt articles on the
> need for public ownership would be printed next to full-page
> advertisements composed in a documentary style, in which steel-
> workers told how they had bought their own houses and television
> sets and industrial journalists gave *ex cathedra* opinions that
> private enterprise and increased exports went necessarily together.
> [*Storyboard,* pp. 91–92.]

The sharp blasts against any form of hypocrisy indicate that
Bowen's point of view is moral and committed as well as comic.

In *After the Rain*, Bowen's commitment takes the form of a
protest against man's tendencies to manufacture absolutes. In
the flood that covers the world in 1966, John Clarke and his
mistress Sonya attach their dinghy to a large raft in order to
survive. The raft, containing eight other people, is controlled
by a man named Arthur who meticulously rations food and tasks
aboard. Arthur, at the beginning, is an agnostic; he relies on
man's conscious and rational activities to work through the
difficult conditions of the flood. The agnostic who runs efficiency
and the spiritual together is played off against the clergyman, Mr.
Banner, who had become ordained because he had not done well
at anything other than rowing at the university, and no institution other than the Church was willing to accept him. Mr.
Banner, pleasant and rambling, is quite willing to defer to
Arthur. But Arthur, the efficient, the practical, the hardheaded,
begins to be carried away by his own success. He starts to elevate
his success to the status of myth:

> I have been thinking about the value of myth. We are, after all,
> in a mythological situation. Our descendants will remember us,
> not simply as the haphazard survivors of a great catastrophe, but
> as the founders, the chosen, the people who came out of the sea

to beget a new race. Indeed, why should they not do so, for that is what we are? . . . For their own self-respect as a people, they must remember us as greater than we are. [P. 155.]

And the other people, with some reservations, begin to worship Arthur, first as leader, then as mythmaker, finally as God. Arthur himself begins to act as a god. He insists on worship, turns what has been routine into ritual, makes himself masks so that he cannot be confronted directly, regards himself as a performer of miracles, calls his raft's log the "Sacred Book," and even murders two men who are no longer useful for the survivial of the others. In his final madness Arthur changes again. He is no longer willing to think of any man, even himself, as God. He feels he is only the chosen emissary, that God is a giant squid they see in the water. Arthur demands that Sonya's unborn baby be sacrificed to propitiate the squid-God. At this point the sane finally revolt and Arthur is killed at the end. But the course of Arthur's madness is the course of superstitious man manufacturing a series of spurious absolutes, from sanctifying his own efficiency and control to abasing himself before mystic horrors he cannot comprehend.

After the protests against political and theological absolutes implicit in the first two novels, Bowen turns to a more directly human statement of commitment in his third novel, *The Centre of the Green.* This novel concerns the Baker family: a retired colonel and his wife living in a cottage in Devonshire; their son Julian, married and working for an advertising agency in London; their son Charles, a single and lonely journalist. Each of the Bakers is essentially lonely and isolated from the others. The colonel, relieved of active command and sent to India to run an officers' candidate school just at the beginning of the war, feels alone and useless, preserves himself through his miniscule routine, his garden, his daily walks. His wife, who brought up their sons during the war, is now addicted to television. Julian, always evasive and unable to face any human relationship, expresses his isolation by attempting to seduce any young girl he can find.

And Charles, honest in his own isolation, tries to commit suicide because he is unable to feel anything deeply and finds no further point in living. Each character tries, in one way or another, to reach the others, but the attempt is either misunderstood or ineffectual. Bowen points out that some of the boys' difficulties originate in their mother's desperate clutching at them while the colonel was in India for four years, but the clutching itself came from her need, her own isolation, and, besides, tracing origins does not necessarily lead to cure. Human personality, whatever the cause, is isolated in individual entities. The story of the Baker family, determined by psychological forces, has many parallels created by either psychological or sociological forces throughout the novel. The landlady who drinks herself into helpless indigence after her husband dies, the girl Charles meets at the cinema who would go to bed with him simply because she has nothing else to do, the resolutely cheerful widow the colonel meets on Majorca —all mirror the loneliness central to human life. As Charles realizes imagistically when, in order to preserve his own emotional detachment (his aim and his curse simultaneously), he looks for silence in the heart of the noisy city:

> It was just a game to begin with, just a device to pass the time. He surveyed the three corners of the Green, and drew an imaginary line bisecting each angle. Where the lines met, the centre would be. Of course, this imaginary calculation could not be exact, but if he were to take it as approximate, and cast around a little, perhaps he might happen on the silence, might fall into it suddenly, that little bubble of silence in the exact centre of the Green.
>
> [Pp. 161–162.]

And, in the midst of the loneliness, all the characters realize that fairness and justice, the usual standards for human judgment, are meaningless.

But in *The Centre of the Green*, despite the central void, man does have some meaningful possibility. The colonel can cultivate his garden and his walks, although he cannot pass these on to his sons. The garden is one of the ways in which the colonel expresses himself, his style. And on his deathbed, as a result of strokes that Julian has maliciously helped to perpetrate, the colonel is aware of style:

> Having children—going to Heaven—carving your name on the door of the bogs—everybody's always trying to be immortal; it's a lot of nonsense. I'll tell you something. We live because we can't help it, and we die because we can't help that either. If we had any choice, we wouldn't die, and we wouldn't be born. Makes chaps feel pretty small sometimes. No choice. Only thing we ever have any choice about is *how* we do things. You know—doing it with style, and all that. That's us—style. The rest is all outside, and we can't control it. Chaps ought to finish well.   [P. 215.]

The colonel does finish well. And both his sons can understand this, can understand that all the human being can do is to do things gracefully, to try. At the end of the novel Julian returns to London and his wife, not because his compulsion is cured, but because he is willing to try to live with himself with grace and style. This theme, central to the novel, is a more contemporary and domesticated version of the Hemingway code, the statement that, in a world where he has no control over the central issues of life, death, and truth, man must try to live with as much exterior grace and dignity as he can muster. The statement, in both the early work of Hemingway and the work of John Bowen, is a statement of both man's limitation and his human possibility.

The use of style, the Hemingway code, takes a slightly different form, although it is equally central, in *Storyboard*. Here Sophia, the young woman who works in the advertising agency, has been disillusioned by Ralph, the academic and hypocritical writer for *The Radical*. Both personally and professionally Ralph has betrayed Sophia, for he has personally sold and professionally distorted information Sophia gave him about advertising. At the end of the novel Sophia cannot change herself or the world around her, cannot relinquish the job she's good at on the basis of some spurious hierarchy of values. She can only keep on living, and wonder:

> Could one help but be what one became? Perhaps a little but it would be difficult, and the effort would never be over. Was it

> worth it? Being something other than what one really was, that
> was just a pretence, just fake. But if there were bits of what one
> was that one didn't like, then one just had to pretend, and hope
> the pretence would stick. One had to keep on pretending, or else
> give in.   [P. 230.]

Sophia does pretend, and makes the conscious effort with dignity
and grace. She herself is personally and professionally (and, in
this novel, the personal and the professional keep running together for all the characters) committed to life.

The story of Sophia and Ralph is constantly connected to the
story of Keith, one of the junior executives at the agency, and his
wife Sylvia. When Ralph thinks of Sophia's career, Keith, in a
scene exactly parallel, thinks of how he might arrange a job for
Sylvia to relieve the drudgery she feels as a Purley housewife.
Keith and Sylvia, however, have been married for a number of
years. Sylvia's pregnancy had forced her to give up teaching and
forced Keith to earn more money by going into advertising.
Sylvia, neurotic, restless, unhappy at the change in their lives
the child caused, has never ceased resenting the child's demands,
and has become increasingly subject to psychosomatic fatigue
and migraine. When Sylvia's petulant fatigue indirectly causes
the child to burn himself, and when her subsequent incompetence
causes the child's death, it would seem that Sylvia has nothing to
live for, that her marriage and her image of herself have both
been destroyed. But Sylvia realizes that she must pretend, must
force her own commitment to something:

> The springs of the bed creaked. Human beings, however they
> might try to be dignified and romantic and all that, spent so much
> of their time behaving like the characters of a dirty joke. It
> couldn't be helped, and it kept things going. Sylvia dabbed cologne
> on her neck and between the cleft of her breasts, and joined her
> husband in bed. One could do things in a cold way, but perhaps
> one got warm doing them.   [Pp. 234–235.]

In the midst of a world in which no absolute or no theory works,
John Bowen's characters are committed to the pretense, the

deliberate attempt to *seem* as human and alive as possible. That is what dignity is.

Although the sense of human dignity is central to Bowen's conception of human character, the characters do not always behave consistently. Even Colonel Baker, the worthy man of style in *The Centre of the Green*, misjudges the plebeian Mr. Monney; he assumes unfairly that Mr. Monney has come only to extract as much money as he can. Here the stuffy pseudoaristocrat leaps to the inaccurate conclusion that the man from a lower class must be a sordid blackmailer. Yet Bowen is, by no means, a systematic defender of the virtues of the lower and middle classes. The bloodthirsty mob riots, smashes cars and people, cries out for hanging in *The Truth Will Not Help Us;* most of the lower classes steal whatever they can find and kill others to ensure their own survival when the flood begins in *After the Rain.* No group or class can provide the measure for dignity or style. In fact, Bowen frequently arranges a deliberate switch, works things so that the unexpected person represents the statement of value in the novel. In *After the Rain,* for example, it is not the intellectual narrator, John Clarke, who finally opposes and defeats the mythmaking God-Arthur. Rather it is Tony, the simple young man who spends all his free time doing calisthenics, flexing his muscles and fishing, who has no theories or capacity to create them, who finally revolts against the cruelty and the abstraction of the god. Both Tony and God-Arthur are killed in the struggle. And the intellectual narrator recognizes his own responsibility for his inactivity, knows that his own doubts, his own intelligence, had rendered him ineffectual in comparison with Tony the bodybuilder:

> But Tony had not been worried by doubts. His horizons were not large; his ambitions were limited. He performed the simple discipline of his exercises; he gave to other people a wide tolerance and respect; he made no moral judgements outside the simple estimate of right and wrong that he applied to himself. Tony was not a noble savage. On the contrary, he fitted very well into a society, asking no more than that it should give him work to do,

respect his privacy, and not require him to do anything that he
believed to be wrong.   [P. 202.]

As soon as a character veers toward too great a simplification,
too abstract a definition, as here the idea of the "noble savage,"
Bowen steers him away.

Frequently Bowen lampoons the cultural abstraction, the
kind of cliché implicit in the characterization of a whole group
or class of people. In *Storyboard*, for example, the "progressive"
young couple think themselves truly radical because they
embrace capitalism, complaining only that capitalism is sometimes so inefficient. Bowen spends a good deal of the novel satirizing *The Radical* and the people who subscribe to it:

> Most of *The Radical*'s readers bought it because they had always
> bought it and its arrival on the doormat every Friday was a re-
> assurance that they still held the liberal opinions they knew they
> ought to hold, but which their way of living (if they allowed
> themselves to think about it) might seem to belie; these did not
> actually get time to read *The Radical*, and placing this week's
> number in the contemporary magazine rack were often horrified
> to find last week's number still there unlooked-at. But simply to
> subscribe to *The Radical* was for them a sign that they had not
> sold out, and was worth the ninepence. Other, younger readers,
> who spent their time more recklessly, bought it as a supplement to
> the Sunday papers, and read it all. And there were still a few
> readers who found in *The Radical* a connection to others of their
> kind. Separated though they might be, some in Newcastle, some in
> Dudley, in Grimsby and in Greenwich, in Tunbridge Wells and
> in Tiverton, probation officers, personnel relations officers, teachers,
> district nurses, dentists, solicitors, keepers of museums, industrial
> consultants—
>
>> Yet, dotted everywhere,
>> Ironic points of light
>> Flash out wherever the Just
>> Exchange their messages:
>
> —and for these (for whom *The Radical* had first been founded)
> it was a mine of fact, a buttress of opinion, another eye to see by,

a living witness, in a world grown corrupt and compliant, that reason and the principles of humanism still had meaning (and a little force) and that it was not yet too late, if only people would take heed, for society to reform itself on lines that were not now exactly Marxist, and certainly not Benthamite, but generally in accordance with enlightened and sensible opinion as far as it could be collated. [Pp. 92-93.]

The exaggerated rhetoric, the pointed quotation from Auden's poem, and the underlying positive approach all echo the strong belief of the liberal of the 'thirties, a phenomenon that Bowen here mocks as dated and hypocritical. *The Radical*, Bowen goes on to point out, is interested only in facts that fit with its pre-established opinions. And, late in the novel, *The Radical*'s violently slanted exposé of advertising is completely ineffectual, for the fuss it creates allows the company to achieve its commercial aim far more easily than it would otherwise have done. The venerable and dedicated institution from the recent past is hollow, phony, and inept. Similarly, in defending advertising, Bowen is reversing the usual occupational generalization. The voice of truth in *Storyboard* is that of a diffident and prissy bachelor who has worked for the advertising agency, without brilliance or distinction, for thirty years. And the usual bantering of terms like "integrity" and "corruption" is questioned, examined, turned around. Bowen's iconoclasm always hits out against the expected abstraction, always preserves the individual and the human from the simplification of the general social explanation.

All four of John Bowen's novels are very consciously and carefully structured. *The Truth Will Not Help Us* begins with an account of the charges against the seamen; shifts into a series of vignettes that show the growing fear, the cruelty, and the lack of logic among the townspeople; breaks into a series of three case histories that demonstrate the origins of the rootless and asocial careers of the three seamen; and then finally coheres in the parody of the ludicrous trial. But the structure is stiff and blocky, a kind of set exercise in contrivance. The futuristic novel, *After the Rain,* begins with the Biblical metaphor of the world-wide flood. In a manner somewhat like that of William Golding, Bowen attempts to use the conventional metaphor in order to reproduce the essential conditions of man's position. But the metaphor is less unique and less striking than those of Golding. And, as Bowen develops his account of human anthropomorphism, the metaphor itself matters less and less. God-Arthur and the sane bodybuilder could battle anywhere, and the relevance of the Biblical metaphor is never made a central part of the novel. Both these novels, despite individual passages of great wit and sharpness, are structurally overloaded. The contrivance of linking the two couples in *Storyboard,* the constant shifts from one couple to another at precisely the same moment, also seem literal and mechanical. The narrative is, too often, a series of parallel points, though the novel gains emphasis from essays like those at the beginning and at the end which defend the role of the advertising agency in contemporary society. All three of these novels are too literal, as if references, points of view, iconoclasms, and attitudes have all hardened around the experience of the novel and withered it. Americanism, too, in reference and in subject matter, is part of the hardened casing, part of the series of deliberate and mechanical impositions that surround the clever and humane centers of the novels. The attack on the illogical cruelty of an investigating committee, the careful account of the place of advertising in commercial society, the texture of American reference and joke—all are, though often contemporary and pungent, somehow stiff and excessively literal, set exercises that seriously reduce the effectiveness of Bowen's writing.

Only *The Centre of the Green* does not suffer from its novelistic paraphernalia. Again, the structure of the novel is very carefully contrived: each of the principal characters is introduced; both brothers are brought from London down to Devonshire at the same time; the same cloudburst (in a way that seems to owe a good deal to Joyce's *Ulysses*) figures in the separate, but parallel, experience of each character. Careful links, throughout the novel, connect one character to another, one story or one problem to another. But here the mechanism is an essential part of the novel, for the characters are connected both by cloudbursts and by the loneliness common to all men. The constant superficial linking of externals is itself an image of the world, a necessary mask for the essential loneliness of human personality. Theme and technique merge. The novel is not artistically perfect: for example, Bowen occasionally uses thick and heavy-handed imagery, like the repeated reference to the vicar's accidental breaking of the bronze chrysanthemum at the funeral of the agnostic, gardening, autumnal colonel. But, for the most part, the technique adequately presents the material of the novel. *The Centre of the Green*, despite its expression of a kind of Hemingway code, also exhibits less American influence than do the other novels. Here Bowen uses fewest American references, fewest set or slightly disguised essays that explain the problems of contemporary Western society. The novel has significantly one less impediment to the artistic presentation and value of the humane.

8

The Moral Center of John Wain's Fiction

FEW CONTEMPOARY BRITISH WRITERS ILLUSTRATE A thematic commitment so consistently as does John Wain. Throughout Wain's first four novels and his one volume of short stories runs a constant commitment to the value of the individual and the personal, a constant assertion of the dignity of the human being. Although frequently describing and satirizing a world of chaotic folly, each of the novels contains a central statement of the moral worth of the individual. These statements are neither grandiose and pious generalizations nor complacent excuses for anything man happens to do. Often they are backed into ironically, and always they are carefully limited and defined against a background in which an ideal or all-consuming morality leads to ridiculous pretense. Yet the statement of man's worth, qualified and limited as it may be, gives both coherence and direction to John Wain's fiction.

John Wain's first novel (published as *Hurry On Down* in Britain in 1953 and, perhaps to underline the outmoded British class structure, as *Born in Captivity* in America in 1954) is mock-picaresque. The hero, Charles Lumley, leaves the university and journeys through contemporary Britain, holding successive jobs as window washer, smuggler, hospital orderly, chauffeur, and bouncer in a shoddy night club. Throughout his wanderings Charles maintains that his aim is to escape all identification with class. Discovering himself can only be impeded by any class designation. Even though he washes windows, he is aware how foolish it would be to regard himself as part of the working class:

> He thought, as he leaned on the parapet of the town's bridge and watched the tiny brown river drifting beneath it, of all the expensive young men of the thirties who had made, or wished to make, or talked of making, a gesture somewhat similar to his own, turning their backs on the setting that had pampered them; and how they had all failed from the start because their rejection was moved by the desire to enter, and be at one with, a vaguely conceived People, whose minds and lives they could not even begin to imagine, and who would in any case, had they ever arrived, have made their lives hell. At least, Charles thought with a sense of self-congratulation, he had always been right about *them*, right to despise them for their idiotic attempt to look through two telescopes at the same time: one fashioned of German psychology and pointed at themselves, the other of Russian economics and directed at the English working class. [Pp. 37–38.]

Charles often seeks to bury himself in occupation or meditation or with a simple girl in one of many similar simple houses, to resist any of the badges of status by which Englishmen recognize one another. On the other side, those who commit themselves to class, who judge others and define themselves by the class structure, are satirized most pointedly throughout the novel. Burge, a young doctor who had known Charles at the university and who finds him working as a hospital orderly, is portrayed as both vicious and idiotic. He attacks Charles directly:

> "That sort of work ought to be done by people who are born to it. You had some sort of education, some sort of upbringing, though I must say you don't bloody well behave like it. You ought to have taken on some decent job, the sort of thing you were brought up and educated to do, and leave this bloody slop-empty-

ing to people who were brought up and educated for slop-
emptying. . . . You're bloody well not catching me out with
your smart questions. It's necessary, and so is emptying bloody
dustbins," cried the educated man, "but there are some classes of
society that are born and bred to it, and ours isn't. If you take
a job like that, you're just——" he fumbled among his small
stock of metaphors, and brought out the inevitable, "letting the
side down. And I don't like people who let the side down."

[P. 174.]

Charles himself is occasionally inclined to make minor versions
of the same mistake. While working as a chauffeur, he gets to
know his employer's son, a boy interested only in motorcycles,
differentials, and valve seats. Charles asks the boy if he would
not rather have been the son of a garage mechanic than the
heir to a wealthy industrialist. But the boy won't bite; he knows
that garage mechanics can have a pretty routine time pumping
petrol and, besides, he wisely refuses to define his genuine interests
in terms of environment.

Yet Charles can neither ignore nor resign from society. Each
of his jobs is involved with society and carries some sort of class
identification. At times, as when he smuggles narcotics into the
country through his work as a driver of cars for export, Charles
realizes that he is dependent on the highly materialistic society he
sought most carefully to avoid. In the paradoxical situations he
works himself into, Charles keeps thinking of a line from a
poem he has read: "And I a twister love what I abhor." Ironically,
Charles finally discovers himself as one of a stable of seven gag-
men for a radio comic. He had realized earlier that he could find
only partial truths in unlikely places, for his attempts to seek
the simple human virtues in a simple setting had all been spoiled
by hidden complexities. When leaving his superficially idyllic
job as chauffeur at the industrialist's Hampshire house, Charles
had mused:

The people he belonged with were ill, disgusting, unsuccessful,
comic, but still alive, still generating some kind of human force.
This expensive bucolic setting had offered nothing more than an

escape down a blind alley, and it had taken a crack-brained mechanic, a nymphomaniac, and a deranged careerist to show him
that. As ever, the serious point had emerged through the machin-
ery of the ludicrous. His life was a dialogue, full of deep and
tragic truths, expressed in hoarse shouts by red-nosed music-hall
comics.   [P. 223.]

Now, working for the radio comic, Charles can preserve his
anonymity as one of seven, avoid the pressure of social definition
that poverty demands, and retain sufficient leisure and independence to realize both what he is and what others are. In other
words, Charles ironically finds that he can best retain the personal
and the humane in the midst of a highly organized and commercial world. And the dignity of the personal and the humane
is the moral value he has been seeking throughout his journey.
He even thinks of his search in terms of a mock allegory:

> The young man (Hopeless) breaks out of the prison of Social
> and Economic Maladjustment; he carries on his back a hundred-
> weight of granite known as Education. After a skirmish with the
> dragon Sex, in which he is aided by a false friend, Giant Crime,
> he comes to the illusory citadel called Renunciation of Ambition.
> And so on.   [Pp. 233–234.]

The gag-writing job is, however, no "Kingdom of Heaven."
Charles's own intelligence, as well as the comic means of presentation, carefully limits the range of value. From an exterior point
of view, in fact, the job establishes Charles as part of the commercial middle class to which, because of his training and education, he honestly belongs. But Charles's journey and acquired
insight, rather than an automatic or inherited designation, have
earned him the right to keep the job and to win the expensive
prize woman.

Edgar Banks, the hero of Wain's second novel (*Living in the
Present*, 1955), also requires a journey, although this one is not
consciously picaresque, in order to discover a reason for living.
At the beginning of the novel Edgar, finding no value in his
society and feeling he belongs to the "second generation of uni-

versal agnosticism," resolves to commit suicide. But even at this point of skepticism, Edgar makes choices on moral grounds, for he decides that before killing himself he will rid the world of the most loathsome creature he knows. Characteristically, he chooses a snide, class-conscious Neo-Fascist as his victim. The process of tracking his victim takes Edgar from London to Switzerland and Italy. Despite all his elaborate plans, however, he is unable to kill either his victim or himself. Something intervenes at every crucial moment in a plot that mocks the serialized cliff hanger, and Edgar's automatic response is to preserve life. He is about to kill his victim when he sees a repulsive child he knows climbing a tree that leans dangerously over a steep precipice. He cannot resist yelling out a warning, a warning that both saves the child and alerts Edgar's chosen victim. He is also unable to crash the car, as planned, in which he is driving his victim over a mountain road. While in pursuit Edgar maintains that he is for the first time "living in the present," open to all emotions and reactions, but uncommitted to any scheme or course of conduct beyond that of rubbing out his victim and himself. But in Italy Edgar meets Tom, an old friend he has always admired, and Catherine, Tom's girl friend. Edgar realizes that some people, without illusion or false gods, get beyond the present:

> Something was terribly wrong with the plan he had been working on. It simply wouldn't do. Standing dumbly by Catherine's side, an empty glass clutched nervously in his hand, he struggled to drag the thing upwards into consciousness. What had happened? That evening in London, when he had begun to live in the present, everything had seemed settled. He had formed his plan, and it had seemed a magnificent one, complete and satisfying. Now, with swift and absolute certainty, he knew that it was so no longer. A really artistic suicide, balanced by a farewell present to life: why had it seemed good then, why did it seem bad, small and empty now?
>
> Tom Straw came bearing the answer in his face, carrying it with the strength of his square body, across the room towards him. He was scowling irritably, but the central core of his goodness and honesty was as plain to Edgar's vision as if it had been made

of some tangible substance. In the presence of this man, the selfishness, the isolation, the foolish theatricality of his original idea stood out revealed. [Pp. 176–177.]

Through Tom and even more through Catherine (for the novel ends with a standard romantic coupling of Edgar and Catherine), Edgar finally finds his own meaning for abstractions like "goodness," "honesty," and love. He also learns that these qualities are of sufficient worth to justify living in the future.

The Contenders (1958), Wain's third and best novel, projects the theme of personal value into a wider area of English society. A narrator, rumpled, fat, easygoing Joe Shaw, tells the story of his two schoolmates, Robert Lamb, the artist, and Ned Roper, the businessman, and their rise to prominence in post World War II England. Each struggles to achieve more than the other, yet both depend on the soundness and the simplicity of Joe Shaw, who still works on the newspaper in the grubby pottery town all three of the characters came from. Although Wain ridicules both complete subservience to Art as a kind of mystical goddess, and the reverence for material success so prevalent in society, neither art nor business in itself is his principal target. Rather, he attacks the spirit of competition that motivates both the artist and the businessman, a spirit instilled by parents, teachers, all of society. And the hero, Joe Shaw, is simply the man in whose clouded chemistry the injection of competition didn't happen to take. Competition, the desire to excel, leads to a kind of involuted egotism and represents the slavish and unthinking adherence to commercial and middle-class values which is examined, in one way or another, in all Wain's fiction. Joe Shaw, when talking with Ned Roper and Stocker, another competitor who is eager only to seduce as many women as he possibly can, realizes the kind of simplification of experience to which the competitive spirit leads:

> I began to see where I was. It was useless, plainly, to argue with either of them, because they were both committed to what was, fundamentally, the same position. They both saw women not

as people but as *instruments*. Stockér saw them as instruments of
pleasure, Ned as instruments of prestige. Stocker's argument was
crude, Ned's—on the surface—more subtle. But in either case
there was only one way of bringing them round, and that was to
get them to see a woman as a *person*. But what was the good? If
I were to tell Ned that an unsuccessful, obscure and unambitious
man might find himself a wife who, *as a human being*, was as good
as anyone available for the most famous and powerful—what
good would that do?   [P. 142.]

Allegiance to the competitive spirit forces both Ned and Robert
to limit themselves to what is visible and acceptable in society.
Ned, the urbane, polished businessman, keeps his private fantasy,
a vast model railroad system that he can control completely,
locked in a private room in his house. The railroad represents
both his escape from society and his desire for control, both
hidden behind a calm, respectable façade. Similarly, Robert's art
acquires the veneer of brittle acceptability as he becomes more
successful, while his acting out of artistic postures prevents him
from holding a woman. The preoccupation with success, a preoccupation handled with deadly irony when Robert gives a toast
to "Success" at the public celebration of Ned's wedding to his
glamorous former wife, keeps both Robert and Ned from getting
beyond the axioms of their society. Paradoxically, Joe Shaw,
superficially far more limited, is able to break through the
limitations of society because he is not racing against a competitive phantom.

In his first three novels Wain used the hero's romance at the
end to indicate his awareness of human value. In contrast, his
fourth novel, *A Travelling Woman* (1959), works entirely
within terms of sexual and romantic relationships. At the beginning a young married man, George Links, bored with his young
wife, arranges for a weekly consultation with a London psychiatrist simply as a means for having an affair with some other
woman. Friends in London encourage him and help him find a
suitable woman, while one of them uses the ensuing complications
to begin an affair with George's wife. The plot of multiple

deception and multiple infidelity finds each character chasing some image of romantic fulfillment. Each thinks his own yearnings and his own difficulties unique, but, as George is shown by his friend Captax, each story fits the same rather sordid design of people trying to avoid the boredom of fidelity. And Captax himself is the man who later deludes himself into thinking that he has found his unique romance with George's wife. George finally realizes that he misses his wife's gentleness and concern, that a single and permanent relationship means more to him than transitory tangles in a world of infidelity. Ironically, it is Cowley, the husband of George's mistress, a man used to disappointment because he'd lost his religious faith just after writing a best seller called *The Discovery of Faith*, who first gives George the message:

> I've only just recovered from something like the same state of disorganization that you're still in. Mine took the form of an intellectual quandary, and to some extent it had intellectual causes, but the differences aren't as important as the resemblances. I wasn't fit to keep my end up in normal human life, any more than you are. My particular kind of disorganization didn't lead me into petty disreputability, as yours has led you, but that's just a difference of temperament. It led me to something worse. After all, it's a peculiar kind of hell to have a wife like Ruth and know that you're not providing her with the kind of love and happiness that she must have. . . . It's something you wouldn't understand, because you don't know, yet, what it is to give your whole allegiance to one person. When you do, you'll be able to imagine what real love is, and then you'll also have an inkling of what genuine failure can be. [Pp. 154–155.]

Both George and his wife recognize that they must give their "allegiance to one person," as Cowley recognizes that he must remain loyal to his best seller and its implications even though he no longer believes it is true. The human being is too limited, both personally and intellectually, to handle the freedom that his powers of logical analysis suggest. He must stick to his commitments, not because they represent some exterior value or truth in themselves, but because man is too feeble to do without them. Man's nature, not some abstract law, requires marital fidelity. As in *Hurry On Down*, Wain uses mock-allegorical terms for his moral fables. When George, repentant, is first rejected by his wife, he thinks of the carpet he is standing on as the "Slough of Despond." Such references, handled comically, underline the differences between traditional Christian morality and the far more secular kind of morality that Wain presents. But the pilgrims progress all the same.

Many of the short stories in the volume called *Nuncle* (1960) revolve around similar moral themes. The young "monster" in "Master Richard" (the awareness of a man of thirty-five housed in the body of a five-year-old) develops elaborate and demonic plans to corrupt the personality of a younger brother, but the plans are foiled because the younger brother quite simply loves him no matter what he does. Personal love can vanquish all the formulations of the intellect. The Oxford student who narrates "A Few Drinks with Alcock and Brown" tries to push aside any thought of the girl he has just jilted and the unopened letter from her in his pocket while he involves himself in ludicrous exterior events concerning the impersonation of a well-known novelist and the dull discussion between a Dutchman and a Swede about an Antwerp prostitute. But the narrator, while deliberately immersing himself in the trivial events going on in the pub, doesn't really fool himself. It is the personal that matters:

> Drinking the rest of his beer, Benlowes thought of this thrush, and had a sudden intuition that it had been the only real thing in his life, and that saying good-bye to Ellen meant saying good-bye to the thrush and everything that the thrush meant.
>
> [*Nuncle*, p. 52.]

The young child in "A Message from the Pig-Man" can get a straight answer from the man who collects garbage, and the answer allays his childish fears. But the child's attempts to understand his mother's divorce, his questions about why his father no longer lives with them, meet only evasion and affectionate condescension. The personal and the emotional are more difficult and more important.

Wain's moral statements are invariably grounded in the contemporary English scene. All the novels contain sociological descriptions of houses populated by different classes, of dingy streets of similar strung-out shops which lead out of industrial cities, of one kind of squalor in grimy pottery towns, of another kind of squalor in mews flats in Chelsea. A number of the short stories even depend primarily on sociological accounts of contemporary phenomena: the emotions in the kind of love affair on which "the refined moon of Kensington" shines in "Rafferty," the way the young television repairman tries to impress the Swiss *au pair* girl in "Christmas at Rillingham's." Although references to specific places and to specific attitudes within society are constant throughout Wain's fiction, there is some change in the values assigned. In the first two novels the moral point involves a kind of acceptance of the dominant patterns of contemporary society. Both Charles Lumley and Edgar Banks, although they find a great deal to satirize and castigate, end by accepting, at least on the outside, the kind of class and social role demanded by their time, place, and training. Both have learned that genuine value is purely personal; both have acquired sufficient insight to realize that a social position expresses only the outline of a person; but both still accept, for its limited worth, the expected social position. Wain's two later novels, on the other hand, provide a more searching examination of the society. In both *The Contenders* and *A Travelling Woman*, the dominant patterns of contemporary society are rejected in favor of the value of an older, more local, tradition. George Links must abandon the whirl of meaningless infidelity in contemporary London and return to his local suburb.

The Contenders, in particular, asserts the value of localism, the traditional English virtue of remaining close to one's original surroundings. A large share of Joe Shaw's worth is based on the fact that he has never really left the pottery town he grew up in, has not become corrupted by the cosmopolitan influences of

London. Although aware of the town's many limitations, Joe is fond of it. He attributes much of Robert's artistic ability to the fact that Robert had been born and brought up there:

> I hadn't realised, yet, that the only reason England has any intellectual and artistic life at all is because men like Robert aren't reared in London. They take their originality with them, and London consumes it all and gives them nothing back. It's because the provinces accept dreariness that London can boast of its brilliance.   [P. 49.]

And Robert himself, when his wife leaves him and he's at his most depressed, returns to the pottery town with Joe in order to recover his talent and his sanity at their source. Joe's mother, who supplies an excessive dose of the kind of wisdom and silent understanding found in the provinces, also looms throughout the novel. She says little but she is never deluded. Man is best, in Wain's fiction, when he sticks with what he knows and can handle, when he avoids the pretense implicit in the cosmopolitan and the universal. In the same way, the narrator of *Hurry On Down*, when meeting a girl friend's family, can respect her working-class father with his pre-1914 habits and manners, but does not respect her younger brother who slurs his speech with smart American locutions and prides himself on his commercial success and his American-style cigarettes. A form of localism, a sticking to what one was born to, is, in the midst of a world becoming rapidly less local, sometimes the best way to retain individual worth and dignity.

But localism is itself a confined and limited value, a value that by its very nature must rule out a good deal of possible human experience in order to assert or establish itself. It is almost more a means of playing safe than an indication of value. Similarly, Wain's heroes are limited, are carefully established as nonheroic. Honest and direct as Charles Lumley sometimes is, he also runs away from any difficult situation as, for example, when he cowers in the lavatory of the train rather than speak with the parents of an old schoolmate. George Links's heroic stature is severely reduced by the consistent presentation of him as an insufferable pedant. Even in the midst of a relevant argument he cannot resist correcting a friend by pointing out the grammatical difference between "imply" and "infer." And Joe Shaw is made fat, elaborately casual, indifferent, and, as his friend Robert once charges him directly, more a spectator of than a participant in human experience. Toward the end of the novel Joe changes. He throws away his pipe, becomes more active, registers emotions himself instead of merely understanding those of others. Yet his ordinary, lumpish character has been so carefully established that the change does not make him into a heroic figure. In addition, because his inactive, provincial, simple qualities have been regarded as valuable and important in the novel, the whole issue of heroism seems out of place. Human character is too contradictory, too difficult, and too limited to allow a word like "hero" to apply.

In fact, although Wain demonstrates the value and the importance of the humane, he also indicates that it is often difficult to understand and explain what the human personality is like. Joe Shaw, for all his home-grown perception, is frequently baffled by what he sees in the people around him and, at several points, abandons futile attempts to communicate with others or with himself. Edgar Banks in *Living in the Present* often cannot understand his own reaction, and wonders why irrational fears attack him whenever he tries to carry out his plan. Several of the short stories confront the mystery at the depths of human personality even more centrally and directly, using the development of a kind of madness as the representation of all that cannot be understood. The man-boy in "Master Richard" has to commit suicide at the end of the story because he cannot understand all the intricacies of his strangely displaced personality. In another story, "Nuncle," the narrator, a former writer now drinking himself to death, tries to reëstablish himself by marrying a placid young girl and moving into her peaceful country cottage. Quite irrationally, he fears his father-in-law who shares the cottage with them. The narrator tries to write again, but cannot. At the same time the father-in-law begins to write stories, and the two arrange a deal whereby he will write stories under the narrator's well-known name. But the practical arrangement leads to a gradual switch in identity; each begins to assume the character of the other and the poor once placid girl doesn't know what kind of allegiance belongs to which man. Finally the narrator must run off to preserve what he can of himself, before identity and personality have been completely swallowed up. The values of the human, the limited, and the local are not abstractly perfect choices; they are, rather, the only sane possibilities in the midst of psychological complexities that the human being only barely comprehends. Deliberate limitation, at least, allows some measure of control.

John Wain frequently uses comedy as another means of limiting and defining the values he asserts. Many scenes in the novels are farcical. In *Hurry On Down*, Charles, somewhat drunk in a pub, offers a man a light and sets fire to his mustache. In another pub, later in the novel, Charles and his friend are first continually interrupted and then driven out choking and gasping for breath by the "ghoulish" smoke from a simple clay pipe. Such scenes are described in enormous and spiraling detail, as are the scenes, in *Living in the Present*, in which Edgar tries to prevent a drunken Scots poet from drinking a bottle of poisoned brandy meant for someone else (the unconsumed bottle is finally broken), or in which Edgar begins telling his employer, over the telephone, why he's not coming to work and ends with a fantastic story about vomiting in a telephone box and being hauled off by the police. Although the later novels contain relatively less farce, Captax' first meeting with George's wife is marked by an incessantly ringing telephone that makes his efforts as a sophisticated seducer and deceiver seem ridiculous. The farce demonstrates the ludicrous quality of man's attempt to seem more in control of his surroundings than he actually is. Another comic device that Wain uses is the conversation at cross-purposes. At one point in *Living in the Present* a group of people are sitting around a table in a Swiss café. Mr. Crabshaw is trying to tell a joke about a man who gave his fiancée a watch; Mirabelle suggests they all switch from wine to black coffee; on the jukebox record, Bessie Smith sings about a faithless lover; Edgar creates a fantasy in which he defends Mr. Crabshaw in a murder trial. All these go on simultaneously, without any connections, in a world in which what one says or thinks has little relationship to what others are thinking or saying.

The diversity of the world that confronts man is also demonstrated by the kind of comic and incongruous image Wain frequently uses. Charles Lumley thinks he's in love, and "his heart lurched over and over in his breast like a cricket ball lobbed along a dry, bumpy pitch" (*Hurry On Down*, p.20). One girl looks at another "as if she were a gall-stone on a X-ray plate" (p. 54), and then the girl turns to look at Charles: "She ran her eyes over him. His spine felt like a row of cotton reels strung on a wire. Then the wire became red hot and melted and the cotton reels clattered to the ground" (p. 55). The contemporary and mechanical images continue in Wain's other work:

> She was wearing leopard-skin trousers and a pair of ear-rings that could have done duty on the front axle of a Ferrari. Her low-cut blouse revealed a cleft between her breasts big enough to hold a bundle of firewood. [*Living in the Present*, p. 241.]

> In the silence that followed, we thought of London, the impossible London of the provincial adolescent, the smoky swamp full of jewelled toads, the dirt-track where racing taxis full of millionaires skid together in a shower of sovereigns, the pallid aviary of bank notes flapping their wings in time to the cunning chimes of Big Ben. [*The Contenders*, p. 39.]

> And with that I set up a fit of coughing that sounded like a concrete-mixer running away down a steep hill. [*Nuncle*, p. 163.]

This kind of image underlines both the comedy and the localism of Wain's prose. At times the comedy is even more severely local, as in the images dependent on reference to fashionable academic figures such as William Empson, logical positivists, and

F. R. Leavis. This kind of comedy, discordant, contemporary, energetic, and often extremely funny, is occasional and decorative rather than central to the kind of statement Wain is making. Yet the frequent comic image and the comic means of presentation help to limit the range of the statement, help to prevent the values endorsed from soaring into absolutes.

John Wain, as demonstrated in his book called *Preliminary Essays* and in his frequent reviews, is an excellent literary critic, intelligent, perceptive, and able to analyze and explain what he sees clearly and cogently. Some of his critical faculty has worked its way into his fiction, for attitudes and points of view are explained and documented with significant and contemporary detail. His observations are accurate and meaningful, his perceptions are intelligently explored and demonstrated. But, if his fiction contains many of the virtues of good literary criticism, it also contains some of the attendant faults. Sometimes Wain over-explains, or repeats a crucial point several times, as, for example, in the frequent reiteration of the folly of self-sufficiency that dissolves the relationship between Tom and Catherine in *Living in the Present*. The prose itself can be drowned by repetition or by elaborately accurate stage directions, as in the two following passages from *Hurry On Down*:

> "I s'pose you've heard all about George's success," said Mr. Hutchins; his voice was bright and confident, but with a curious undertone of bewilderment and pathos. "He's got a Fellowship," he added, using the strange word in inverted commas, grafting it like some strange twig on to the stunted trunk of his artisan's vocabulary.   [P. 13.]

> "I suppose you wanted to speak to Father" (thank Heaven at least she did not refer to the yellowed scarecrow as "Daddy"), "now that you've taken your degree you'll be wanting to put everything into a bit better order, I suppose." (An oblique, but not too oblique, reference to his haphazard approach to life.) "He's been wondering when you'd show up." (Implying that he had been skulking out of the way of his responsibilities.)   [P. 17.]

The parenthetical stage directions in the second passage seem to show only that Charles is aware of what is being implied by the person he's speaking with, an awareness already apparent in the novel. Similarly, in *A Travelling Woman,* George Links takes several pages to define and categorize, in fairly standard terms, every feature of the woman he is pursuing. The artifice is sometimes too much for the material it should present. *Living in the Present,* organized around Edgar's plan to commit justifiable murder and suicide, ultimately breaks down because the gimmick, the artifice, is too heavy and too static and tends, by the end of the novel, to squelch the sense of experience and discovery central to the novel.

Each of Wain's first three novels ends with the hero, limited and restricted as he is, finding himself and his place. In each the hero also gets the girl as prize. In one way this kind of ending seems sentimental; the equation between value and reward seems a little too pat and soft. Yet the value, the moral center of Wain's work, is, in its insistence on the dignity of the humane and the personal, a sentimental value. In a world where man has little understanding and less control, he can at least make personal choices and at least recognize what and where he is. This is essentially a sentimental doctrine because the choices and the recognition are endowed with more emotion than they structurally or logically warrant. Man, as Wain sees him, is a creature full of complex and reverberating emotion. Depositing all this on the carefully limited and the personal is almost bound to seem sentimental, to seem as if the happy romance at the end is an unjustifiable gesture. Wain's attempts to avoid sentimentality have not been notably successful. The accidental resolution of *A Travelling Woman,* the simple mistake in identity that prevents George Links from going off with still another woman, or the ironic switches obviously fabricated to save some of the short stories from sentimentality, are simply reversals that do not alter the sentimental content. Wain's comic devices are often too brittle, too decorative, and too occasional to prevent the weight of the emotion from seeping through. Wain needs a richer, more central kind of comedy, a fundamental perspective that can hold the limited and local value without seeming to invest it so heavily with emotion. Perhaps Joe Shaw shouldn't have a mother, or perhaps the simple Italian girl should really want to set up an espresso bar in the pottery town; at any rate, some wider aesthetic use of comedy seems necessary. For the kind of point Wain is making about the contemporary world that he depicts with such specificity, force, and intelligence, he does require some tangible expression of the value of the personal and the humane. But the form of expression often lacks a comic richness that would avoid both the brittle gimmick and the heavy sediment of emotion.

9

Angus Wilson's
Qualified Nationalism

ANGUS WILSON HAS DEALT WITH A WIDE RANGE AND
variety of contemporary experience. He has developed several
different techniques in becoming, in his last three books, the most
skillful and comprehensive novelist writing in England today.
Because many of his works seem to originate from, though not to
reproduce, earlier works, I should like to examine his development in a roughly chronological order.

Angus Wilson's first two volumes of published short stories
(*The Wrong Set*, 1949, and *Such Darling Dodos*, 1950) contain
a good many scathing portraits of British society. Most of the
stories depict, with precision and detachment, the delusions and
the pretense under which people operate. In many stories characters reveal, although they do not admit, the hatred they feel
for those they live with; frequently the character's behavior
contradicts his professed attitudes or codes. Wilson often satirizes
his characters sharply, as in "Crazy Crowd," where he shows the
egotism and the emotional self-indulgence of a country family
that prides itself on its difference from others, its unconvention-
ality, its jolly "craziness." The satire is presented through the
clash of different points of view, and, in many of Wilson's early

stories, all the material is developed in the same way. In "Et Dona Ferentes," for example, the attraction between the middle-aged father of a family and a young Swedish boy staying with the family on an exchange visit is developed through a series of interior monologues, as the father himself, his wife, his sharp old mother-in-law, his bookish son, his adolescent daughter, and even the callous young Swedish boy alternate in viewing the events at a family picnic. People, in Wilson's stories, seldom understand one another. In "What do Hippo's Eat?" a seedy middle-aged major, without money or job, takes his shrewd, young Cockney landlady to the zoo for a day's visit. Each has plans for the other: the major is trying to charm his landlady into giving him money to set up a business; the landlady, fully aware of his incompetence and shallowness, simply wants to keep him for his tarnished charm without investing any money in him. The relationship between the two can work out, but only if each deludes himself about the other's motives. What goes on on the surface is rarely matched by the motives or the attitudes of the people involved.

When Wilson's early stories are more dependent on plot, the plot is usually a simple reversal. A young man of twenty-five feels enormously rebellious when confronted with his mother's hearty protection, but he feels terribly lost and lonely when she dies. A young research student feels a great sympathy for her middle-aged professor who is, she feels, imprisoned by a dissatisfied and alcoholic wife. The student insists on probing the truth of the situation and making the older couple acknowledge it, but, in the process, the professor himself, not his wife, is destroyed. In still another story an elegant couple who pride themselves on their humane liberalism cannot act on their humane principles when confronted by the wife's military, ex-prisoner brother. Social grace takes easy precedence over principle. On the whole, these stories, dependent on simple reversals or on crashing hypocrisies, even though deftly done, show Wilson at his weakest and trickiest. These early stories are also permeated with a kind of naked malice that works both ways, both within and toward the character concerned. A successful businessman ruthlessly takes over the management of an art gallery, and Wilson ruthlessly exposes him. In another story ("Totentanz," which appears in both of the first two volumes) a young academic wife utterly fails to become the London social success she planned. Her failure receives no compassion, either from the author or from the wives of her husband's former Scottish colleagues. The Scottish wives, in turn, judge her mercilessly and are themselves mercilessly judged by the author. The whole story, done with precision and sharpness, is a radiating ring of concentric malice.

Not all Wilson's early stories deal with British society since the end of World War II. One story, "Union Reunion," describes the feelings of a couple returning to colonial society in South Africa in 1924, having spent the previous twenty years in England. Looking at their relatives who have remained colonials, the couple brilliantly document, in a page or so, the colonial feelings of pride, fear, and racial anxiety that occupy Doris Lessing for about a third of a novel. Another story, "Saturnalia," is concerned with the social and personal tensions at a New Year's Eve party to bring in 1932 at a South Kensington hotel. Wilson frequently deals with the historical or the sociological generalization. In "Such Darling Dodos," a fading dandy, loyal to his "happy chromium-plated 1920's," is always uneasy when he visits his scholarly and progressive relatives, creatures of the serious 1930's, in Oxford. But on his last visit the dandy is pleased to discover that his own attitudes, his skepticism about learning and progress, have returned to fashion in Oxford after World War II. He can now patronize his more sober relatives.

The historical and sociological point plays a relatively larger part in Wilson's most recent collection of short stories, *A Bit Off the Map* (1957). One story, "A Flat Country Christmas," shows two young married couples who try to avoid their political differences as they get together for a Christmas drink. But behind the political differences is only the nothingness of the new, post-war housing estates, and one of the men ends the evening in tears of desperation. In another story a young contemporary

woman who wants both security and excitement must choose
between her stuffy, though dependable, husband in publishing
and their lodger, an irresponsible and dishonest, though appealing, writer. The young woman, made representative of many
young women in the 1950's, has a short affair with the lodger,
but remains with her husband. The stories in this volume, though
still written with enormous economy and point, are both less
tricky and less simply malicious than those in the first two
volumes. The title story traces a young, retarded denizen of the
coffee bars as he listens to conversations assailing society which he
is unable to comprehend and as he dedicates himself to discovering "Truth." Using a number of different points of view and
satirizing demonically "angry young men" along the way,
Wilson shows how the feeble-minded boy is led to seek his
"Truth" by killing a strange old man on Hampstead Heath in the
middle of the night. Yet here the multiple points of view yield
a combination of horror and compassion. Similarly complex is
another story called "After the Show." In this story an intelligent
seventeen-year-old Jewish boy, the only member of the family
who is available, is called suddenly when his uncle's mistress tries
to commit suicide. The boy attempts to comfort the mistress,
imagines himself a hero, but really learns from her a good deal
of the pain and loneliness of experience. They are able to communicate, but the next day the girl is still a "mistress" and the
boy still an awkward adolescent, though they remember their
talk the night before. Communication is partial, momentary,
yet it does exist. Other stories, such as "Ten Minutes to Twelve,"
deal with the questions of government and of attitudes toward
political and social power. Wilson's fictional world in *A Bit Off
the Map* has become wider and more emotionally complicated.

The theme of conflict between generations representing
different social and political ideas, central to stories like "Such
Darling Dodos" and "Ten Minutes to Twelve," is also the central
issue of Wilson's play, *The Mulberry Bush* (first produced in
1955 and published in 1956). In the play an old liberal couple,

a retiring master of an Oxbridge college and his wife, watch as their family degenerates into a smooth, cricket-playing, head-prefect young barrister and a guilty, frightened young girl. In addition, all the old couple's worthy projects, both public and private, turn sour. The mastership is to be handed over to a cold, rising fund raiser; the German refugee they supported and trained cruelly calculates his own material gain; the social world of tolerance and rationality they tried to create is impossible; their worthy son, an eminent social scientist now dead, had a secret mistress for years and once unjustly fired a man and ruined his career. Throughout the play eminent figures topple from their pedestals and circle, like everyone else, around the mulberry bushes of their own egos. At the end of the play the old man realizes that even his tolerant liberalism has been, in a way, a manifestation of his own ego, and has in part created the misery, the coldness, and the unhappiness his children and grand-children face. But, given the fact that all people are, to some degree, locked within their own egos, Wilson shows a good deal of sympathy for the old couple who tried to formulate a kind of liberal and rational code for human behavior. No codes work, but the outmoded liberal code, a kind of vague Fabian socialism mixed with the advocacy of birth control, equal rights for all colors and races, and homes for unwed mothers, is, at least, more humane and more concerned with others than are the purely self-seeking attitudes of the current generation. And one grand-child, the young girl, along with a young history don she intends to marry, is able to recognize the kind of tolerance and humanity represented by the old code. The play, however, is not effective. It is excessively talky, sometimes dull, and the symbols of the pedestal and the mulberry bush burst incongruously into the fabric of the talk. The play also, in trying to parallel public and private issues, often falls into melodramatic contrivance. Wilson's subtle connection of personal morality with public position requires a form less striking and obvious than the drama. Wilson's connections, often understated, are interior, and seem to require the multiple perspectives and the careful shaded relationships among what one thinks and says and does which the novel form provides.

Angus Wilson is primarily a novelist. His first novel, *Hemlock and After,* was published in 1952. Like many of his short stories, it frequently details character in terms of sociological and historical reference. For example, James, the pompous barrister who is the son of the novelist hero, Bernard Sands, is ticked off as one of those who enjoy wallowing in the new rage for Anouilh's period 1913 plays. Another character, a huge and vicious countrywoman who tries to blackmail the hero, gives large parties where everyone gathers sentimentally around the piano to sing "Pack Up Your Troubles" and "The White Cliffs of Dover." A more complex character, Bernard's sister, is also characterized almost entirely in terms of history. A spinster professor who teaches English, although she feels that literature is less important than "Life," retains, in 1951, an unswerving allegiance to the cause of the Spanish Loyalists. She never grumbles about rationing and deplores the new conservatism of the London School of Economics. Bernard himself, a successful novelist engaged in getting the government to use a stately home as a place where young writer's can, at government expense, be free to write, also thinks of his friends and his career in historical terms. He has a circle of friends from the 1920's, some high in the government, who chat about art and theater at mannered cocktail parties; he recalls his progressive friends and platforms from the 1930's, thinking of them as rather "dowdy remnants"; he travels in the smart and flippant world of contemporary theatrical homosexuals, although he avoids the hard, smart world of advertising and fashion magazines in which his daughter is engaged.

Yet Bernard is not simply a public figure. His attempt to set up the government scheme to support young writers is endangered by his own personal behavior. Since his wife, Ella, lapsed into a kind of psychotic withdrawal and indifference some years earlier (and he feels guilty about that, too), Bernard has had two homosexual affairs, and exposure of his behavior threatens at one point to undermine the public project. In addition, Bernard, as a homosexual and a public figure, feels enormously guilty when he witnesses a young man arrested for crudely soliciting him in Leicester Square. In other words, Bernard is riddled by conscience in a constant effort to make the public and the private sides of his behavior fit each other, to be responsible, humane, and inclusive. Bernard's effort to understand, to help, to sympathize, is not common to all people. His son, James, for one, mocks him:

> All this universal understanding, this Dostoyevskeyan emotional brotherhood, and, at bottom, he had nothing but utter contempt for nine-tenths of humanity; as for the other tenth he probably hated their guts for not being susceptible to his patronage. Thank God, thought James, *he* never aimed at understanding humanity. Indeed, the whole appeal of the law, his forte as a barrister, lay in his belief in justice. If people were too weak or too stupid to cope with life as it was, they had to be taught. [P. 21.]

Although Bernard's home for writers is established as he wants it, despite misunderstanding and hostility at the opening ceremony, and although Bernard is able to convince a fey young friend that he ought to live independently, the conclusion is far from victorious. Bernard, always troubled with conscience about his acts and their motives, worries himself into a fatal heart attack. And, within a year the writers at the home themselves choose to have it administered by a professional administrator (one of the things Bernard feared most) simply to save time and trouble. Toward the end of Bernard's struggle Ella recovers from her psychic withdrawal and actively helps him. They examine their past, and realize that they have significantly failed to help both their children. Perhaps private failure is part of the price of public eminence; Bernard has never been able to manage control over both the personal and the public sides of his nature simultaneously. Although the theme of various conflicting responsibilities is never fully worked out (Bernard's sister's conversion to his point of view at the end seems gratuitous), Wilson's statement of the problems confronting the public figure in contemporary society reaches, even in this first novel, a complexity and a degree of thoughtful, individual examination far beyond that demonstrated in the more famous Lewis Eliot series by C. P. Snow.

Hemlock and After is not, however, without flaws. Some of the incidents, like the arrest in Leicester Square and the attempt to sell a placid young virgin to the local architect, are made excessively melodramatic. The disastrous opening-day ceremony is prepared for with a long and ominous introduction which outlines the action that is shortly to take place. The evil woman who sells young virgins and who tries to use blackmail to defeat Bernard's scheme is semisymbolic in a novel without other symbolic content. The novel also contains a good deal of the naked malice evident in Wilson's early stories: one whole chapter, in the center of the novel, appropriately called "Camp Fire Cameos," consists of a series of catty interchanges among a number of homosexuals. Yet, despite all these excesses, the novel develops a complex set of problems through a number of well-articulated points of view. As Bernard wins in some ways, but loses in others, so other characters work toward partial resolutions. Bernard's brittle daughter, Elizabeth, is able to break through her smart shell sufficiently to have an affair with Terence, Bernard's first boy friend. Though each gains something from the affair, the relationship cannot become permanent. And Bernard's younger friend, Eric, is able to leave his beloved mother and move to London on his own, although his departure is effected only by mutual misunderstanding. Communication, again, is possible, but invariably incomplete or inconsequential.

Wilson's skillful handling of multiple points of view reaches its culmination in his second novel, *Anglo-Saxon Attitudes* (1956). The novel begins with a series of tableaux, static yet interconnected scenes in which each of a number of characters is introduced through his attitudes, thoughts, and statements concerning an important lecture on medieval history. The lecture, in turn, refers to the crucial public event of the novel:

the unearthing, in East Anglia, forty years before the novel's action begins, of a seventh-century bishop's tomb, including both bishop and an incongruous pagan fertility idol. The historians have all, in one way or another, been influenced by the discovery. In the tableaux Wilson not only develops each attitude toward the historical event and characterizes each historian both personally and professionally, but focuses each scene on the character's view of Gerald Middleton, the sixty-two-year-old professor, the last surviving historian present at the discovery (although he was incapacitated by a sprained ankle when the discovery actually took place), and the central figure of the novel. Gerald, a figure of detachment and dignity, has retired prematurely and has never done the brilliant historical work expected of him. Although still strong and perceptive, he spends most of his time collecting drawings. The second section of the novel, in another series of static scenes, follows Gerald's personal life. Here again Gerald has been a failure. He lives apart from his gushing, sentimental Scandinavian wife and is essentially estranged from all three of his children: Robin, a forceful and competent industrialist who manages the Middleton family business; Kay, a shy girl with a withered hand who has married Donald, an intense, shabby, and unsuccessful academic; John, a charming homosexual and former member of Parliament who leads television campaigns for righteousness against the evils of government bureaucracy. Gerald finds Robin pompous, Kay dull and dowdy, and John careless and intellectually dishonest. Similarly, all the children find Gerald removed and ineffectual; they are far closer to their warm and approving mother, Inge. During the aimless talk that follows Inge's large Christmas dinner, Gerald, in a series of flashbacks, reveals many of the causes of his estrangement from his family. He thinks of his mistress, Dollie, whom he loved but had abandoned "for the sake of the children," of the day Kay's hand was burned in the fire, of his decision not to go into the family business. Yet the themes of the personal and the professional are connected, for Dollie was the wife of Gerald's friend Gilbert, who was killed in World War

I and was the son of the professor who published the findings of
the bishop's tomb. Gerald, in his reflections, begins to realize that
his failure as a historian is, in some way, connected with his
failure as a husband and a father.

After Wilson has presented this vast background with skill and
depth, Gerald begins to try to create some order and meaning
out of his life. He involves himself with a vast number of people,
cutting across all levels of British society. He meets spivs and
homosexuals on the fringes of London's criminal world, acid-
ulous little scholars who break truth into tiny, footnoted frag-
ments, and earnest young garage mechanics who listen to *Salome*
on the gramaphone in surburban semidetached houses. Wilson
portrays all these varied characters with memorable sharpness and
force. Gerald finds, in his increasing involvment with contemporary society, that his professional contacts are invariably connected with his personal ones. The attractive young girl who is
the granddaughter of the old actress Gerald stayed with when the
bishop's tomb was discovered is also Robin's mistress and John's
secretary. The market gardener victimized by the government,
whose cause John so theatrically embraces on television, is married to a woman who was a maid in the house at the time of the
archeological discovery. Her father, still alive though speechless
from a stroke, is the only survivor who actually does know what
happened when the bishop's tomb was opened. Robin's wife is
related to the caretaker of the old actress. All these twined connections operate more and more forcefully on Gerald, as he
realizes that he will have to sort out truth from error within
the mazes of both his personal and his professional past.

The whole novel is, in one way, a highly complicated statement on the nature of truth. Gerald recognizes that he has
evaded the truth for most of his life:

> It recalled too vividly the whole pattern of his family life: a world
> of indulgent sweetness and syrupy intimacy. He had done nothing
> to reform it all these years; he could do nothing now. Neverthe-
> less, the failure of his family life added to his preoccupation with
> his professional death and closed him round in a dense fog of self-

disgust. It seemed to him that his whole life had grown pale and futile because it was rooted in evasion.

[*Anglo-Saxon Attitudes*, p. 108.]

Gerald remembers that Gilbert, just before he was killed, had, while drunk, bitterly attacked scholarship and claimed that he had planted the pagan fertility idol in the bishop's tomb as a malicious joke. Gerald had always, in respect for his dead friend and for the scholarly reputation of the dead friend's father, refused to check the story, just as he had refused to check his suspicion that Inge, in a fit of rage and frustration, had deliberately burned Kay's hand. Gerald decides to uncover the truth both about the fraud and about his wife's action, a decision that leads him into the centers of experience he has avoided for years. He even agrees to edit a new compilation of articles on medieval history.

Throughout the novel Wilson satirizes various forms of the quest for truth. Silly scholars constantly converge in exotic places to forward the "interchange of ideas," although only pleasant banalities are interchanged at the scholarly meetings. Publicists like John Middleton expose the government with fanfare and rhetoric, but Wilson shows that John succeeds only in having a competent civil servant discharged and making an amiable, though incompetent, market gardener miserable. Inge transposes all experience into sentimental fairy stories coated with love and refuses to acknowledge anything unpleasant, even the criminal homosexual, invited by John, who steals her jewelry. The market gardener, Cressett, spends all his time reading encyclopedias, convinced that truth resides in the minute accumulation of fact, while he is unwittingly victimized by the civil service, by John Middleton, and by his wife. Young Timothy, Gerald's grandson, with all the assurance of his sixteen years, is sure that truth consists of simply putting every detail into the right place. For Donald, Gerald's unpleasant son-in-law, truth consists in revealing family scandal in public. All these searches for truth are ludicrous, malicious, or inadequate. Only Gerald's search, the comprehensive examination of the individual's whole experience, his profession, his past, his family, his relationships, can yield meaningful truth.

Gerald does find the truth. He discovers that the pagan idol was a fraud planted in the bishop's tomb, and he announces his discovery, despite the pain it causes him, to the historical world. He confronts Inge with his suspicions about Kay's hand, and she acknowledges that they are true. He finds Dollie, who had become an alcoholic under the stress of her relationship with him, and tells her that he ought never to have left her. But truth is not always useful. Gerald cannot compensate Dollie for thirty years. His children are not impressed with his revelation about Inge, for John, crippled now, and Kay still revere their false, affectionate mother. And although historians respect Gerald's findings about the fraud in the bishop's tomb, a number of them still regard him as a dilettante who has wasted most of his talents. Truth is also not transferable. At one point Gerald becomes honest and direct with Robin. Knowing that Robin is troubled because he is married to one woman and in love with another, Gerald tells him of his love for Dollie and the mistake he made in sacrificing that for his children. Robin gruffly replies: "My case is a little different, you know. Marie Hélène can't give me a divorce, she's a Roman Catholic" (p. 258). Gerald never becomes a hero operating forcefully and effectively in society. But he does stand at the apex of the novel, unifying a massive amount of contemporary material, giving focus and direction to Wilson's treatment of the nature of human truth. The novel itself, a complex series of attitudes and points of view, is developed into a diverse and profound statement about man in contemporary society.

Instead of a construction of multiple prisms flashing against one another, Angus Wilson's next novel, *The Middle Age of Mrs. Eliot* (1958), is almost entirely the careful development of a single character. The novel, without tricks or the slightest hint of melodrama, is a novel of sensibility in an almost Jamesian sense. The heroine, forty-three-year-old Meg Eliot, is, at the beginning of the novel, the contented wife of a successful

London barrister. Despite the fact that they have no children, Meg feels in control of herself and her world, able to manage the things and people she sees around her: her friends, her committees, her collection of ceramics. As she and her husband, Bill, are about to leave on a trip around the world, partly for pleasure and partly for a case that Bill must try in Singapore, Meg summarizes her good fortune:

> She recited carefully to herself their personal beatitudes; and blessings they were indeed—good health, energy, a proper income, a decent social conscience, wide interests, humour shared, sufficient humour indeed to accept large parts of life unshared, and, through it all, complete happiness together. It was simply superstitious fear of hubris that threatened to gnaw through such a fabric; and for atavistic, puritan superstition there was no cure like the months of wonderful new interests, the days of lazy ease that now lay ahead of them. [P. 39.]

Meg gives a party the evening before they leave. At the party she manages people superbly, without stuffiness or coldness or contempt, and she thinks of herself as a combination of Glencora Palliser, Oriane de Guermantes, and Clarissa Dalloway.

On one of the first stops of the trip, however, at Srem Panh in Badai, Bill is shot by some students at the airport terminal who had intended to kill the Badai Minister of Education. Bill had made a heroic gesture to protect the official, and had stopped the bullet. Within a few moments Bill dies, and Meg's world collapses. After resting for a few weeks she returns to London to find that Bill had left her only debts and their house (he had, under the pressure of hard-working success, gambled a great deal). Meg now needs both to earn her living and to develop a new set of feelings, attitudes, and allegiances with which to continue living. Bill had always protected her completely. She must now create something meaningful on her own.

The whole novel traces Meg's attempts to create her own existence, to choose values and to develop her own attitudes and consciousness. At first, she is surprised to find that others' attitudes toward her change because her position has changed: the helpful, once deferential Miss Gorres, the clerk in the antique shop, makes a pass at Meg under the guise of friendly discussion between two women; Mr. Darlington, the young permanent secretary of the welfare committee of which Meg had been chairman, now patronizes her and points out her lack of qualifications for social work. Clearly her old activities must be abandoned, and Meg enrolls in a secretarial school to learn shorthand. Depressed by lonely bed-sitting-rooms, she tries living with some of her old friends, people poorer than she had been whom she was always willing to help. But economic equality and old friendship are not enough. One friend keeps inviting Bill's executor for dinner and giving Meg unwanted advice (in addition, this friend's young son mistakes Meg's kindly auntlike interest in him for sexual passion); another friend suggests Meg join her in a life of wild parties and elegant prostitution; a third friend, also a widow, resents the fact that Meg charms her truculent son-in-law and orders Meg to leave the flat. At this point, having just received her shorthand certificate, Meg breaks down. She has fully learned how little of her old life and her old sympathies can be patched together again.

In order to recover Meg visits her brother David, who runs a large nursery in the South Downs. David's partner and friend, Gordon, has just died so that David also is lonely. Unlike Meg, however, David has both money and occupation, along with a more certain formulation of his own undemonstrative pacifistic values. A homosexual and a conscientious objector, David is also more accustomed to working out his own attitudes. At the nursery Meg recovers and becomes useful as part-time secretary, bookkeeper, and household manager. She and David also begin to build up a relationship of concern for each other which they had never had before. As far as David is concerned, Meg could stay at the nursery permanently. Yet, slowly, Meg begins to realize that she is dominating David, changing his peaceful life as any intense relationship changes people. David begins, with Meg's help, to return to literary research (he had been a young fellow at a college before World War II) instead of working on the series of garden books that he and Gordon had started together. Because she fears she is destroying David, Meg leaves, this time fully able to establish her own life in London.

Meg's independence is neither simply financial nor a kind of empty bravado. She has, like a heroine in a Henry James novel, learned her own possibilities and limitations in the midst of a world from which her husband had previously protected her. Her responses have become more acute, her perceptions sharper, her knowledge of politics and people much greater, although she must now accept her sexless middle age. She is able, at the end, to make a genuine and difficult judgment, and to know why she is making it. The style, more interior and developing much more slowly than the style of Wilson's earlier works, also reflects the growth of Meg's sensitive and moral consciousness. Whereas *Anglo-Saxon Attitudes* flashed words, events, and thoughts against one another in a complicated pattern, *The Middle Age of Mrs. Eliot* unfolds slowly as it carefully exhausts every thought or reaction that passes through Meg's mind. References to art, literature, and music are frequent, as the intelligent woman, again like a Jamesian heroine, uses all forms of art to enhance her own awareness of experience. This novel, although entirely different, is as complete and as totally satisfying as is *Anglo-Saxon Attitudes*.

Angus Wilson's most recent novel is entirely different from either of its predecessors. *The Old Men at the Zoo* (1961) is a fable, a story of the management of the zoo at Regent's Park which becomes a story of the care and management of human beings. The link between the animals and human beings is quickly and constantly made. Each office occupied by the managers is called a cage and each of the officials is described in terms of a characteristic animal. One curator is called a "sick old puma" who later becomes a "sleek, handsome young leopard" when his ideas momentarily triumph; another curator, the man in charge of birds, has a nose like a beak; the president of the society, a man high in the government, is called a "fat, lost old bear" or a "wise old bear"; the young narrator, at first detached and ironic, is referred to as a camel. Later in the novel, as all rational control of society seems to break down, the identity between man and beast becomes even more complete. Crowds gather outside the zoo to protest the attempt to save the animals (a war is going on at the time) and carry placards reading "Men not Beasts." But it is almost impossible to tell one from another: "The hoarse roar seemed to engulf the silence of the Zoo, though here and there the cry or scream of an animal or bird joined the human din" (p. 295). The action of the book begins when an apparently gentle giraffe, ill with a tumor, suddenly kills a keeper, emasculating him in the process. Rational and ordered society has been upset by the unsuspected violence and tumescence of the creature.

All the officials recognize, in the face of possible violence, the necessity for some sort of control over the animals. The first director, Edwin Leacock, favoring a doctrine of "limited liberty," wants the establishment of a reserve on the Welsh border where the animals can roam over a wide area of woods and hills with few checks on their freedom. He argues that the reserve will permit both man and animal to keep some of the valuable "life of the instinct" so frequently lost in contemporary society. Leacock is a publicist and a crusader, using the contemporary medium of television to popularize his idea. He wins the backing of the influential president, Lord Godmanchester, the donor of the land for the reserve. Godmanchester's motives, however, are quite different from Leacock's, for Godmanchester is sure that a war is coming (the novel begins in 1970) and wants safe control of the animals on his own land. Leacock begins to move the animals to the reserve, but the doctrine of "limited liberty" doesn't work. The creature is unable to limit his own liberty, and a few animals escape from the reserve and frighten the nearby villagers. Leacock is unable to handle the problem. He arranges a public execution for an erring lynx (the lynx had done no harm in escaping), an example that creates far more terror than it assuages. Leacock is ultimately a bad director, for he insists on punishing fiercely whatever breaks from his lenient control, as he is merciless toward his nymphomaniac daughter whom he cannot silence or control. His personal and professional limitations coalesce, for his daughter, his subject, is raped and killed by the animal she has provoked. "Limited liberty" leads to disaster for the creature, and the reserve is abandoned.

The next director, the elegant explorer Sir Bobby Falcon, believes in restricting liberty much more severely. With all the animals back at Regent's Park, he favors a return to the Victorian concept of the zoo—animals herded together in pretty cages, barrel organs and brass bands, colored lights and patriotic slogans. He plans a grand opening for his revival of older zoos for British Day and regards himself as the last powerful survivor of an old order, a happier and more colorful time for Britain. The war interrupts his plans for the grand opening, but, just before the bombs actually fall, Sir Bobby turns on all his gala lights and recordings of "Home Sweet Home." As the animals roar and howl in the unnatural light, Sir Bobby screeches, "They'll all go out in their grey dreariness. We'll go out as a high old, rare old, bloody beautiful joke." Sir Bobby is a similarly valiant poseur in his private life. His wife, interested in the theater, sees him rarely, and he is continually trying to be unfaithful. Yet, at moments of crisis, they appear together to make a brave, public stand, and each has a good deal of respect for the other's allegiance to a more noble, happier time.

After the war is over, the zoo becomes sinister. The new director, the cosmopolitan Uni-European, Englander, establishes a zoo in which the conventional difference between man and animal is diabolically reversed. He sets up an exhibit with a chained, shoddy Russian bear and a caged, miserable American eagle. He then invites the mob of Uni-Europeans to tear the bear and the eagle to pieces. The leader of the Uni-European party, Blanchard-White, plans an exhibition in which political prisoners will be pitted against wild beasts in the revival of a grand old European spectacle. All rational control has, at this point, vanished from society; control is simply the violent abstraction of total irrationality.

All these changes in government and administration are seen from the point of view of Simon Carter, the young secretary of the zoo. Although Simon tends to favor Leacock's position, he remains detached through most of the early conflicts. He is the only one at the zoo able to come home without smelling like one of the animals. He is careful and critical, interested in research and examination, and able to doubt Leacock's certainties even though he substantially agrees with him. He worries about motives and responsibility, and is frequently called a "prig" by others when he will not fall in with their schemes easily and enthusiastically. The war forces Simon out of his intellectual detachment. He tries to save the animals, but can only barely save himself. When the Uni-Europeans take control, Simon tries to work with them, feeling that any zoo, any control, may be better than extinction or anarchy. But his American wife, loyal throughout the other changes, leaves him after she sees the mob rip apart the eagle and the bear. Simon finally realizes the horror of the Uni-Europeans, protests, regains his wife, and is sent to a concentration camp. Inexplicably, sane government is restored at the end of the novel. The Uni-Europeans are defeated and jailed, while Simon and the few remaining responsible administrators are liberated. Yet Simon, at the end, is chastened; he is less arrogant, priggish, and detached. During the war he could keep alive only by trapping and eating badgers, the animals he had once protected as his principal zoölogical interest. He has been forced to recognize the atavism at the center of even the most responsible of human beings.

All the changes in the zoo's administration reflect possible perspectives on the government of human society. Leacock's "limited liberty" reflects the uneasy control and neurotic administration of a government that would allow the maximum liberty commensurate with national security. Sir Bobby's Victorian fanfare represents the conservative and impossible return to a more ordered and settled way of life. The Uni-Europeans represent the irrational and irresponsible mob, those who glorify their instincts and follow any violent slogan. The novel is set in 1970 in order to objectify, more easily, tendencies and attitudes already manifest within contemporary society. *The Old Men at the Zoo* is not, however, a prediction; fables are never that specific. Rather, the novel is an exaggerated objectification of current society, a logical extension of attitudes, slogans, and perspectives that Wilson finds currently visible. The novel is also different from *1984*. Orwell's novel is a melodramatic warning, sensationally exaggerating the dangers of a specific form of government; Wilson's novel is a fable, making an exaggerated statement about the nature of the creature in contemporary society, a wider and more complex statement relevant to all forms of government. Within the context of his fable Wilson also demonstrates his allegiance to a kind of rational control. Simon, the intellectual, the administrator, is also, in a way, the hero. Man can survive, in terms of the novel, only if he recognizes his own animalism but attempts, as intelligently as he can, to govern this brutality rationally and wisely. He cannot establish programs or return to rigid, narrow codes of the past, but he can try to exercise some control over the beast, over himself. And, as in Wilson's other novels, the personal control and the professional control are equated. Simon's relationship with his wife invariably mirrors the appropriateness of his response to the given professional issue. The worthy man, to Wilson, cannot easily separate his worth into categories marked job, bed, or indulgent father.

The limited and perceptive rationality that the hero manifests is, in Wilson's work, a peculiarly British virtue. Obviously Wilson does not beat the drum in order to acclaim the superiority of everything British, but the man of intelligence and responsibility who tries to exercise some control over the bestial is, like Simon Carter and Gerald Middleton and Bernard Sands, invariably British. On the other hand, principal villains have usually immigrated from foreign countries. In *The Old Men at the Zoo*, Sir Bobby Falcon's British Day may be outmoded and ridiculous, but it is neither so sinister nor so despicable as the celebration of the Uni-European movement. The Uni-European leader states his aims quite openly:

> To see justice done and to have a little fun. I don't think they're such incompatible aims really. In fact, quite the contrary, quite the contrary, particularly if, in throwing off the puritan legacy, we get closer to the rich vein of Mediterranean brutality on which our European legacy so much depends. [P. 317.]

Inge Middleton's muddled softness and Marie Hélène's calculated hardness are both alien intrusions; Bill Eliot is killed in the bestial governmental squabbles in Srem Panh. But Meg Eliot, working out her own future; Gerald Middleton, examining the truth of his past; and Simon Carter, responsibly concerned with the nature of man in society, are all thoroughly and sensibly British.

Angus Wilson is the best contemporary English novelist. Each of his last three novels is an entirely different attempt to present significant issues in contemporary society. No other contemporary has treated so vast a range of social and intellectual problems or controlled so diverse material from an intelligent and coherent perspective. In addition, no other contemporary has used so various and effective techniques—a prismatic series of interconnecting mirrors, a novel of sensibility, and a striking fable—to represent the many sides of the human creature.

10

Comedy and Understatement

WHILE ALAN SILLITOE DEPICTS THE ATTITUDES OF THE
worker in a Nottingham bicycle factory and Kingsley Amis
deals with the young man in the red-brick university or provincial library, other novelists during the past decade have
continued to describe social attitudes and manners in more
familiar patterns. Roger Longrigg has written four comic novels
centered on young men in advertising who live in Chelsea mews
houses, on horse racing, or on Mt. Everest parties among the
ex-debutantes who roam between Hyde Park and the Thames.
Hugh Thomas has written a novel (*The World's Game*, 1957)
describing the Foreign Office and the people, old and empty or
young and disillusioned, who work there. Honor Tracy has
written a number of novels in which the sane and logical Englishman comes into conflict with a shoddily romantic and irresponsible Ireland. In one of these comedies, *The Straight and Narrow
Path* (1956), a young scholar reports that a group of Irish nuns
have celebrated midsummer by jumping over fires in their own
version of an ancient fertility rite, and almost all of Ireland is
scandalized when the report appears in an English newspaper.
The whole novel develops reactions and complications from the

single incident. But none of these recent novels is concerned with
the lower or the lower middle classes, with the social issues that
develop from a breaking down of the English class structure.

Andrew Sinclair's novels treat class more explicitly than do
those of Longrigg, Thomas, and Honor Tracy, yet Sinclair's
heroes are far from Sillitoe's workers or from Lucky Jim. In
Sinclair's first novel, *The Breaking of Bumbo* (1959), the young
hero, from an unspecified segment of the middle classes, has gone
through Eton on scholarship and is, during the course of the
novel, in the battalion of Guards stationed in London. He tries
to live the guardsman's elegant bachelor life: Rugby matches,
drinking until dawn, debutante parties throughout the season.
The hero of Sinclair's second novel, *My Friend Judas* (1959),
is a student at Cambridge who pretends to come from a lower
class than he does and uses class and class attitudes as material
for mockery throughout his undergraduate career. Although
the villain of the novel is a rightist snob whose affectations parody
those of Evelyn Waugh's undergraduates in the 'twenties, the
hero really feels that class is irrelevant. Toward the end of the
novel he thinks about the subject of class:

> I mean, take this whole class-racket that worries me stiff. I don't
> mean class, in the jokey Mitford sense; I mean class, a joe's place
> in his set-up. Even then, it's not all that. I know that I, good old
> bourgeois Ben Birt, buzz round pretending to be more of a
> prole than I am, so I can spit in the eye of the richer bourgeois,
> who try to look like aristos. But we're both wrong. Maybe, like
> the porters who try to be porters, we should just try to be stu-
> dents, and do our jobs. Class being doing your job well. Class
> being knowing where you are and why. Class being more than
> schooling, accent, lolly, looks; . . . class being a fair idea of what
> you can do and what you can't, and saying that's that. Though it's
> a fact that most joes don't know what they can't do. They don't
> know their class. Or maybe they do know their class, but they
> don't think it's where they are.   [Pp. 205–206.]

Despite his lack of snobbery, Ben Birt regards getting rid of the
usual preoccupations and designations of class as something far

easier than the heroes of Wain, Amis, Osborne, or Sillitoe would ever acknowledge them to be.

Roger Longrigg often satirizes those preoccupied by class issues or the dislocated who try to rise from prior class affiliations. In his first novel, *A High-pitched Buzz* (1956), the posh people who work in the advertising agency all laugh at the one girl in the art department who is not a part of their elegant world:

> She had wispy, dry, reddish hair, pulled back into a pony's tail (at *that* late date a pony's tail); a heavy reddish face; a style of dress in which Bohemianism and the terrible orthodoxy of her background strove in sad and inconclusive conflict, like two very weak old ladies hitting at each other with broken parasols.
>
> [Pp. 63–64.]

Longrigg also satirizes the jumbled foreign and discordant influences in contemporary coffee bars. *Switchboard* (1957) again mocks the secretaries in advertising offices who are not so well-bred or so sophisticated as their bosses are, and spends a good deal of time satirizing the rigid, nonconformist family that one of the principal characters marries into. In Longrigg's third novel, *Wrong Number* (1959), his hero, a young Oxford don, complains that some of his new fellow dons are "uncouth physicists from the Black Country" and "furious economists from London." Later in the novel the hero stays at a country house in order to write and produce a musical for charity. He uses Marlowe's *Dr. Faustus* as the framework for his parody, characterizing "Wrath" as one of the "Angry Young Men" who retains his anger despite the fact that his books are selling extremely well.

Honor Tracy satirizes not only the irresponsible stage Irishman, but also any form of the progressive or the do-gooder. One of her more recent novels, *A Number of Things* (1960), relates the trip of a young writer, Henry Lamb, to the West Indies in order to write a series of impressions for a liberal magazine. Young Henry, unpretentious, honest, and well-bred, quickly discovers the hypocrisy of the liberal magazine (the editor, lisping and sentimental, will not print Henry's accounts because they conflict with his preconceived notion of West Indian nobility and "rhythm"). Miss Tracy ridicules almost everyone Henry encounters: Orlando Figgis, the primitive West Indian turned Shakespearean commentator; the self-sacrificing Miss Perowne who wishes to break down all class barriers on board the ship and prides herself on her enthusiasm for discovering and encouraging native talent; Candida Firebrace, the spirited native who enjoys religion so much that she dedicates herself to both the Pilgrim Zeal from Minnesota and the Catholic Church; the sententious editor who cheats Henry of the money he's promised him; George Bernard Singh, the native hotelkeeper who persists in raising Henry's rent and in hiding his letters from him. The West Indies, for Miss Tracy, represents a new world gone mad, a whole set of irresponsible people suddenly given money and power by deluded fools. Only the well-bred young man, the man who represents the virtues of the old English society, can remain sane in the midst of the contemporary chaos. Andrew Sinclair has little veneration for the special virtue of any class, but he also mocks much that is contemporary: the coffee bars, the new skepticism about all politics, the "Angry Young Men." Ben Birt, in *My Friend Judas,* makes fun of all the realistic and committed undergraduate writers and deliberately sets himself to compose "romantic muck" for an anti-anti-Establishment Cambridge paper. He constantly derides the self-pity of those students who talk and write about class and about social problems.

These writers—Longrigg, Sinclair, Honor Tracy, and Thomas —do not, however, simply represent a conservative or upperclass reaction to the work of writers like Osborne and Wain. Rather, they satirize the Establishment just as forcefully as they deride the poor Bohemian in the advertising agency or the young man from the Black Country at Oxford or Cambridge. Honor Tracy burlesques Henry Lamb's vegetable-growing parson father who is completely removed from the contemporary world, the hypocritical British colonial administration in the West Indies, the priggish Englishman wherever she finds him, and the ineffectual little lord who periodically cannot control his whim to run naked through his Irish woods. And Miss Tracy seems to reserve her greatest contempt, in all her novels, for the newspapers, for those vast classless organizations that distort the facts simply to fit their own policies and prejudices. Andrew Sinclair mocks the Guards with their military stiffness and their belief in useless hardship as a form of good training, the shallow debutantes who go through endlessly repetitious parties in order to capture a husband, and the viciousness of the conscious aristocrat. Roger Longrigg balances his satire of the grubby or the dislocated with comic treatment of wealthy old men in clubs, well-bred young girls who continue their school language by talking of everything in initials at parties, the wealthy county ladies with their charities and their love affairs, the fashions in taste that demand that every young Londoner prove his contemporaneity by admiring Kipling, and the sameness of the young advertising men who live in similar mews houses in Chelsea. Longrigg's most recent novel, *Daughters of Mulberry* (1961), adds farce to his comic methods, for, in this story of an old man's attempt to make enough money to buy a comfortable estate by judicious betting at the horse races, Longrigg has long scenes where his characters try to assemble the models of ships or airplanes given away with breakfast flakes or escape from the police by strategically placing flashlight batteries on the stairs. Hugh Thomas also satirizes the Establishment. He depicts the Foreign Office ensnared in meaningless protocol and sententious, noncommittal language. Most of the officials, important though their positions and decisions are, spend their time worrying about the social life in the capital on their next tour of duty or the complexities of the "fag-prefect relationship" in the structure of the Foreign Office. Thomas also describes a disarmament conference in which the participants are more interested in the image they present to the newspapers than in disarmament and a House of Commons in which the members are interested only in oratorical tricks. With the exception of Thomas, these writers satirize all class or group entities in contemporary England. Although the heroes are usually well-mannered, the authors are unwilling to allow them to make a special plea for the virtue of a particular class. The satire, quick, extensive, sharp-minded, dominates the novels.

These four writers, however, despite satire and despite constant understatement, place some value in the character of the hero. Longrigg, Thomas, and Honor Tracy have little to do with the tradition of the bumbling, equivocal antihero who figures in the comic fiction of Wain and Amis. All Longrigg's heroes are loyal: loyal to their bosses despite the incessant political maneuvering within the advertising agency, loyal to their women despite the constant complexity of sexual attraction. In *A High-pitched Buzz* the mocking young hero is even willing to risk losing advancement within the agency (at first, his only apparent aim) by defending his boring, petty, tyrannical boss. Simon Smith, the young hero in Thomas' *The World's Game,* maintains an unsatirized faith in the possibility that political action can improve man's condition amidst what he feels is the decadent skepticism of the Foreign Office. Although sometimes naïve, Simon preserves his independent political judgment and his honest reactions throughout the novel.

Honor Tracy's heroes are all distinguished by a remarkable adherence to common sense in a zany, senseless world. Henry Lamb tries to report what he sees in the West Indies, and, although he never defends the eternal rightness of British colonial administration, he refuses to join other contemporaries in long wails of national self-recrimination or to praise anything he sees simply because it's authentically native. Andrew Butler, in *The Straight and Narrow Path,* begins as a somewhat priggish young man of principle caught by mystical Irish nonsense. Yet he is shrewd enough, once he discovers that the Irish simply use their nonsense to gain whatever they can for themselves, to fabricate a story about a ghost haunting the canon's house in order to serve his own end. Principle is never so important, for Miss Tracy, as seeing the world with clear intelligence. In another novel, *The Prospects Are Pleasing* (1958), she has her witty and materialistic English hero win out against the ineptitude of the proud, mystic, and irrational Irish. The Englishman even has to steal the painting that represents Ireland's cause, simply by walking into the National Gallery and taking the picture from the wall, while the frightened Irishman hides and then runs away.

Andrew Sinclair's hero in *My Friend Judas* is more limited and closer to the antihero than are the heroes of Longrigg, Thomas, or Honor Tracy. Ben Birt begins with a sense of his own limitation, commenting on his minute place in the scheme of things and acknowledging that he is more comfortable in the admiration of his home town than in the midst of Cambridge's scholarship and sophistication. Yet, when genuinely moved, he is capable of disinterested action simply to help other people. He tells a white lie in order to save his tutor's marriage, and he remains with an unattractive girl throughout the May Week Ball. He also comes, through the course of the novel, to value Cambridge, to see the university not simply as a pleasant way to spend three years without responsibility, but as a social force that stands against the world of "the Big Dirt and the Great Muck." Through the university he has developed a set of allegiances, almost, as he indicates on the last page, a morality in spite of himself. Throughout the novel Ben tells his college porter, Doggie, that he, Ben, is really an aristocrat, a lord. Thinking Doggie an implacable old Tory, Ben assumes that his lies have been responsible for the many favors that Doggie has done for him. At the end, however, Doggie reveals that he always knew that Ben was lying but liked him anyhow. He gives Ben his reasons:

> But you, sir, you was friendly or not as you felt. And you'd have your bit of fun, and share it around like. And that's what we like, them as shares their fun like the old gentlemen did before the new lot came in. They're all so serious now, sir. They mind so

much. Haven't got a civil word in their head for those they
think is worser. Not like the old gentlemen, sir, and you, sir.
You've always got your little joke, and that's what I like. *Lord
Birt*, I've laughed over that many a time.   [Pp. 204–205.]

Ben then thinks: "He was an old Tory, but that's how he wanted
it. And he saw through me more than I saw through myself, the
lousy spy. I liked Doggie" (p. 205). Sinclair's hero, though
treated somewhat sentimentally, has, through the university,
progressed from amoral honesty to some appreciation of the
humane and responsible tradition the university represents.

In addition to Sinclair's commitment to the traditional values
of Cambridge, these writers also allow for commitment to particular political issues. The hero, somewhat more sure of himself
than is the antihero, feels that he can afford to risk himself and
his career for a particular belief. Sinclair's guardsman, Bumbo,
for example, is removed from his battalion because he advocates
refusing to fight if he is sent to Suez. He even attempts, while
drunk and tired after an exhausting Rugby match, to persuade
the enlisted men on his team that the English cause in Suez is
unjust and that Eden's government has acted only out of pique
and pride. The events concerning Suez in 1956 seem to have
elicited stronger convictions and reactions within the British
Establishment than has any other event within the past decade.
Hugh Thomas' hero, Simon Smith, endorses the other side.
During the events leading up to the Israeli invasion of Egypt,
Simon becomes more and more upset by the anti-Semitism and
the refusal of all the well-bred members of the Foreign Office
staff to understand Egypt's moral guilt. Simon regards Israel as
a liberal democracy battling "an unholy junta of authoritarian
powers," and he feels that Britain will exercise no power or
influence. Finally, in disgust with his job, his associates, and his
class, Simon resigns from the Foreign Office and plans to go to
Israel. Although Simon and Bumbo support different sides in
an issue that is both political and moral, each hero does commit

himself, to his immediate practical disadvantage, on a political issue. The antihero, in comparison, is never sufficiently certain, either of himself or of his world, to form so direct an attachment to a political cause.

Particularly in the work of Sinclair, however, the commitment to a political cause is invariably understated, as are the commitments in the work of Longrigg and Honor Tracy. These are all comic novels (with the exception of *The World's Game*), and comic in a quick, almost desperate way that precludes lingering on a point or stretching out an issue. Longrigg specializes in a kind of clipped style, using a large number of short scenes with comic juxtapositions and sudden leaps from one topic to another. Every crucial conversation in his novels is broken by the nonsense that someone at the next table is talking or interrupted by a seemingly irrelevant detail or a piece of social commentary. *Switchboard* contains a whole middle section of one-line conversations, all demonstrating the development of the hero's illness, as only the sharpest details of experience pierce through his growing delirium. In *Daughters of Mulberry*, as the novel turns into a chase to disclose a deliberate switch of horses, Longrigg develops the suspense through the cinematic device of alternating quick scenes among several locations. Sinclair's comedy, though less standard than that of *Daughters of Mulberry*, is also quick. *The Breaking of Bumbo* is full of interrupted conversations, sudden social comment in the background, and guardsmen's chatter. *My Friend Judas* uses these same devices but also adds a rich and imagistic monologue through which Ben Birt often mocks the world around him. In the work of both Longrigg and Sinclair, all the comedy functions so as to provide a kind of understated commitment, made but quickly hushed up lest it sound pretentious or sentimental. Engaging as they are, these novels are too slight to take any more deliberate or extensive statement.

Even as it stands, the work of Longrigg, Thomas, Sinclair, and Honor Tracy sometimes seems not quick or agile enough. In Longrigg's first two novels, any dire event, such as an infidelity, is grimly foreshadowed. The hero keeps preparing for the disaster with statements like, "If only I had noticed." The hero of the first novel, *A High-pitched Buzz*, is, as a minor character in the second novel, reunited with the girl he had lost. The ending, the losing of the girl, is logical for the events of *A High-pitched Buzz*, and the subsequent reunion, never explained, seems more suitable to a woman's magazine serial. Then, too, Longrigg's two most recent novels are less interesting than his earlier satiric treatments of contemporary London. *Wrong Number* contains some fine satire of county theatricals, but the love affairs that make up a good share of the novel seem stilted and empty. And *Daughters of Mulberry* becomes a semicomic thriller, as the old racegoer eventually unravels the fraud. Honor Tracy's novels, for all their wit, intelligence, and clarity, seem always to rest on the same central point: the man of common sense and logic surrounded by pretentious folly and malicious delusion. Andrew Sinclair, perhaps the best of these novelists, tends to sentimentalize and to repeat, over and over again, some of his best devices. Ben Birt's mocking, imagistic monologues give *My Friend Judas* much of its richness, but some of them seem to go on and on. At one point Ben goes to a party and describes the room:

> Pearl's room is a real tiara. Illumination shines at you out of every nook and cranny. Rarefied taste bongs you on the conk from every facet. Costly knick-knacks jostle discreet gee-gaws. Bijoux of ormulu are piled on porcelain figurines. Jade, alabaster, amber and onyx rub their shiny skins together. Yellow marble buddhas eternally contemplate their navels, in which fresh rose-buds have been newly placed. A stuffed retriever lies on the Indian rug; he'll bark if you fondle his tummy. Glossy photos of Pearl, in dressing-gown or beard or armour or brief loin-cloth, consider each other with grave appreciation and the content of Narcissus. Marlowe Society posters say in big, plain letters AS YOU LIKE IT or OTHELLO or EDWARD THE SECOND. According to custom, the actors' names aren't mentioned. But the posters being on Pearl's wall betray their careful anonymity. Lack of advertisement can never lick a Pearl. He is his own hoarding.
>
> [Pp. 32-33.]

Hugh Thomas is a more sober writer. But his careful discussions of the organization, the waste, and the inefficiency of the Foreign Office are mapped out with laborious detail. He also falls easily into literary clichés: his Americans, Russians, Britons, and Frenchmen around the conference table seem taken directly from a Peter Ustinov play; the images he uses for personal emotions seem drawn from standard imagistic compilations. In short, none of these novels is the work of a great writer. Yet each novel is dealing with the contemporary world in some meaningful way outside the framework of the preoccupations of the most significant writers of the past decade. All these novels are slight, in one way or another. Yet the very slightness of the heroic commitment, of the novel in which the hero can achieve some publicly meaningful action, is in itself significant.

To some extent Longrigg, Thomas, and Sinclair share a common theme. In the work of all three the hero, faithful to his principle or to his superiors, is isolated from most of his society. He can control his own actions, but he cannot command support or approval. And often he is deceived by those in whom he placed the most faith. The women the hero encounters, in the work of these three writers, are invariably unfaithful. The girl Bumbo loves, a young model, soon becomes interested in other men, wanting to keep Bumbo around as her "really *deep*" and wholly spiritual relationship. Bumbo himself, broken from the Guards, finally marries a witless debutante, who is pregnant by another man, simply as a vaguely generous gesture. *My Friend Judas* also deals with an unfaithful girl: Ben's great love, Judy, cannot resist changing men weekly and finally marries one of Ben's naïve and scholarly friends. Simon Smith, the hero of *The World's Game*, is passionately in love with his chief's wife and is unaware, until the very end of the novel, that she is habitually unfaithful to her husband. Longrigg's women are also not to be trusted. The hero's girl in *A High-pitched Buzz* deserts him, and one of the principal girls in *Switchboard*, a sharp middle-class young lady who has captured the wealthy director of the advertising agency, lands in bed with her husband's godson. *Wrong*

Number deals with all the predatory county wives, always anxious to deceive their husbands with younger or more handsome men. In each of these novels the hero is left alone at the end, deserted by his woman and misunderstood by most of those around him. Although Bumbo has made his stand on Suez, he is now trapped in a loveless marriage. Simon Smith is off for Israel, his friends thinking him crazy and his illusions about both love and government completely shattered. Even the old hero in *Daughters of Mulberry*, having uncovered the crooked horse switch, suffers more than anyone else in the novel. The fortune he has tried to amass in forty years at the track is gone, and he goes back to the bar, alone, to try to figure out the winner of the next race.

Within their isolation most of these heroes become wiser people than they were before. They learn how little any of us knows of what another thinks or feels. Ben Birt in *My Friend Judas* not only learns that he has trusted the wrong people, but also that he must falsify what he knows about Judy, his Judas, so that her marriage with his friend will have some chance to work. His knowledge, and the necessity for keeping it to himself, only reinforce his isolation, an isolation that he has always noticed in the American fiction of Hemingway, Salinger, and Nathaniel West. Bumbo, too, is misunderstood. His fellow officers cannot imagine that anyone would hold a conviction, so they assume that Bumbo has been broken because he is a homosexual and a coward. His new wife's family assume he has married simply to gain their superior connections in society and business. Similarly, Hugh Thomas' hero cannot connect with the world of the Foreign Office. When the chief's wife discovers that Simon is headed for Israel, she assumes that his unrequited love for her has driven him to exile himself, and she even, for the first time, wants him to kiss her. She is incapable of understanding that his decision is moral and political, for such decisions are entirely alien to the Foreign Office crowd that Thomas portrays. Longrigg's heroes also learn through experience, as the hero of *A High-pitched Buzz* finds, on a visit to his boss's home, how easily and superficially he has judged whatever did not fit into his tiny advertising and Knightsbridge world. For each of these heroes something of the assured world and the clubby trust of the fortunate Briton has been lost. The hero remains, more like a figure in the tradition of American fiction, the tradition of Hawthorne, Melville, and Hemingway, still keeping faith with himself, but wiser and more lonely in his heroism.

Yet the lonely heroism is slight and almost always understated. Longrigg and Sinclair, in particular, surround their heroes with constant verbal jokes and comic references. Yet, like Hugh Thomas, they portray the contemporary world in which man frequently finds himself alone, unable to attach himself to a meaningful group or society. They retain the hero; they do not question that far. Yet, from the established positions in society, these writers comically, sometimes diffidently, often gracefully, develop statements concerning the enormous difficulty involved in understanding and relating to the chaotic contemporary world. They define the irrelevance of the older traditions they admire, of loyalty, of adherence to principle, of humane concern for others. They work their way through to positions that other writers as diverse as Iris Murdoch, Alan Sillitoe, John Wain, and Angus Wilson assume as axiomatic.

11

Images of Illusion in the Work of Iris Murdoch

EACH OF IRIS MURDOCH'S FIRST FOUR NOVELS HAS, AS its title, an image of the kind of illusion its characters face. The first novel, *Under the Net* (1954), tells the story of Jake Donaghue's wanderings about Bohemian London and Paris as he attempts to find or construct a satisfactory way of life. But planned ways of life are nets, traps, no matter how carefully or rationally the net is woven, and Jake discovers that none of these narrow paths really works. The nets in the novel range from logical-positivist philosophy and left-wing politics through miming theatricals to film scripts and sophisticated blackmail. In the second novel, *The Flight from the Enchanter* (1956), Miss Murdoch deals with a different sort of illusion. All the characters are under spells, enchantments, held in a kind of emotional captivity by another person or force. The principal agent of enchantment, an ephemeral cosmopolite named Mischa Fox, exercises a spell over a number of the other characters in the novel; yet he feels no responsibility for the effects of the spells he exercises and the spells provide no real meaning or satisfaction for the characters caught in them. Emotional enchantment works no better than the weaving of conscious and rational nets, and the characters are eventually forced, by their own natures, to flee enchantment as they must unravel nets. The third novel is called *The Sandcastle* (1957). The title is emblematic of the love affair a married, fortyish schoolteacher tries to build with a young artist named Rain. But the affair cannot last; it is a castle of sand. As Rain explains, when talking about her Mediterranean background, she has known only dry, dirty sand, unsuitable for building castles of any shape or form. From the schoolteacher's point of view, Rain provides too much energy, too much vitality, for him to cope with in his circumscribed world, as a deluge of rain can wash away a sandcastle. And, significantly, there is a torrential rain on the day when the school teacher displays his inability to deal with all the complications of the affair. The elements of the affair—the grains of sand and the moisture—exist, but the sand is either too dry or too wet. Human beings are unable to control the moisture, to build a lasting shape out of the illusory dream, and the castle either crumbles or is washed away.

In Miss Murdoch's fourth novel, *The Bell* (1958), a group of people in a lay religious community attempt to place a bell on the tower of a nearby abbey. The bell is a postulant, a means of entering the religious life for each of the people involved. But the bridge leading to the abbey has been tampered with and, in its journey, the bell topples into the lake. The bell itself, the effort of human beings to construct and particularize their own means of salvation, is undermined by human action, emotion, and behavior. At the same time the traditional bell, the bell that once actually pealed from the abbey tower, is recovered from the lake by two of the least devout characters and sent to the British Museum as a historical curiosity. The tradition of the past is meaningful only for antiquarians, is removed from the central issues of experience, while the contemporary bell is another illusion, the image of another unsuccessful human attempt.

Most of the images in Miss Murdoch's titles are relative. For example, while the bell is a postulant for the religious life for many of the characters, it is a different kind of postulant for each. The athletic Christian, James Tayper Pace, gives a sermon saying that the bell represents purity, candor, innocence; for Michael, the leader of the religious community, the bell combines this innocence with the wisdom of the serpent and represents a kind of saving self-knowledge. What each person sees in the bell is a reflection of himself and his ideals. Similarly, in the other novels, there is not simply one net or one enchantment. People build their own traps from their own minds and feelings, and the traps, the illusions, are all stated in different terms. Only in *The Sandcastle* is the title an image for a single illusion or relationship. In the other novels, each of the characters fabricates himself into an illusion expressed in terms related to those of other illusions. But the illusions are really different for different people: Michael's bell is much more complex than James's, Annette's enchantment is more romantic and juvenile and very different from Rosa's. Each of the novels, however, does collect the various illusions under a general set of terms, terms that are somewhat different for each of the four novels. Each novel gives a symbolic identity to the characters' desire to manufacture form and direction out of their disparate experience. And, in each novel, this attempt on the part of the characters to manufacture form and direction is unsuccessful; the general structure suggested by the title cannot meaningfully operate in the fragmented, relative world. ·

Against these images of man-made structures, Miss Murdoch frequently poses images of the natural world. In *The Flight from the Enchanter,* for example, references to fish are often indications of the natural forces man tries to capture, possess, construct. When Rainborough, an unsatisfied civil servant, attempts to prove and define himself by trying to seduce young Annette, he thinks of her in terms of fish:

> It was like hunting fish with an underwater gun, a sport which he had once been foolish enough to try. At one moment there is the fish—graceful, mysterious, desirable, and free—and the next moment there is nothing but struggling and blood and confusion.
>
> [Pp. 135–136.]

Possession spoils the sense of being of the fish, the animate quality that makes it desirable. Similarly, Mischa, the principal enchanter, keeps a large bowl of colored fish in the ballroom of his elegant house. In a moment of jealous fury, at a wild party, Rosa hurls a paperweight and smashes the fish bowl. The fish cannot survive. Once imprisoned, the fish cannot survive liberation, as many of the people in the novel, once enchanted, can break away only by enormous effort and suffering. Possession does not, however, always involve death, and enchantment is not always that decisive, that final. Near the end of the novel, when Rosa is about to break away from the spell of Mischa's enchantment, they are talking at sunset in Mischa's garden in Italy:

> A lizard came suddenly on to the parapet near to Mischa. It stood tensely still, and in the horizontal sunlight its small body cast a big shadow. With an easy sweep of the hand Mischa caught it and drew it on to his knee and held it for a moment with both hands cupped. His face lit up with animation and pleasure as he looked down at the panting belly of the lizard. It lay still in his hands.
>
> "Give him to me!" said Rosa. She stretched out her free hand.
>
> "Be careful how you hold him," said Mischa, and he put the lizard into her palm.
>
> Rosa's fingers closed upon it maladroitly. In an instant, with a quick twist, the lizard had sprung away from her on to the ground, leaving its writhing tail behind in her grasp. With a cry Rosa dropped the tail upon the gravel. It lay there still twisting and writhing. Mischa picked it up quickly and threw it over the parapet. They looked at each other wide-eyed with a sudden fright and distress.
>
> "He'll soon grow another one," said Mischa, and his voice was trembling. [Pp. 299–300.]

The natural, the vital, sometimes has a recuperative power that possession or enchantment, those emotional artifices, cannot wholly efface. And Rosa herself, battered by her relationship with Mischa as well as by her relationship with two diabolic Polish brothers, can break enchantments, leave part of herself with them, but still escape and survive.

In *Under the Net,* Miss Murdoch also uses natural creatures as symbols of some animate and essential quality. In one of his many schemes Jake Donaghue kidnaps Mars, an aging dog who has starred in films. Mars is caged when Jake steals him, and Jake goes through a difficult and elaborate process to release him. But, once Jake possesses Mars, he finds that his plan to exchange the kidnaped Mars for the return of a manuscript he believes stolen from him misfires. No one intended to keep the manuscript from him and the original owners no longer want Mars. But Mars still exists, is still a form of being no longer amenable to human purposes and machinations. And, at the end of the novel, when all Jake's nets have been unraveled, he returns to his shrine (Mrs. Tinckham's disorderly, cluttered sweetshop) to find that Maggie, the cat, has given birth to four kittens. The birth of the kittens does not point out a means of salvation for Jake; it simply serves as an animate fact (the fact on which the novel ends) in contrast to all the specious illusions of man's conscious attempts. *The Bell* also makes use of a dog. Nick, a sort of devil in the religious community, the man whose action specifically prevents the bell from reaching the abbey, has a dog, Murphy, who very much resembles him. They roam the woods together, live the same sort of lawless existence. But Murphy is a dog, Nick a man, and Murphy can escape the torments, the human traps and ideas and forms, that finally drive Nick to suicide. Although Nick first talked of "training" Murphy, it is Murphy who is left to howl in agony at the end. As Nick attempts to train Murphy, so other members of the religious community try to recognize, classify, impose order upon the birds in the woods near their house. But the birds outlast the community, flying freely despite the light metal bands human beings have tied upon their legs. The unconscious creature survives where the conscious human venture fails, as, in *The Bell,* Dora, the most creaturelike of human beings, the woman uninterested in bells, salvation, ultimate meaning, is the one who survives.

A dog serves a similar function in *The Sandcastle.* The school-teacher, Mor, and his family owned a dog who is now dead. But the dog survives in the mind of Mor's daughter, Felicity, as she sees the spirit of the dog possess the bodies of the people around her. For Felicity, the dog's spirit is a natural and understanding force in the midst of a complex, structured world of relationships which she can neither understand nor fully cope with. She wonders whether her older brother really believes in the dog's spirit or has become too limited by adult facts and adult constructions. Here the dog is a symbol of illusion when posed against the common-sense world; but it is also ironically a symbol of a natural creature when posed against all the mundane fabrications men build, and the unhappiness these fabrications cause, in the world of the novel. The dog also serves for Mor and his wife. The memory of the dog, attached to their feeling for their garden, is the only point of emotional contact that Mor and his wife share. And none of Mor's consciousness of his affair with Rain, nothing of his artificial sandcastle, can destroy either his or his family's memory of the dog. The wandering, formless creature also appears in *The Sandcastle* in the form of a gypsy present at crucial moments in the relationship between Rain and Mor. The gypsy becomes a vague image of the way things are going, of the impending disastrous end to the affair. Mor, after he has passed the gypsy at several different times, tries to find him, control him, and make him part of the understandable universe. But the gypsy is deaf, and, like the lizard or the dog, represents something beyond human communication or control, some animate force not subject to human construction or illusion.

The vital nonhuman is also posed against the charts of human beings in another way, for Miss Murdoch makes frequent use of gardens and woods in her novels. Sometimes the garden is suggestive, as in *The Sandcastle* where Mor and Rain first sense their affair in a rose garden when they touch. The garden communicates something that each of them needs and finds in the other. Where they fail is in their ability to retain and control the feelings of the garden in a world of human beings and human responsibilities. At various points in the novel Mor returns to the garden, watching Rain's window (lights of human activity and concern) from the midst of his garden, his love. The garden has affected man, but man cannot preserve, make permanent, the spirit that emanates from the garden. Sometimes, too, the garden is more profuse. Not only can man not capture it, but he can be lost in it. Jake Donaghue in *Under the Net* chases Anna, his vision of meaningful romance, through the Tuileries on Bastille Day, losing her among the trees, the statues, and celebrating lovers. The garden, like the world, is part natural and part man-made, but exists in such profusion that man loses himself and his vision in the tangle. Sometimes the garden is better ordered, as is the beautiful and carefully isolated garden attached to the abbey in *The Bell*. But this is the garden of those who have already entered the religious life and it is significantly their graveyard as well. In contrast, in the lay religious community in *The Bell*, the woods frequently impinge upon the efforts of man, as the remnants of an older civilization at Imber were crowded out by woods and grass and growth. The postulant community, unlike the final and lifeless abbey, is the human attempt to capture space, form, meaning from the country wilderness, as it is the attempt, ultimately unsuccessful, to give meaningful direction to chaotic human experience.

Gardens are also used by man in order to create something out of the wilderness. Rainborough, in *The Flight from the Enchanter*, is proud of his garden, but the hospital behind claims some of the land and knocks down his wall in order to possess it. Other man-made institutions can spoil the garden. In *The Bell*, the inhabitants of the religious community cultivate a market garden as one of their most important projects. Here the garden is an image for the conscious direction man attempts to give to his experience. The garden works for a time, thrives and is profitable, but it does not outlive the collapse of the community that created it. Only the wilderness survives the failure to place the bell on the tower; the wilderness and Dora, the formless, flourish. Michael notices: "He watched Dora, turning towards life and happiness like a strong plant towards the sun, assimilating all that lay in her way" (p. 335). The market garden, mechanically cultivated, decays.

Human actions and aspirations are represented in the houses and the structures human beings build as well as in their attempts to cultivate the land. Imber Court, for example, the long, clean, aseptic manor house in *The Bell*, represents the clean and pure existence its inhabitants want to lead in order to gain religious meaning and direction. The sexual deviations that wreck the community stem from the woods (where Dora and Michael see Toby swimming, where Catherine runs wild) and the corruption of the pub in town. The court itself represents the human chart, the human attempt, the human illusion that doesn't fit the facts of experience. Similarly, in *The Sandcastle*, Demoyte's house (where Rain lives) represents, with its large library and gracious proportions, a sensible and humane tradition. The books and the fire show ease, wisdom, comfort. But the treacherous garden, at least treacherous for Mor, lies just outside the window, and the house is not strong enough to prevent the garden's impact. Mischa Fox's house in *The Flight from the Enchanter* represents the kind of prefabricated enchantment with which Mischa holds other people. For his large party, "A carpet had been laid upon the steps, and there were flowers on either side of the door, metallic blue and red in the crystalline light from the doorway, and swaying slightly in the evening breeze" (p. 200). The house itself also reflects Mischa's personality, the labyrinthine quality that helps make him so mysterious and attractive to others.

> Mischa had had the fantasy of buying four houses in Kensington, two adjoining in one road, and two adjoining in the next road, and standing back to back with the first two. He had joined this block of four houses into one by building a square structure to span the gap. Within this strange *palazzo*, so rumour said, the walls and ceilings and stairs had been so much altered, improved and removed that very little remained of the original interiors. By now, it was reported, there were no corridors and no continuous stairways. The rooms, which were covered with thick

carpets upon which the master of the house was accustomed to walk barefoot, opened directly out of each other like a set of boxes; and the floors were joined at irregular intervals by staircases, often themselves antiques which had been ripped out of other buildings. The central structure, which, it was noticed, had few windows, excited yet wilder speculation. Some people said that it housed a laboratory, others that it contained a covered courtyard with a fountain, and others again that it was a storehouse for art treasures which had been procured illicitly by Mischa and which were so well known that his possession of them had to be kept a secret. [Pp. 200–201.]

This detailed, structural description is by no means unusual in Miss Murdoch's novels. Man's plans to build, man's plans to achieve something are frequently given exhaustively thorough and precise treatment with all the engineering and the architecture involved fully described. Two boys' attempt to climb the tower of the school in *The Sandcastle*, Jake's trials and engineering difficulties in stealing the dog in *Under the Net*, and Toby and Dora's reclamation of the old bell in *The Bell* are fully detailed. But all these engineering projects, as well as all the houses represent, are either unsuccessful or useless. The boys cannot prove themselves by climbing the tower (one of them is nearly killed) and the reclamation of the bell serves no meaningful purpose. Human achievement, human construction, never really does what it has been designed to do. Although characters change during the course of the novels, they seldom can carry through a deliberate plan or a conscious intention. The conscious construction is all, like the masks for the mimers in Anna's prop room in *Under the Net*, a form, a face, a pose that does not represent either a means of salvation or the essential feelings of the central figures in the novel.

Man's interest in structure is, in Miss Murdoch's novels, part of his interest in precision, in defining himself and his world. Almost all the characters in the novels seek some form of definition, some means of coherently explaining what they are. Even the enigmatic hero, Mischa, wants the tangible and the precise. He keeps photographs of scenes important to his childhood with the scholar, Peter, and he uses photographs, much as a black-mailer does, to keep his hold, his enchantment, over others. Photographs frequently appear as images of the precise, of man's attempt to control something around him: Annette keeps a pho-tograph of her brother as her only apparent tie to family and background; Michael, in *The Bell*, photographs all the birds he has captured and catalogued. And man is able to use a camera, is able to fix formless experience at given points, is able to make contact, in limited time and space, with other people and other things. It is only when man attempts to make the precise into a wider system of precision, to fit the formless into a pattern (like a net or an enchantment or a sandcastle or a bell), that the system turns into an unworkable illusion. As Jake, in a dialogue he's written, has his friend Hugo say (and Hugo, character-istically and ironically, disclaims all knowledge of the actual statement):

> If by expressing a theory you mean that someone else could make a theory about what you do, of course that is true and uninterest-ing. What I speak of is the real decision as we experience it; and here the movement away from theory and generality is the move-ment toward truth. All theorizing is flight. We must be ruled by the situation itself and this is unutterably particular. Indeed it is something to which we can never get close enough, however hard we may try as it were to crawl under the net.   [P. 91.]

The net is verbal and theoretical. Any meaningful human pos-sibility must be direct, active, concrete, limited to a particular situation. Hugo himself has failed to find satisfaction and mean-ing in the theoretical roles he has constructed: a patron of the arts, a film producer, and a sort of Undershaftian maker of armaments. He has a somewhat better chance at the end of the novel, for he plans to engage in concrete and limited work, to become an apprentice to a watchmaker in Nottingham. Jake, too, after his grandiose schemes for power, fortune, and literary eminence have failed, achieves a kind of independent value, a concrete though limited meaning, as a hospital orderly.

Almost all the characters try to make their desires for definition into some kind of system, and the system fails. Annette's wish to learn in the "school of life" becomes a system, a *mystique*, and she is forced to return to the more limited precision of the shelter of her family. Catherine, in *The Bell,* wants to define her spiritual impulses by the attempt to become a nun, but the rigid structure of the road to the sisterhood becomes too much for her nature. Mor, in *The Sandcastle,* defined as a schoolmaster already, tries to turn his wandering impulses into the pattern of a grand passion. The large definition, man's attempt to make himself part of a theory, doesn't work.

All the novels include one or more God-images, characters of wisdom and insight to whom the other characters turn for advice. Hugo and Mrs. Tinckham in *Under the Net,* Peter Saward in *The Flight from the Enchanter,* Demoyte and the jeweler leader of the local Labour party in *The Sandcastle,* Michael and the Abbess in *The Bell,* all at one time or another serve in this god-like role. But the God-figure never really works in the structure of the novel. The advice turns out wrong or the God-figure never meant at all what the character thought he meant or the God-figure himself is equally perplexed. Ironically, it is Calvin Blick, a flunky, an unsavory blackmailer, a man who had defined himself in a limited, unsystematic way, who comes closest to stating the general truth in *The Flight from the Enchanter.* He tells Rosa: "You will never know the truth, and you will read the signs in accordance with your deepest wishes. That is what we humans always have to do. Reality is a cipher with many solutions, all of them the right ones" (pp. 304–305). And the God-figures, those who abstract reality into a theory or a message, invariably miss or contradict the point.

Iris Murdoch's images frequently place the formless against the precise, the fish or the woods against the architecturally devised or the man-made cage. And when the man-made image, the reflection of the human attempt to impose order on its world, is made into a generalization or a system, that system fails to operate for human beings, becomes a rational or emotional illusion. Man, in Iris Murdoch's world, is part creature, part rational and conscious being. He has a strong need for the definition, the precision, his conscious nature can provide. But he also needs to limit the definition, to recognize that elaborate definitions, generalizations, make splendid targets for the shafts of the creature, the separate and particular and often unconscious situations that make up human experience.

Throughout Miss Murdoch's first four novels, the creature is given form primarily through its opposition to other more precise, elaborate, or bizarre forms. The creature is often articulated by what it is not, by the nets or traps or enchantments it avoids. In Miss Murdoch's fifth novel, *A Severed Head* (1961), however, the primitive human creature, avoiding the traps and the generalizations most human beings succumb to, is given a forceful, dramatic, and bizarre presence in the figure of Honor Klein. In the midst of a group of urbane Londoners, characters who drift into and out of numerous love affairs, who constantly define and redefine themselves and their emotions, Honor Klein, an anthropology don at Cambridge, represents a primitive, permanent human force that all the other characters no longer recognize in themselves. She sees through the pretenses of others, she cannot be appeased by the accepted banter of a civilized society, and she recognizes the violence and the force of the unconscious in the nature of man. The novel itself is seen from the point of view of Martin Lynch-Gibbon, polite, educated, the head of a small firm that imports claret, an amateur military historian. At the beginning of the novel Martin is content both with his charming, social wife and with his young mistress who lectures in economics at the University of London. Martin is able to divide his relationships quite neatly, to manage a comfortable and undemanding existence with ease and éclat. He is proud of his distance from the barbaric centers of human feeling. But when his wife suddenly falls in love with her psychiatrist, Palmer

Anderson, who is Honor Klein's half brother, she sets off a chain of new allegiances and new definitions which destroys Martin's little formula for comfort. Throughout the shifting alliances and infidelities, Martin becomes more and more drawn to Honor Klein, sensing the magnetic force of this superficially unattractive woman. Even at their first meeting Martin had been struck by Honor's presence:

> Divested of her shapeless coat she seemed taller and more dignified. But it was her expression that struck me. She stood there in the doorway, her gaze fixed upon the golden pair by the fire, her head thrown back, her face exceedingly pale; and she appeared to me for a second like some insolent and powerful captain, returning booted and spurred from a field of triumph, the dust of battle yet upon him, confronting the sovereign powers which he was now ready if need be to bend to his will.   [Pp. 67–68.]

As a military historian Martin would think of power in military terms, and the military image, complete with a samurai sword and blunt commands, continues throughout the novel.

Like Miss Murdoch's other novels, *A Severed Head* mocks the spurious kind of rationality man invents for himself. When Martin is first told of his wife's affair with Palmer Anderson, he is asked to be rational and understanding, specifically to remain friendly with the pair, to dine with them often and join them for drinks in their bedroom. Rationality, in this society, is close to sterility, a form of gentle behavior that refuses to make any distinctions among various human entanglements. When Martin's wife, Antonia, after leaving Palmer and returning to her husband, again announces that she is having an affair, this time with Martin's brother, she repeats her request that Martin be rational. She still wants Martin to hang around, to share the furniture and the intimate luncheon conversations. Antonia is the emotionally self-centered person who uses words like "rationality," "tolerance," and "understanding" as only half-conscious guises for a desire to possess simultaneously all the men she knows. But the rationality itself, in Miss Murdoch's world, is always false, always an enchanting abstraction by means of which the human being, either deliberately or accidentally, deludes both others and himself. The rational approach is also made ludicrous through the person of Palmer Anderson, a psychiatrist. Palmer, to whom Martin is also attracted, is announced as a man who can liberate people from the restrictive patterns in which they were brought up, but his liberations, in fact, consist of a series of clichés: he talks often of his love that is "something bigger than ourselves"; he is determined to "understand" everyone and everything, assuming that, once understood, a problem or a relationship is solved; he approaches all human relationships with a wide-eyed frankness that invariably misses the point. Through Palmer and his psychiatry, Miss Murdoch points out the lack of perception involved in applying rational formulas to the behavior of human beings.

Images of the head, the focal point of the rational, appear throughout the novel. At the very beginning Martin is pleased because his mistress, Georgie, is so sensible and rational. He simply means that she makes no demands upon him. He finds her head particularly attractive, and keeps repeating that each finds comfort or pleasure by looking at the head and face of the other. This sensible affair, along with other sensible relationships and Georgie's past sensible abortion, drives Georgie to an attempt at suicide. Yet Martin's interest in heads continues. He constantly pictures Palmer and Antonia as heads, Palmer's a distinguished gray crewcut and Antonia's a warm and fading cloud of golden hair. Martin's brother Alexander, a man who derivatively echoes Martin in choosing his women in this shifting and directionless system of sexual alliances, shares the interest in heads. As a sculptor, Alexander feels that the head is the most important part of the human being. Alexander, Georgie, Palmer, and Antonia, each man living with each woman at some point in the novel, are all part of the society that deludes itself, that talks of the head or the rational under the assumption that the human being is able to control and to formulate something crucial about his own experience.

In contrast, Honor Klein, shapeless, baggy, seeming to Martin like a "headless sack" when he first meets her at Liverpool Street station on a foggy London evening, displays little interest in rationality. She recognizes the folly of understanding, of human definitions of human love, of endless discussions within the civilized modes of behavior. When Martin becomes entranced by her, she explains:

> Because of what I am and because of what you saw I am a terrible object of fascination for you. I am a severed head such as primitive tribes and old alchemists used to use, anointing it with oil and putting a morsel of gold upon its tongue to make it utter prophecies. And who knows but that long acquaintance with a severed head might not lead to strange knowledge. For such knowledge one would have paid enough. But that is remote from love and remote from ordinary life. As real people we do not exist for each other. [P. 221.]

And Martin, as he becomes more deeply involved with Honor Klein, loses his connection with the urbane, diffuse, and scattered world, becomes himself "a severed head." The title, like those of most of Miss Murdoch's other novels, works in more than one way: Honor Klein, compelling, magnetic, standing for a central emotional force and able to see through the rational pretense of the other characters, is "a severed head"; Martin, in coming to value Honor's force, to regard it as something more worthwhile and more deeply committed than his old casual contentment, becomes himself "a severed head." Yet the body cannot function when the head is severed, and Honor knows that no relationship between her and Martin can really exist. As paralyzing an illusion as the head may be, no human being can survive without one.

Honor, "a severed head," a representation of primal human force without the addition of civilization or rationality, is the id. As Martin loses hold of the complex and superficial network of his comfortable alliances, he is drawn in, further and further, to the simple and emotional center of being, to the id. But the id, the strong and irrational quality of the creature, is no solution, no final answer for man. Honor and Martin cannot exist in a human relationship, for each is "a severed head," an incomplete human being. Perhaps the id would have been sufficient had man never developed, never been conscious of any other possibilities for controlling human experience. But having attempted various rational formulations about human behavior, man cannot happily return to the unstructured and purely emotional response, cannot retreat into the id. Martin is maimed permanently, "a severed head."

The egos, the civilized characters that cluster around the id, whirl in a circle of purposeless activity. As engineering and architectural processes were described in great detail in the earlier novels, so in *A Severed Head* are the multiple buildings of love affairs, of human relationships, detailed extensively to demonstrate human effort. The effort never creates a lasting structure; it is always as temporary and as inconsequential as the various households that Antonia and Martin establish. Antonia and Martin break up their house and establish others twice in the course of the novel. Each move, with the consequent division of property, is lavishly explained; each new chip on the prized Carlton House writing table is noticed and located. The long lists of belongings and the appearance of removal men indicate the elaborate and purposeless activity into which man is thrown by his spurious self-definition and sexual realignments. Man immerses himself in the trivia he can control so that he need not face the enormity he cannot control.

Most of the illusions—romantic love, the power of reason, the permanence of the man-made structure—that trap people in Miss Murdoch's other novels trap them in *A Severed Head* as well. The novel also contains a God-figure, as, for Martin, Honor Klein's representation as a primitive, nonrational id stands for a kind of transcendent honesty and intensity. Martin has always been attracted to the false *mystique:* in the first scene of the novel, he and Georgie burn incense to glamorize their love; toward the end of the novel, Martin worships the force that surrounds Honor Klein and elevates the id far beyond the status of his old doctrines of wine-sampling comfort. Miss Murdoch is, however, careful to distinguish Honor's function as a God-figure for Martin from any hint of conventional Christianity. Honor Klein is a Jew, and, as she demonstrates the brutal power of her samurai sword to a fascinated Martin, Miss Murdoch adds that "in the distance the church bells continued their mathematical jargoning." The church is part of the world of complex, illusory, and rational relationships. Honor is a representation, bizarre and terrifying, of one side of human experience, the primal force of the id. And because she is only one side of human experience, Honor, as God-figure, holds no ultimately meaningful or saving message for man. In addition, at a crucial point in the novel, Martin discovers Honor in bed with Palmer Anderson, her half brother and the psychiatrist addicted to the most obvious forms of rationalist clichés. The God-figure and the Devil meet in human experience, for each is only a simplification of one side of human experience. Although Martin, forced by the collapse of his comfortable world, continues to worship Honor, Miss Murdoch makes it clear that "a severed head" is a ludicrous and ironic god.

In Miss Murdoch's first four novels the God-figure was set against the idea of the simple, spontaneous, unstructured creature. The God-figure, connected to all man's machinations to achieve some sort of structure and permanence, was mocked, was demolished comically as a futile though understandable fabrication. But the idea of the creature, the formless center of the human being, remained inviolate. A Severed Head makes even that possibility ludicrous. The God-figure, less systematic, crystallizes and implicitly satirizes the idea of the creature. The creature is, after all, the id, and Miss Murdoch, in inflating the id to a mock God-figure and endowing it with samurai swords, relentless force, and an excessive knowledge of human relationships, mocks the very faith in the creature that pervaded her earlier novels. Martin, the man in modern society, loses his head over this abstraction, this God-figure, to a greater extent than did comparable heroes over their abstractions in any of the earlier novels.

Miss Murdoch has, in this novel, added another dimension to her depiction of contemporary society. Her rich, imagistic, highly suggestive prose still mocks man's effort to formulate precise codes, man's ratiocinative pretense. But what was, in the earlier novels, simply value as antithesis is, in *A Severed Head*, given its own imagistic and bizarre presence, and mocked in turn. Honor is a black God-figure, black because her divinity is not in the rational and conventional abstractions with which man deludes himself: rather, her divinity, her power, and her horror exist deeply and centrally within the nature of the deluding and deluded creature himself.

12

"Gimmick" and Metaphor in the
Novels of William Golding

WILLIAM GOLDING HAS WRITTEN FOUR NOVELS: *Lord of the Flies* (1954); *The Inheritors* (1955); *Pincher Martin* (1956); *Free Fall* (1959). Each of the first three demonstrates the use of unusual and striking literary devices. Each is governed by a massive metaphorical structure—a man clinging for survival to a rock in the Atlantic Ocean or an excursion into the mind of man's evolutionary antecedent—designed to assert something permanent and significant about human nature. The metaphors are intensive, far-reaching; they permeate all the details and events of the novels. Yet at the end of each novel the metaphors, unique and striking as they are, turn into "gimmicks," into clever tricks that shift the focus or the emphasis of the novel as a whole. And, in each instance, the "gimmick" seems to work against the novel, to contradict or to limit the range of reference and meaning that Golding has already established metaphorically. The turn from metaphor to "gimmick" (and "gimmick" is the word that Golding himself has applied to his own endings) raises questions concerning the unity and, perhaps more important, the meaning of the novels.

Golding's first novel, *Lord of the Flies,* tells the story of a group of English schoolboys, between the ages of six and twelve, who survive a plane crash on a tropical island. The boys were apparently evacuated during a destructive atomic war and are left, with no adult control anywhere about, to build their own society on the island. The chance to create a new paradise is clear enough, but Golding quickly indicates that the boys are products of and intrinsically parts of current human society. Even on the very first page: "The fair boy stopped and jerked his stockings with an automatic gesture that made the jungle seem for a moment like the Home Counties." The island provides food, plenty of opportunity for swimming, and "fun." But a conflict quickly develops between the boys, led by Ralph, who would keep a fire going (they cherish some hope of rescue) and build adequate shelters, and those, led by Jack, originally members of a choir, who would hunt wild pigs and give full reign to their predatory and savage instincts. In the first, democratic meeting Ralph wins most of the boys' votes and is elected the leader of the island. But the rational democracy is not able to cope very well with the fears of the younger boys, the occasional tendency to rash mob action, the terror of the unexplained "beast" which fills the night. Gradually Jack gains more followers. He paints himself in savage colors, neglects to tend the fire because he is mercilessly tracking down a wild pig, establishes a wild and ritualistic dance that fascinates the boys. When one of the boys, having discovered the rational truth of the "beast" at the top of the mountain (the "beast" is a dead man in his parachute, dropped from a battle ten miles above the island), stumbles into the ritualistic dance, he is forced by Jack to enact the role of the pig. The boy is never given the time or the opportunity to make the rational truth clear, for the dancers, cloaked in frenzy and darkness, kill him. Ralph is unable to stop the others, and even, to his shame, recognizes some of the same dark frenzy at the center of his own being. And Piggy, Ralph's "brain trust" though always unattractive and unpopular, the boy whose glasses got the fire going in the first place, is killed by Jack's principal lieutenant. Jack is victorious. His dogmatic authority, his cruelty, and his barbaric frenzy have a deeper hold on the nature of man than do Ralph's sensible regulations. The forces of light and reason fail to alleviate the predatory brutality and the dark, primeval fear at the center of man.

But the metaphor of the society the boys construct is not left to do its work alone. Just when the savage forces led by Jack are tracking down Ralph and burning the whole island to find him, a British naval officer arrives to rescue the boys. Ironically, the smoke of barbaric fury, not the smoke of conscious effort, has led to rescue. Throughout the novel, frequent references to possible rescue and to the sanity of the adult world seemed the delusions of the rational innocent. Ralph and Piggy often appealed to adult sanity in their futile attempt to control their world, but, suddenly and inconsistently at the end of the novel, adult sanity really exists. The horror of the boys' experience on the island was, after all, really a childish game, though a particularly vicious one. The British officer turns into a public school master: "I should have thought that a pack of British boys—you're all British aren't you?—would have been able to put up a better show than that" (p. 248). The officer's density is apparent, but the range of the whole metaphor has been severely limited. Certainly the whole issue, the whole statement about man, is not contradicted by the ending, for, as Golding directly points out, Ralph has learned from the experience: "And in the middle of them, with filthy body, matted hair, and unwiped nose, Ralph wept for the end of innocence, the darkness of man's heart, and the fall through the air of the true, wise friend called Piggy" (p. 248). But the rescue is ultimately a "gimmick," a trick, a means of cutting down or softening the implications built up within the structure of the boys' society on the island.

Golding's second novel, *The Inheritors*, relates the story of the last family of man's ancestors, conquered and supplanted by man. The family of "people" (Golding's word for the heavy, hairy, apelike forerunners of man) migrate to their spring home and slowly realize that things have changed, slowly discover the encroachments of a tribe of "others" (men). The "people" are not capable of thinking, of abstraction, or of forming rational connections. They simply act by instinct and "have pictures," many of which they do not understand. Yet, for all their perceptual and intellectual limitations, the "people" have a code of ethics (they will not kill other animals, though they do eat the meat of animals already killed), a deep and humble sense of their own limitations, and a faith in the divine power and goodness of the earth. In addition, the "people" enjoy a family life free from fighting, guilt, and emotional squabbling. Each has his function, carefully defined and limited, each his respect for the other members of the family. The novel is the process of man conquering the "people," capturing or killing them one by one. The last of the "people" is able to watch man, to understand dimly man's power and victory. But this last survivor of the "people" is also able to sense in what ways man is a creature different from the "people." He watches man brawl and fight, steal other men's mates, suffer guilt and anxiety, tear himself apart between his real ability and his failure to exceed his limitations. The novel carries the implication that man's unique power to reason and think carries with it his propensity toward pride and sin and guilt, toward those qualities that cause him pain and misery.

Most of the novel is told from the point of view of the last of the "people," a humble creature who depicts the issues without fully understanding them. The last chapter, however, provides a switch in point of view, for it is seen through the eyes of one of the men after the "people," the "devils" in human terminology, have been wiped out. The theme does not change: man sees himself as a being tortured by pride and guilt, one who has faith in his power but continually runs into conflict with other men and with his own limitations. Here, the "gimmick" does not change or vitiate the point of the novel. Rather, the "gimmick," the switch in point of view, merely repeats what the rest of the novel has already demonstrated. Awareness and rational intelligence are still inextricably connected with human sin, and the "gimmick" at the end of the novel breaks the unity without adding relevant perspective. The contrast between the "people" and men is more effectively detailed, made more sharply applicable and relevant, when dimly apprehended by the last of the "people."

Man's capacity to reason is again ineffectual in Golding's third novel, *Pincher Martin*. Christopher Martin ("Pincher" because he has presumably stolen almost everything he's ever had), a naval officer, is blown into the North Atlantic when a submarine attacks his ship. Fighting the water and shrieking for rescue, he eventually finds a rock in the middle of the ocean. He laboriously makes his way to the surface of the rock. Convinced of his health, his education, and his intelligence, he consciously sets about organizing his routine, naming places, gathering food, doing all that rational man can do to insure his survival and rescue, his ultimate salvation. But time and weather, forces stronger than he, in addition to his guilty consciousness of past sins (brought up through his memory of his past as actor, seducer, pincher of whatever his friends had), wear down the rational man. All his rational efforts fail and he is pushed by nature, both external and internal, toward death and damnation.

The conflict between survival and extinction is extended by a consistent use of microcosmic imagery. When Martin first sees the rock, Golding writes: "A single point of rock, peak of a mountain range, one tooth set in the ancient jaw of a sunken world, projecting through the inconceivable vastness of the whole ocean" (p. 30). The rock is constantly compared with a tooth of the world; the struggles taking place on the rock are a mirror of the struggles taking place all over the world. Martin's battle for survival is imagistically made the battle of all men for salvation, a battle in which reason, sanity, and careful order are not enough. As the rock is imagistically linked to the larger world, so is Martin himself made a kind of universal focus. His head is frequently a "globe," his own teeth are linked to the shape of the rock:

> His tongue was remembering. It pried into the gap between the teeth and re-created the old, aching shape. It touched the rough

edge of the cliff, traced the slope down, trench after aching trench
. . . understood what was so hauntingly familiar and painful
about an isolated and decaying rock in the middle of the sea.

[P. 174.]

Similarly, the issues of Martin's salvation or damnation are
presented within his own body. He sometimes feels his "center"
in conflict with the memory of his loins. His eyes are "windows."
The forces of nature that defeat him are linked to forces within
himself. Ocean currents are tongues; the mind is a "stirred
pudding":

. . . how can the stirred pudding keep constant? Tugged at by
the pull of the earth, infected by the white stroke that engraved
the book, furrowed, lines burned through it by hardship and
torment and terror-unbalanced, brain-sick, at your last gasp on
a rock in the sea, the pudding has boiled over and you are no
worse than raving mad. [Pp. 190–191.]

The microcosmic imagery, connecting the man to the rock to
the universe, becomes a vast metaphor to convey the futility of
man's sanity, of man's careful and calculated attempts to achieve
salvation.

The "gimmick" in *Pincher Martin* occurs in the final chapter.
His body is washed ashore and the naval officer who comes to
identify him points out that Martin couldn't have suffered long
because he didn't even have time to kick off his sea boots. Supposedly, in the narrative itself, the first thing Martin did, before
he even sighted the rock, was to kick his sea boots off. In other
words, the final scene shows that the whole drama on the rock
was but a momentary flash in Martin's mind. The dimension of
time has been removed and all the microcosmic metaphor is but
an instantaneous, apocalyptic vision. In the ultimate sense this
revelation enhances the microcosm, compresses all the issues into
a single instant in time. But the revelation, in fact, makes the
situation too complete, too contrived, seems to carry the development of the microcosm to the point of parodying itself. One can
accept the struggle of forces on the rock as emblematic of a
constant human struggle, but, when the dimension of time is

removed, when the struggle is distilled to an instantaneous flash, one immediately thinks of parody in which the struggle was not significant at all. Here the "gimmick" extends the technique, but so magnifies and exaggerates the extension that the novel ends by supplying its own parody.

In his most recent novel, *Free Fall,* Golding also deals with the limitation and the folly of the assumption that man can control his universe rationally, but here the futility of rationalism is not the central issue of the novel. The novel, anchored in social probability more securely than is any of the others, tells the story of Sammy Mountjoy who rose from the slums of Rotten Row to become a successful artist. Sammy, telling his own story, searches for the moment at which he lost his freedom, at which he made a crucial decision that inescapably hardened his natural propensity toward sin. The metaphor is Faustian: at what point and for what reason was this soul given over to Satan? Sammy, guilt-ridden, traces his career looking for the point and the reason. He quickly dismisses the poverty of his background, his illegitimate birth, his youthful blasphemy against the Church, his early membership in the Communist party—most of these were external and Sammy was essentially innocent then. He waves aside his seduction and subsequent desertion of the dependent Beatrice, his willingness to betray his comrades when a prisoner of war in Germany, his dishonesty—these were not causes, but effects, the patterns established by a man already irrevocably fallen. He examines his attraction to the rationalism preached by an early science teacher, but decides that this was not the cause, for, though the doctrine was shoddy and incomplete, the teacher himself was a man of principles deeper than those he avowed, and Sammy had always preferred the man to the doctrine. Finally, Sammy localizes his loss of freedom in his early decision to pursue Beatrice at whatever cost. He had, while at school, drawn a picture of her and given it to one of his less talented friends to hand in as his own. The picture was highly praised; none of Sammy's other drawings received the recognition that this one did, and this one was publicly credited to someone else. Sammy kept trying, unsuccessfully, to draw Beatrice again. She then became an obsession for him; he had to track her down, pursue her, possess her, sacrifice everything in order to gain her. And this decision, taken as he left school, marks Sammy's loss of freedom. The decision, the willingness to sacrifice everything to achieve his aim, is an indication of human pride and egoism, the conscious human impulse to abandon concern for others, freedom of action, salvation itself, for the satisfaction of one's own end. Sammy relentlessly pursues and possesses Beatrice, overcoming her apathy and gentility by sheer energy and force. She does not satisfy him, for the appetite of human pride is endless, and he deserts her. Like Faust, Sammy loses his freedom when he is willing to stake everything on the satisfaction of his human pride.

At the end of the novel, when Sammy has discovered his sin, the reader suddenly learns that Beatrice has been in a mental institution ever since Sammy deserted her seven years earlier. Sammy visits her, but she will not speak to him and she urinates, in fright, on the floor when he tries to force her to acknowledge his existence. The doctor later tells him that Beatrice is incurable. When Sammy seeks to pin down just how guilty he is, the doctor replies:

> "You probably tipped her over. But perhaps she would have tipped over anyway. Perhaps she would have tipped over a year earlier if you hadn't been there to give her something to think about. You may have given her an extra year of sanity and— whatever you did give her. You may have taken a lifetime of happiness away from her. Now you know the chances as accurately as a specialist."   [Pp. 248–249.]

Here the "gimmick," the final scene at the mental institution, both exaggerates and palliates the metaphorical structure of the novel. The fact that Beatrice is in an institution at all magnifies the external consequences of Sammy's sin and becomes, in Beatrice's unfortunate behavior, almost a parody of the damage caused by human pride. The novel shifts from Sammy's self-examination to the disastrous effect of his pride on others. After Sammy's sin is externalized, the doctor's sensible comment questions the possibility of directly charging one person with the responsibility for another and, to some measure, cuts down Sammy's guilt. But the novel was originally concerned with Sammy's loss of freedom, with this individual and interior issue, reflected by implication inside other human beings. By making the issue exterior, the ending both exaggerates and simplifies the description of the nature of man involved, both softens and hedges concerning man's guilt. The Faust legend loses much of its power if Faust is to be charged with preaching sedition to his students or if Faust is to wonder about his share of guilt when his students break church windows. The final "gimmick" in *Free Fall*, in making interior issues exterior, changes some of the meaning, dissipates some of the force and relevance, of the novel.

In each novel the final "gimmick" provides a twist that, in one way or another, palliates the force and the unity of the original metaphor. In each instance Golding seems to be backing down from the implications of the metaphor itself, never really contradicting the metaphor, but adding a twist that makes the metaphor less sure, less permanently applicable. The metaphors are steered away from what would seem to be their relentless and inevitable conclusions, prevented, at the very last moment, from hardening into the complete form of allegory. In one sense, each "gimmick" seems to widen the area of the artist's perception as it undoubtedly lessens the force of the imaginative concept. The "gimmicks" supply a wider perspective that makes each of the following questions relevant: If the adult world rescues the boys in *Lord of the Flies*, are the depravity and the brutality of human nature so complete? How adequate is *Pincher Martin*'s microcosmic synthesis, if it all flashes by in a microsecond? Can Sammy Mountjoy, living in a world that includes others, talking to them, sleeping with them, helped by them, keep his guilt and the problem of his freedom all to himself? Is the Faust legend an adequate expression of the problems of contemporary man? All these relevant questions are implicit in the "gimmicks" Golding uses, "gimmicks" that qualify the universality of the metaphors, question the pretense that the metaphors contain complete truth. But this qualification is achieved at the expense of artistic form, for the "gimmicks" also palliate and trick, force the reader to regard the issues somewhat more superficially even though they widen the range of suggestion. The "gimmicks" are ultimately unsatisfactory modifiers, for, in the kind of qualification they provide, they reduce the issues of the novels to a simpler and trickier plane of experience.

Golding's metaphors can all be read as orthodox and traditional Christian statements about the nature of man. Each metaphor underlines man's depravity, pride, the futility of his reason. The novels are permeated with the sense of man's sin and guilt, and the images depict these qualities in conventional Christian terms. The "gimmicks," however, back down from the finality of the theologically orthodox statements. In an age when many other writers view man's experience as disparate, impossible to codify, existential, Golding's metaphors are at least sufficiently unique to suggest the reality, the permanence of the traditional Christian explanation of the nature of man. But, then, the "gimmicks" seem to provide some concession to contemporary man's fear of generalized absolutes, to his existential attitude. This is not to suggest that Golding reverses his metaphors with these slender "gimmicks," that the novels ultimately demonstrate the failure of the orthodox explanations. Rather, the metaphors still stand; the orthodox Christian versions of man's depravity and limitations, in Golding's world, still convey a great deal that is relevant and permanent. But they do not convey everything. The "gimmicks" suggest that the orthodox Christian explanations are not quite adequate for contemporary man, although they are too tricky and slender to do more than suggest. The "gimmicks," precisely because they are "gimmicks," fail to define or to articulate fully just how Golding's metaphors are to be qualified, directed, shaped in contemporary and meaningful terms. The "gimmicks" tend to simplify and to palliate, rather than to enrich and intensify the experience of the novels. For all his unique brilliance and his striking metaphors, Golding has not yet worked out a novelistic form adequate for the full tonal and doctrinal range of his perception.

13

Some Current Fads

MOST OF THE BRITISH FICTION OF THE PAST DECADE has been highly popular and publicized. Reviews in newspapers and magazines, articles in literary journals, and interviews on radio or television have been concerned with many of the works and their authors. With all this attention, in both Britain and America, popular judgment has not always been sound or discriminating. Several writers have, in the course of the public enthusiasm for contemporary British writing, developed reputations far beyond anything merited by either their statements concerning contemporary problems or their literary skill. Among the writers I find most overrated are C. P. Snow, Lawrence Durrell, and Colin Wilson.

C. P. Snow has published a series of eight sober novels under the general title of *Strangers and Brothers* (this is also the title of the first novel of the series, published in 1940). These novels record, in the first person, the experiences of a lawyer and government administrator named Lewis Eliot, dealing with his background, his struggles, his friends, his college at Cambridge, and the complicated society he lives in. Lewis Eliot, like Snow himself born in 1905, details his experiences and his impressions of society from 1914 until the middle 'fifties. The course of Eliot's career demonstrates a drift from the optimism of a poor young man viewing a world of almost limitless possibility in the middle 'twenties, to the measured judgments of a middle-aged and responsible government administrator. One of Lewis' friends, George Passant, a vital and enthusiastic young solicitor in a small town, represents this optimism. George, who believes strongly in progress, has the liberal's faith that the poor boy, by intelligence and hard work, can rise swiftly in the more mobile British society of the early 'twenties. He encourages others (including Lewis Eliot) to learn and study, and forms a "group" of young and spirited people who talk about free lives and envision the possibility of a better world. This optimism is attached to science in *The Search* (a novel first published in 1934, then rewritten and reissued in 1958, that is not part of the *Strangers and Brothers* series), in which the young hero, Arthur Miles, believes that science contains the key to all the wonderful and liberating possibilities in the universe. Placing this optimism and faith in progress in the 'twenties may be one reason for Snow's enormous popularity among his own generation in America. Vast numbers of Americans, the second generation of the large immigrations between 1880 and 1910, felt that the 'twenties offered new possibilities for freedom, science, and unrestricted human effort. Their families, like those of Snow's characters, had been held back by poverty and more rigid social conventions before World War I, and the young intellectuals could hardly have predicted Spain, Nazi Germany, and the hydrogen bomb.

Snow's characters find, in later years, little to justify their optimistic assumptions. George Passant, save for three years during World War II when he works in Lewis Eliot's government office, never leaves the solicitor's office in the small Midlands city. He never even advances beyond the job of chief clerk, beaten by his enthusiasm for causes and his unwillingness to compromise his optimistic faith. Arthur Miles, the scientist, finally leaves science recognizing that the field is full of compromises and politics, that his own contributions, though competent enough, are not apocalyptic revelations, that he has lost his original dedication. And Lewis Eliot, Snow's central character, trades his early faith for a secure and responsible niche within the Establishment, a job that is constantly involved in compromises and committee meetings. When, in *Homecomings* (1956), one of the characters mentions that he intends to vote Conservative for the first time in his life in the 1951 general election, Lewis Eliot, still professing leftist sentiments, fully understands. Eliot adds that in the last thirty years, on the whole, things have "gone worse than we could possibly have imagined."

Lewis Eliot feels that he has no genuine choice. He defends his career by repeating that, because government contains the only power in a mass society, concerned and responsible men must join the government and sit on endless haggling committees in order to help wield the power as justly as possible. At times Eliot defends the Establishment with a kind of irascible petulance directed at those who question, but without full explanations. In this way, in *The New Men* (1954), he tries to cut off criticism and to assert secret governmental authority. In *Homecomings*, he repeats bland assurances that the government was wise to prosecute a man severely for passing atomic secrets without explaining, upon a responsible protest, the nature or the importance of the offense. Yet in other ways Eliot is an old liberal still. He complains that the class structure has become more rigid during his lifetime because the forces of loud protest and of skepticism have died down. And he satirizes the officials "with their moral certainties, their comfortable, conforming indignation" who refuse to keep George Passant in a government office at the end of the war. The mature Eliot is always concerned, in one way or another, with the Establishment:

> People of my sort have only two choices in this situation, one is to keep outside and let others do the dirty work, the other is to stay inside and try to keep off the worst horrors and know all the time we shan't come out with clean hands. Neither way is very

good for one, and if I had a son I should advise him to do what you did, and choose a luckier time and place to be born.

[*Homecomings*, p. 250.]

Snow seems, through Eliot, to oversimplify the problem. It is not that Snow takes a one-sided view of the Establishment, but, rather, that he views all social problems in large and grandiose political terms. One either accepts or rejects the government; no other alternatives are possible; matters of social conviction or attitude are invariably expressed in reference to practical political power. Throughout the Lewis Eliot novels, Snow continually illustrates some form of the conflict between individual conscience and political power. He does not make the primary oversimplification that one of these is always good and the other always bad. But he does, consistently, fall into the secondary oversimplification, the assumption that the conflict between conscience and power serves as an adequate statement for all man's social and political dilemmas. Perhaps Snow's kind of oversimplification can be clarified by reference to his recent address entitled "The Two Cultures." In this Snow distinguishes the scientific culture from the literary and humane, claiming that each is ignorant of the other and that education must find some way of joining them. But Snow's distinction barely scratches the surface of the problem: Would he have scientists each take four courses in literature? Should literary students, then, take courses in the theories of modern physics when they cannot understand the calculus? And, more important, how does Snow's educational reform affect the problem of the educated man's control over the mass society? What is the point in dedicating science or literature to the reform of the society when the most effectively advertised image captures the largest number of votes? Similarly, Snow's questions to demonstrate that the scientist and the literary man are each ignorant of the other's tradition (the scientists were asked who Shakespeare was, and the literary men were asked to name the second law of thermodynamics) seem about as relevant to the problems of knowledge, insight, and culture as were the television quiz shows.

In addition to the oversimplifications Snow imposes upon the novels, Lewis Eliot, as narrator, demonstrates other difficulties. He is portrayed as a detached, rational, careful man, able to hide his feelings and operate graciously among many different people. Yet, at the same time, everyone is anxious to confide the most intimate details of his personal or professional life to Lewis, as if he were the warmest and most understanding of men. In all the novels except *The Light and the Dark* (1947) and *Time of Hope* (1949), Lewis is given little warmth and his understanding is almost entirely theoretical, but both men and women rush to pour their troubles and their secrets upon him. This unconvincing character often seems simply a mechanical device to hold the novels together. As a young man, in *Time of Hope*, Lewis falls deeply in love with a neurotic young girl named Sheila. He courts her for years, and wins her confidence although he never wins her love. She falls in love with another man, Hugh, as weak and uncertain as she is herself. Lewis, in order to have Sheila to himself, convinces Hugh that she's entirely mad and Hugh, always anxious to avoid complications, disappears from the novel. Sheila, deprived of the only man she could love, turns to Lewis in desperation and marries him because she has no one else. Lewis quite openly assumes the responsibility for her, yet, even by the end of the novel, he begins to complain that attention to Sheila has begun to ruin his career as a barrister. In the novels that deal with his later life, Lewis frequently repeats the theme that he has sacrificed his career for Sheila, acknowledging, less and less as time goes on, his responsibility for her. Yet he makes a great many sententious judgments about the responsibilities of others, of women, of government officials, of fellows in colleges. He demonstrates how and why others fail: George Passant, Jago in *The Masters* (1951). I do not mean to suggest that a narrator must himself be admirable or must not allow time to push him into hypocritical positions. But Snow never develops any meaningful fictional distance between author and narrator, never creates a solid point of view through which Lewis Eliot can be consistently seen. Rather, Snow uses his narrator for the purpose of the moment: lovesick young man, enterprising barrister, cool and intelligent government official, compassionate family man with his second wife. These purposes are not necessarily consistent, and Snow relies solely on a chameleonlike narrator to express his point of view through a series of eight novels.

Despite the fact that the novels lack meaningful control over point of view, other elements in the novels seem far too rigidly under control. The same issues, indeed the same conversations, sometimes appear at length in more than one novel. Lewis Eliot is able to hire George Passant as his assistant, over the objections of Hector Rose, in both *Homecomings* and *Strangers and Brothers*; Lewis holds almost identical conversations with a lawyer named Eden about George's trial in both *Strangers and Brothers* and *Time of Hope*. The senior fellow of the college is, at great length, the same tedious combination of senility and lucidity in both *The Masters* and in a novel whose action presumably takes place seventeen years later, *The Affair* (1960). Slices occupying a few pages in one novel often become the major theme and terms for another, as, in *Time of Hope*, Snow describes the March family and its attitudes in exactly the same terms that make up the principal theme of *The Conscience of the Rich* (1958). Similar plot devices keep reappearing throughout the novels. Both his first wife, Sheila, and his second wife, Margaret, jilt Lewis Eliot under identical circumstances. Each time he goes away on holiday or on business, apparently secure, and returns to find that his love has promised to marry or has married someone else. In exactly the same way, the cold, distant hero of *The Search* is jilted when he goes to Munich to do research for three months. The sameness of these passages and devices gives a sense of sterility to Snow's fictional world.

At times Snow's writing is wooden. Often, particularly in *The Affair*, the least effective of the eight novels, Snow introduces a character by explaining prosaically what the character is supposed to illustrate rather than by credibly showing the character's speech and action. At the very beginning Tom Orbell is called suspicious and self-seeking, although he seems, from all objective description, innocuously amiable and flat. Howard, the principal victim in the novel, is called rude and truculent over and over again, although these qualities are barely demonstrated. At a party early in the novel all conversation centers around the issue Snow wishes to develop, the case of scientific forgery that splits the college's fellows into factions, and one can hardly believe that a Christmas Eve party is in progress. The party becomes, blatantly, a simple excuse for demonstrating a variety of views and reactions concerning the forgery. Characterization is often inadequate. Margaret, Lewis Eliot's second wife, is a composite of all possible virtues; she even tries to break down Lewis' enormous reserve. Charles March is kind and charming, a benevolent member of a wealthy family, but, although he is one of the principal characters in *The Conscience of the Rich*, he is never really developed. His sister Katherine and her husband, Francis Getliffe, a scientist of both principle and compassion, appear in several novels but are never fully explored. Character is often sacrificed to the summary of minutes in the long committee meeting or the careful reporting of the legal brief.

Sometimes, too, in the work of C. P. Snow, character is sacrificed for melodrama. For example, Paul Jago, the leading candidate and the one Lewis Eliot supports in *The Masters*, is described as an unusually warm and humane man. The warmth is never depicted, simply explained and discussed by other people. Through the long controversy about who is to become the next master of the college, another side of Jago gradually begins to appear. He is erratic, somewhat unstable, apt to fly into a rage over trivia, and these qualities are depicted thoroughly and skillfully. His unpredictable rages, as well as his Conservative politics, lose him the election that seemed almost certain at the beginning of the novel. But the warmth and the humanity were simply a blind, simply a preparation for a melodramatic shift rather than a part of the man's character. Jago is, however, redeemed in *The Affair*. Although he has kept away from the college for the intervening seventeen years, he reappears at the crucial moment, demonstrating, this time quite specifically, all his warmth and force and humanity, to see that justice is done. Character is the vehicle for melodramatic tricks rather than an attempt to probe the nature of man. Many of Snow's novels are melodramatic thrillers. *The Masters* builds on the suspense of the college election. *The Affair*, full of parallels to the Dreyfus case, vindicates justice after a long struggle with the forces of reaction. *Strangers and Brothers* ends with Lewis Eliot, now a lawyer, helping to contrive a dramatic acquittal for George Passant and some of his friends on a charge of fraud. Though acquitted, George is never entirely redeemed by the society, but he has had his moment of drama and remains a naïve but noble hero. All these novels are full of trial scenes, startling revelations, and dramatic reversals which even Lewis Eliot's measured calm cannot quite tone down. *The Search* also ends on a note of high drama. Arthur Miles, no longer a practicing scientist, has tried to help an old friend, an inferior scientist who married Arthur's first love, by giving him some scientific data. But the friend, Sheriff, cannot wait for the slow success that Arthur's data offer. Sheriff picks up some experiments and fudges the results in order to obtain quick publication. Only Arthur has the information to demonstrate that Sheriff has been dishonest, and the novel becomes the struggle, in Arthur's mind, between loyalty to his friend and the dedication to science that would demand he publish the fraud. Arthur is torn, but finally decides not to expose the fraud, knowing that he has simultaneously killed any possibility for his own return to science.

Snow's novels are most effective when they rely on a kind of nostalgic social history. Generally, the best novels are those dealing with the early days in Lewis Eliot's career: the accounts of his father and his boyhood in *Time of Hope;* the long descriptions of melancholy cricket matches in both *Time of Hope* and *The Light and the Dark;* Lewis' fascination with the rich familial traditions of London's Jewish aristocracy in *The Conscience of the Rich.* Snow describes scenes like these with the ease, the fondness, and the rich detail that are almost invariably absent from his novels more dependent on melodramatic triumphs of justice or on sober and qualified defenses of the government. Even *The Search*, though not a good novel, contains some effective passages describing cricket matches and the political conservatism of an old scientist in the 'twenties. But Snow's talent for evoking social history seems to be limited to some time before World War II. Lewis Eliot, as he narrates *The Affair*, which takes place in 1954, seems completely out of touch. He tries to describe the new fellows in the postwar Cambridge college, but recognizes how far he is removed from them. He uses a young English don named Ince as one of his principal examples. He is shocked at Ince's iconoclasm, his lack of interest in politics, his desire to seem more lower-class than he is, his devotion to the analysis of a single novel by Conrad, his preferences for beer and jazz. But the details, accurate as they are about a phenomenon of the 'fifties, are not enough for Snow. He somehow seems compelled to make Ince completely irresponsible about college justice (and, as such, one of the principal villains of the novel) simply because Ince is bluntly indifferent to the squabbling about the grand issues of Church and State. Snow's work seems curiously out of date. In addition to the oversimplification, the woodenness, and the melodrama that mar some of the writing, C. P. Snow's novels are limited by perspectives relevant only to the 'twenties and the 'thirties, perspectives that can evoke the past nostalgically but seem quaint and superficial when applied to Britain since 1945.

Although he had previously published novels, travel books, essays, and poetry, Lawrence Durrell became well known and widely read only with the recent publication of his Alexandria Quartet. The Alexandria Quartet consists of *Justine* (1957), *Balthazar* (1958), *Mountolive* (1958), and *Clea* (1960), all of which presumably deal with the theme of modern love. In the preface to *Balthazar*, Durrell explains that the first three novels are intended to be "siblings," equal spatial situations, and that the fourth novel adds the dimension of time. With the help of a characteristic image, Durrell explains:

> Modern literature offers us no Unities, so I have turned to science and am trying to complete a four-decker novel whose form is based on the relativity proposition. Three sides of space and one of time constitute the soup-mix recipe of a continuum. The four novels follow this pattern.

The "three sides of space" are not, however, genuine or equal "siblings," for each of the first three novels is, in a way, a separate point of view, and the second and third novels successively reverse the point of view of the novel preceding. For example, in *Justine*, Darley, a young and naïve novelist living in Alexandria, falls in love with the strange and sophisticated socialite, Justine. They have an affair, and Darley assumes that Justine is motivated by an ungovernable passion for him. In *Balthazar*, a novel in which Darley's point of view is elaborated by the additions of Balthazar, a rational and homosexual doctor, Darley learns that Justine has merely used him as a decoy. She apparently had an affair with him simply to focus her husband's suspicions, while at the same time she was really in love with another novelist, Pursewarden. In *Mountolive*, Justine and her husband discuss her infidelities. He has, of course, known about them all along, and Justine has obviously enjoyed deluding Darley. In the final novel, which takes place some years later, after Justine has been defeated and imprisoned, she uses Darley simply as an old friend who comforts her and understands. The relationship between Justine and her husband, Nessim, goes through similar gyrations. At first she seems merely an unfaithful wife. Gradually Durrell reveals that this improbable marriage between a poor and beautiful Jewess and an aristocratic Copt has been arranged for some political purpose. Only in the next novel, *Mountolive*, told from the point of view of the British ambassador in Egypt, does it become clear that Justine and Nessim are part of an anti-British plot to smuggle arms into

Palestine. And the mutual intrigue gives Justine, for the first time, a genuine feeling for Nessim:

> The passion of their embraces came from *complicity*, from something deeper, more wicked, than the wayward temptings of the flesh or the mind. He had conquered her in offering her a married life which was both a pretence and yet at the same time informed by a purpose which might lead them both to *death!* This was all that sex could mean to her now! How thrilling, sexually thrilling, was the expectation of their death! [P. 206.]

And in the final novel, after their intrigue is discovered, Justine regards Nessim as a "father," a kind and compassionate man. These changes are all, in a way, further explanations of a spatial continuum, yet they are all tricks. Each novel seems to establish and to elaborate relationships that simply anticipate the reversal in the next novel.

Another major character, in Durrell's Alexandria before World War II, is the novelist Pursewarden. More successful and more intelligent than Darley, he also works for the British Foreign Office. Pursewarden commits suicide. In *Balthazar*, he seems to have committed suicide because he had been unable to transcend his art, to see more deeply into experience through the facts of his novels. But *Mountolive* offers a much more tangible reason: Pursewarden has been duped by his friend, Nessim. He had refused to believe that his friend could be working against the British and now cannot face the acknowledgment that all his dispatches to London were wrong. In *Clea*, however, Pursewarden's blind sister comes to Alexandria. She reveals that she and her brother had been lovers, had even had a child. His love for her had ruined his marriage to another woman back in England, some years past. He therefore kills himself in order to free his sister to love another man, Mountolive, who can marry her. All the separate motives for suicide represent a theory of relativity, but it is a relativity developed by magician's methods. The object changes each time the cloak is flapped in front of it.

In addition, as the stories of Justine and Pursewarden demonstrate, intrigue and politics are at least as important as love. Durrell's kind of trickiness pervades the whole Alexandria Quartet, sometimes in even more blatant and obvious ways. Through the first three novels, Clea, the beautiful artist, is given a number of reasons to avoid any sexual relationship: a dedication to her painting; a sophisticated father whom she adores; a close friendship with Justine so that she can see the debilitating results of sexual excess; a friendship with Melissa, Darley's old mistress, so that she can understand how constantly men are unfaithful. All this seems a build-up for the surprise of having Clea suddenly become Darley's mistress in the final novel. Similarly, all the novels develop the complete contrast between the elegant Nessim and his ugly, primitive brother, Narouz, simply as preparation for the fact that Nessim has Narouz murdered for political purposes. Tricky, violent, surprising stories are constantly pushed into the novels. One minor character, an old transvestite, tells the story of his father's death. His father was driving in an early road race when his veil was drawn into the axle of the car and he was dragged, choking, out into the road. The story is a very slightly altered account of the famous death of Isadora Duncan.

Justine is written from Darley's point of view. The second novel, *Balthazar*, is also from Darley's point of view, although additional information is communicated by the device of having Balthazar edit and comment on Darley's manuscript. Balthazar keeps going over the same incidents, adding, changing, philosophizing about Darley's naïveté. Darley refers to Balthazar's constructions as the "great Interlinear." But the insertions also include letters, journals, and frequent quotations from the other characters. The point of view is constantly interleaved by reference to what Clea said or what Pursewarden wrote in his notebooks or what Justine's first husband thought. Even in *Mountolive*, the public puzzle–solving book written from Mountolive's more careful and objective point of view, other characters' letters and quotations frequently interrupt the perspective. Point of view becomes, in the Alexandria Quartet, a device to furnish startling or unusual information rather than a means of carefully exploring the range and the limitations of human perspective.

Durrell has often been praised for the richness and the neo-romantic quality of his prose. Yet, frequently, the prose sounds both overblown and trite. One of Durrell's more moderate and less colorful descriptive passages sounds like a cultured and sophisticated travelogue:

> It was a fine day and shallow draught boats were coursing among the beanfields towards the river tributaries, with their long curved spines of mast, lateen rigs bent like bows in the freshets. Somewhere a boatman sang and kept time on a finger-drum, his voice mixing with the sighing of *sakkias* and the distant village bangings of wheelwrights and carpenters manufacturing disc-wheels for wagons or the shallow-bladed ploughs which worked the alluvial riverside holdings.
>
> Brilliant kingfishers hunted the shallows like thunderbolts, their wings slurring, while here and there the small brown owls, having forgotten the night habits of their kind, flew between the banks, or nestled together in songless couples among the trees.
>
> The fields had begun to spread away on either side of the little cavalcade now, green and scented with their rich crops of *bercim* and beanrows, though the road still obstinately followed along the banks of the river so that their reflections rode with them.
>
> [*Balthazar*, p. 70.]

More obvious is the excess of the following passage:

> A message which was to draw me back inexorably to the one city which for me always hovered between illusion and reality, between the substance and the poetic images which its very name aroused in me. A memory, I told myself, which had been falsified by the desires and intuitions only as yet half-realized on paper. Alexandria, the capital of memory! All the writing which I had borrowed from the living and the dead, until I myself had become a sort of postscript to a letter which was never ended, never posted. . . .
>
> [*Clea*, p. 11.]

Both these passages are written from Darley's point of view, and Darley is certainly the most consistent purveyor of the over-elaborate. Yet the other novelist, Pursewarden, Darley's alterego, is apt to be equally elaborate in puncturing Darley's pretense. Pursewarden is, at least, aware of the kind of prose he writes: "I know my prose is touched with plum pudding, but then all the prose belonging to the poetic continuum is; it is intended to give a stereoscopic effect to character" (Balthazar, p. 245). And Mountolive, too, the objective and factual man, lets the colors transport him every time he describes the Egyptian landscape. Durrell also demonstrates a fondness for words such as "etio-lated" and "desuetude" throughout the novels. References are continually made to other writers, to Stendhal, Blake, Marvell, Whitman, Eliot, Auden, Lawrence, and their styles are capsul-ized in striking images ("Eliot puts a cool chloroform pad upon a spirit too tightly braced by the information it has gathered") and argued about by the various characters.

Durrell has developed a particular kind of discordant image that figures prominently throughout the Alexandria Quartet. Like the "soup-mix recipe" in the middle of the portentous preface to Balthazar, these images throw the very mundane detail into the heavy or romantic description. The cliché of the rhythm of the earth becomes "the earth's own systole and dias-tole"; Darley, in the midst of a melancholy speculation about the excessive pain that love has brought him, compares himself to a dry-cell battery; an airy description of the clouds, the minarets, and the sea of Alexandria is disrupted by "the snouts of foreign men-of-war" in the harbor; as Narouz dies, "the great voice thinned softly into the burring comb-and-paper sound of a long death rattle"; ships in the harbor, in the midst of the activity of loading and unloading, expose "their steaming intestines" and are "laid open in Caesarian section." All these images, as if given license by the theories enlarging the range of poetic diction at the beginning of the twentieth century, push the discordant almost as far as it can go. These images use the discordant as a contrivance simply to palliate the overblown richness of the surrounding prose, not to demonstrate anything about the incident or the experience itself. Durrell's prose is curiously involuted, concerned only with its own balances and modifying discords, unconcerned with its supposed subject matter. And this involution emphasizes the overelaborate quality. Other images in Durrell's work are clichés. Seas "lick" piers and characters feel "the tug of memory's heavy plumb-line" in the elaboration of a cliché. The brutal and exotic quality of the city of Alexandria is also done in images, images that seem to combine the cliché and the elaborately discordant:

> Voices of girls, stabbing of Arab quarter-tones, and from the synagogue a metallic drone punctuated by the jingle of a sistrum. On the floor of the Bourse they were screaming like one huge animal in pain. The money-changers were arranging their currencies like sweets upon the big squared boards. Pashas in scarlet flower-pots reclining in immense cars like gleaming sarcophagi. A dwarf playing a mandolin. An immense eunuch with a carbuncle the size of a brooch eating pastry. A legless man propped on a trolley, dribbling. [*Clea*, p. 66.]

The intricacy of the imagery almost hides the description of the dirt of Alexandria.

Durrell's novels are also marred by long and pretentious speculations about the eternal verities. Darley cautions himself endlessly about making human judgments, wonders what the nature of truth or the nature of art is, and philosophizes about the dichotomy between body and soul which he feels in his own experience. Like the prose, these speculations are elaborate wisps. Pursewarden mocks Darley's devotion to "Beauty and Truth," but he, too, indulges in long, and equally airy, disquisitions on the nature of art. Pursewarden keeps developing his theory of the novel as a series of "sliding panels," a series of impressions, facts, and theories, individually disjointed, which compose a work of art as a whole. Seldom have so many notebooks and quotations been necessary to explain impressionism. Durrell's theorizing, like his prose, seems excessively elaborate decoration contrived simply to disguise or ennoble what is essentially a series of startling tricks and reversals. Durrell has really written "adult" thrillers in the exotic setting of a corrupt Alexandria. But sometimes I wonder. Is the whole Alexandria Quartet really an elaborate hoax, calculated to satirize the lavish praise that all the overblown prose and the pompous theorizing has received? This seems to me barely possible, though unlikely. If so, if Durrell is really deliberately overdecorating his thrillers to spoof a public concerned with art, sensitivity, culture, and fine writing, I applaud his achievement. He then has fooled me, too.

Since the initial praise that welcomed Colin Wilson's pseudo-philosophical treatment of his reading in *The Outsider* in 1956, most of his reputation as a profound commentator on his time has died down. Yet Colin Wilson has continued to write. And, in two recent novels, *Ritual in the Dark* (1960) and *Adrift in Soho* (1961), he has represented one possible attitude toward contemporary experience. Wilson's novels demonstrate a fascination with the irrational and the demonic, with the deeply destructive influences at work within the society. The hero of *Ritual in the Dark*, Gerard Sorme, feels himself a rebel against all of society:

> I disliked those students because they seemed a sloppy and undisci-
> plined mob of adolescents. That makes me an authoritarian. But
> I detest the authorities when they stand about in uniforms and
> give orders. So I dare say I'm an anarchist. An authoritarian
> anarchist!   [P. 121.]

Similarly, the hero of *Adrift in Soho*, a young man trying to write a book in London, scorns both the provincial Midlands society he came from and the empty Bohemianism he finds in Soho and Notting Hill. Wilson's heroes frequently voice indiscriminate resentment against almost all other people and groups.

Wilson's antisocial heroes are also fascinated by the perverted. Gerard Sorme, almost friendless when the novel begins, soon finds himself highly interested in the actions of Austin Nunne, a homosexual, a sadist, and finally a murderer. The story of

Austin Nunne is actually the story of Jack the Ripper set in contemporary London, and Wilson points out the parallel a number of times. As Gerard slowly realizes that Austin is a mad criminal, he becomes closer to him and loses no opportunity to try to understand how Austin operates. Gerard concludes that Austin's insanity is typical and represents the insanity of the whole age. In the course of the novel Gerard also meets and becomes friendly with Oliver Glasp, a painter who is in love with a twelve-year-old girl. Glasp's love is pure and, when he discovers that the girl, one of seven children living in a slum, has already lost her virginity, he becomes so broken up that he moves away. The theme of Jack the Ripper indicates a fascination with violence as well as with perversion. Gerard, though outwardly mild, walks the streets of London thinking of how he would like to exterminate the masses, and he immediately recognizes incipient violence in both others and himself. Even Harry, the more quiet hero of *Adrift in Soho*, relishes the details of famous murder cases and recalls several times that Jack the Ripper was a distant relative.

The irrational and violent qualities of Wilson's heroes, however, are docile suburban attitudes when compared to those manifest in another contemporary novel, *The Divine and the Decay* (1957), by Wilson's friend, Bill Hopkins. Hopkins' hero, Plowart, is the young candidate for Parliament of an extreme rightest party, a Neo-Fascist who has gone to one of the Channel Islands to provide an alibi for a murder he's arranged. Plowart is a maniac who worships power, who is certain that he alone can control a corrupt and decadent society. He storms about the island, vicious to others, anxious only to impress the young dame, Claremont Capothy. Yet Claremont, like the author, is obviously attracted to Plowart, admires his force and power. In what is surely one of the most incredible suicides in literature, Claremont is willing to join Plowart in jumping off the island's craggy rocks into the whirling water. For her, though she realizes that Plowart cannot rule the world, this irrational immolation is preferable to any form of life. Hopkins also demonstrates a violent contempt for any form of physical weakness. He makes Christopher Lumas, a cripple at whose home Plowart stays while on the island, a wheedling idiot. Lumas alternately condones his wife's infidelity by childishly begging her to remain with him at any cost and sets elaborate infantile traps to catch her lover. He is treated without the slightest shred of dignity or compassion. All the endless rhetoric of the novel, all the crags and depths and praises of brute force, are applied to the examination of the mindless maniac. And that examination is made from the point of view of pure and mindless fascination.

In contrast, Colin Wilson's heroes are innocents, seeking to understand all the violence and irrationality they find around them. They are invariably interested in "visions," in religion, in finding an ultimate meaning behind the chaotic society they see. Gerard Sorme confines both his yearnings and his suspicions about Austin to an aging, bedridden priest. He shows no shame at the simplicity of calling himself an "existentialist" as he wanders about searching for a God to make everything come right. Harry, in *Adrift in Soho*, is trying to write a book that will explain all of both secular and spiritual experience. The naïveté is so thorough, so undiluted by sarcasm or another point of view, that it seems unintentionally charming. Wilson's innocence is also evident in another way. All women in both novels are, when the hero meets them, either pure virgins or depraved girls who will sleep with any man available. Gerard encounters Gertrude, Austin's aunt, and Caroline, a young relative of Gertrude's. Both Gertrude, a spinster near forty, who is interested in evangelical religion, and Caroline, a frank creature of seventeen, succumb to Gerard's male power within a fortnight, yet both have been entirely virginal before. Similarly, in *Adrift in Soho*, Harry meets an attractive Australian girl named Doreen. Although Harry and Doreen wander, entranced and disapproving, through the Bohemian world for weeks and share the same bed almost every night, they confine themselves to chaste cuddles and affectionate kisses on the cheek. They approve of the Bohemian's revolt from society on an abstract level, but they are puritanically shocked at the usual Bohemian's behavior. Harry, in one scene in the reading room of the British Museum, is seriously disappointed with himself because he notices an attractive girl's slip when he should be paying attention to his books on the origins of Christianity.

Wilson's two novels are less appealing when the long, pretentious essays of documentation are added to support the hero's theories. Gerard Sorme drags in Tolstoy, Shaw, and Dostoyevsky to support his frequent arguments; Harry, somewhat less belligerent, is fond of explaining his ideas through Shaw, Nietzsche, and Thomas Mann. One feels that each of the heroes has just finished a term paper in an elementary university course called Basic Humanities. The novels are also full of clichés. When Harry and Doreen live among the Bohemian group, with its chaotic sleeping arrangements, in Notting Hill, they are very careful to make their little room clean, homey, and ordered. They admire the artist, Ricky Prelati, who secludes himself in the attic to paint, ignoring the wild parties that go on below. Ricky, a man of order and control, is also a genuine artist, as the whole world of television, press, and criticism immediately acknowledges as soon as it sees his paintings. The search for order and meaning, direct and explicit, also motivates Gerard in *Ritual in the Dark*. Slowly, painfully, he becomes aware that Austin's perversion and violence are linked to shadows of the same qualities in many superficially stable and solid citizens within the society.

Colin Wilson is not far enough from his heroes to see them clearly or to use them to provide any intelligent or meaningful statement about the society. Yet, for all their naïveté, his heroes do reflect something about contemporary Britain: the interest in violence and perversion; the disillusion with the notion that permissive freedom is the best possible condition for the adolescent; the search for order and stability; the feeling that organized society is shallow and hypocritical. Yet Wilson's work simply reflects. It lacks both the intelligence and the literary distinction to do anything more.

14

Identity and the Existential

A GREAT DEAL OF CONTEMPORARY FICTION AND DRAMA
confronts the problem of identity. Contemporary man is often
involved in a search for his identity, an examination of the
possible personal, social, religious, or doctrinal affiliations by
means of which he can define himself. He longs for the security
a specific affiliation can give him, while he finds that the complexity within both himself and his world cannot be easily
expressed through any definable affiliation. In this way, heroes
of the work of Wain and Amis examine the class structure of
contemporary Britain, although they are usually unable and
unwilling to become a tangible part of it. Iris Murdoch's
characters search for definition, try to reduce experience to the
manageable and comprehensible, but none of the definitions,
none of the identities, provide any meaningful satisfaction.
Similarly, the revival of the mock-picaresque, evident in a novel
like John Wain's *Hurry On Down*, demonstrates the interest
in the problem of identity. The hero, originally uncommitted,
wanders throughout the society looking for some value to which
he can attach himself, seeking to discover who and what he is.
The enormous frequency, in comic works like those of Amis

and Keith Waterhouse, of naming or tagging people or things for satirical purposes provides further evidence of contemporary man's concern with identity. The tag is the affiliation too easily made, the security of definition made ludicrous because it has been purchased at the price of a more general and intangible understanding.

One recent novel locked within the problem of identity in terms of both theme and plot is Nigel Dennis' *Cards of Identity* (1955). Dennis later dramatized the novel which has been produced and published as a play. The novel begins when three characters, members of the Identity Club in London, move into an abandoned country manor house. The three characters, simply by pretending to be sure of themselves, manage to assert their position and their right to the house. They accumulate a staff from among the local residents: a middle-aged man with military bearing and a clipped mustache who reveres the traditions of the country and the aristocracy; his devoted and patient sister; a harassed and overworked doctor; a brisk and competent nurse; an ordinary workingwoman intimidated by the impersonality of the National Health Service and of ration books (the novel takes place in 1951). The three inhabitants of the house give these five local characters new identities, persuade them that they are and always have been other than they seem. The man with the military mustache becomes a butler, even allowing a disreputable past as a seaman to be invented for him; his sister, who no longer recognizes her brother, becomes the housekeeper and, under the guidance of her identity-creating employers, believes she is mourning a husband that she, in fact, never had. The ease with which these people are willing to undergo changes in identity provides Dennis with an opportunity for satire. For example, the leader of the three zany club members, called Captain Mallet, says of the local doctor, easily transformed into his gardener, "His is the insanity of the phlegmatic, Britain-can-take-it type. He has gone on taking it for so long that he no longer knows exactly what it is he is taking." But, in addition to the easy satire, the device of casually switching the identities of ordinary people becomes Dennis' depiction of a contemporary world in which people are so desperately unsure of themselves that they require constant exterior confirmation of who and what they think they are.

Captain Mallet and his cronies are also crooks, supporting the house on funds ingeniously swindled from the staff. After the manor house is running smoothly, the captain invites all the other members of the Identity Club for a conference. The Identity Club consists of people who, convinced that the theory of identity is the only meaningful theory in modern life, seek to rule the world by imposing identities on the people they encounter. The club's meeting consists of a series of case histories of switches in identity: the young war veteran who ends his search for ethical and spiritual values with which to attack contemporary materialism by becoming a warden to protect badgers; the young man, brought up not to fear sex because his parents ran about naked, who is never thereafter sure whether he is a man or a woman; the former Communist who recants and enters an abbey, subsequently earning a fortune from the large sales of his frequently rewritten confessions. Dennis uses these case histories as a means of satirizing contemporary hypocrisy, lack of direction, and lack of value. The confusion of identity represents all the confusions of contemporary man. At the end of the novel the police come to investigate the ownership of the manor house. The members of the club quickly escape, leaving the five indentured identities to wobble their ways back to their feeble original selves. The club was merely a device to demonstrate how easily contemporary man can be enslaved.

Cards of Identity is a limited novel. The case histories become repetitious, each reinforcing the confused and directionless plight of contemporary man. The jokes soon become stale and predictable, for they all depend on the victim's never being aware of who or what he is. The style is a somewhat uneven pastiche: sometimes it is quick and conversational; at other times it is long-winded and involved, as if the author is slowly removing himself from his material; at still other times it is entirely impersonal in order to satirize all characters. Occasionally Dennis becomes directly explanatory and essayistic. Toward the end of the novel he even adds a long pseudo-Shakespearean play (an entertainment that the servants put on for the members of the Identity Club) which is merely an exercise underlining the same problems of confusion in different terms. Within the welter of styles, however, Dennis keeps hammering the same point over and over again. Contemporary man's problems center on his confusion about his own social, political, and personal identity; man was better off, in past eras, when he knew who and what he was. Yet, despite all these limitations, the novel is useful because it underlines, so abstractly and insistently, what many contemporary writers regard as a crucial issue for man.

In a recent first novel, the search for identity is made even more intense. Jennifer Dawson, in *The Ha-Ha* (1961), describes the schizophrenia of a reserved young girl on scholarship at Oxford. The novel begins in a mental institution where Josephine Traughton is recovering from a breakdown she suffered when her mother, the only person with whom she could make contact, died because of a defective electric blanket. Josephine begins to discover herself through an affair with one of the other patients, a young man named Alasdair. But when Alasdair is discharged from the institution and leaves without warning, Josephine falls apart again. She escapes from the hospital and, pervaded by a feeling of extraordinary lightness, wanders about the countryside trying to touch, to feel, to make contact with some reality outside her nebulous self. In her wanderings, a confused combination of trees, railway bridges, sex, and country inns, she constantly searches for some meaningful human contact through which to define herself. The whole course of this second breakdown, brilliantly written, is, in one way, made an analogue for the problems all people of Josephine's generation face: the need for tangible identity, for reassurance of meaningful human existence. Madness occurs when the sensitive individual is no longer able to find her own identity in the midst of a bewildering and uncertain world.

British novels and plays are not direct dramatizations of specific existentialist doctrines, like the problem of identity, in the same sense that Sartre has specifically dramatized his philosophy in his literary work, but, rather, many British writers have adopted attitudes similar to those of the existentialists. The existentialists, too, have frequently used the problem of identity as one of the crucial issues man faces. Sartre often wonders how human beings define themselves and points out that we often accept the formulations and definitions of ourselves that other beings thrust upon us, however uneasy or incomplete that acceptance is. We have a difficult time defining ourselves within a vacuum, and sometimes can only define ourselves in opposition to others, as the members of the French Resistance could define themselves only in opposition to the Nazis. Camus's heroes also have a great deal of difficulty discovering who they are, as Meursault, the hero of *The Stranger,* can only begin to understand himself in objection to society's impingements upon him. Other existentialists, such as the Catholic, Marcel, also talk of the breakdown of personality and identity in the twentieth century, a breakdown that leaves the individual in uncertainty and confusion.

The collapse of public labels, public ties that would help the individual define himself, leads to man's necessary reliance on himself as the only means available. All the existentialists, from Kierkegaard on, hold to the doctrine that man must see things himself, that all genuine perceptions are subjective. Contemporary British writers often express a similar feeling about the subjectivity of all genuine perception by expressing, through their novels, numerous different points of view. Iris Murdoch (who also has written a helpful and informative critical book about Sartre) and Angus Wilson frequently express a wide variety of contradictory points of view in their novels. The clash of points of view, the impact of contradictory definitions, underlines the complexity and confusion of the world the individual faces. He can only, subjectively and individually, try to work his own way through it. No objective or absolute truth lingers behind the system of Sartre or Camus, as no single point of view can explain the multiplicity of experience and attitude in the fictional world of Iris Murdoch or Angus Wilson.

The principal foundation of existentialism is the idea that existence is prior to essence, that a person must assume his existence and the existence of other things and people rather than posit abstract and "essential" natures of people and things. In other words, the existentialists insist on dealing with the concrete facts of experience, multiple and unsystematic though they may be, rather than theorizing about the general nature of essences. Certainly other older doctrines, such as pragmatism, have maintained a similar insistence on the facts of experience. Yet pragmatism, in the work of people like Dewey or William James, while avoiding any notion of the ideal or the absolute, tends to regard facts as the material for scientific constructions. Pragmatism often assumes that man can sort out the facts of his experience and reach meaningful, though qualified, general conclusions from them. In contrast, most existentialists tend to regard facts as less certain, less amenable to sorting and arranging, more a welter of perplexing and easily distorted images. Under both philosophies, man has the theoretical possibility of controlling the facts of experience for his own good. But the existentialist is a good deal less sure of both the control and the good than is the pragmatist. For most contemporary British writers, existence is also prior to essence. In the work of Sillitoe, Amis, and Iris Murdoch, the sensible man must deal with experience concretely whereas the man who fits experience into an abstract essence is made ludicrous or vicious. Of these writers, Amis presents perhaps the most pragmatic world. With the exception of the hero in *That Uncertain Feeling*, his heroes do manage to work their way, concretely and successfully, through a world of fallacious essences. The heroes in Sillitoe, Iris Murdoch, or Angus Wilson do not find the virtue of simple perception quite so rewarding. Their worlds are more difficult, their facts harder to understand and arrange. Man, for these writers, as for the existentialists, is caught between his vast possibilities and his enormous limitations.

Although there are Christian existentialists, such as Karl Jaspers and Gabriel Marcel, most existentialists do not believe in the existence of a supreme being (Sartre has even attempted to prove that God cannot exist). For most existentialists, the individual must work his way through his concrete experience because there are no immutable or certain standards for the human being. And there are no such standards because there is no God, no realizable essence that can suggest immutable standards or values. The same point of view is implicit in a good deal of contemporary fiction and drama. The work of Amis and Wain shows man working through himself and his society, but no God illuminates his path or stands remote to assign him to ultimate salvation or damnation. For Iris Murdoch, representations of various gods, various abstractions that purport to guide the human being, invariably give irrelevant or mistaken advice. As soon as any perspective begins to assume absolute attributes, Miss Murdoch quickly switches events to ridicule the God-figure. For most of these writers (with the exception of William Golding, who uses Christian metaphors meaningfully and directly), God would seem to represent the fallacious essence, the abstraction that clouds clear and accurate perception of the facts of experience. Alan Sillitoe is more explicit. In *The Writer's Dilemma*, the essays first printed in the *Times Literary Supplement* as "Limits of Control," Sillitoe develops the theory that the idea of God, the human persistence in adhering to an abstraction, has done enormous harm to society:

> The idea of God is man's fatal neurosis, and war, as one sort of psychoanalysis, has certainly failed to cure him of it—though the next one might not. As soon as God is disregarded, and human contest becomes one of man against nature, then the battles between men will cease, and be replaced by the simple problem of getting enough food and shelter for everybody.   [Pp. 68–69.]

Angus Wilson, in four long novels that explore almost every conceivable aspect of human thought and activity, seems never to deal centrally with God or with a superhuman abstraction at all.

According to Sartre, man is free, both in spite of and because of the fact that God does not exist, to create his own values. Man even has the responsibility to make sure that his freedom does not impinge upon the meaningful freedom of others. Camus, too, talks of the free man committing himself, despite the fact that the things he commits himself to never achieve the status of absolute authorities. And, for both Sartre and Camus, commitment or engagement can be social and political as well as personal. Contemporary British writers tend to stress the possibility of commitment to values within a world where no absolute values exist. Writers as diverse as Angus Wilson, Doris Lessing, and John Bowen all emphasize the personal value of meaningful commitment. Unlike Sartre and Camus, a number of the British writers, such as Wain, Nigel Dennis, and Doris Lessing, sometimes find value in the past, in some set of attitudes ruled out by change and history. The evocation of the past can lead to a degree of sentimentality usually absent in the best of contemporary writers, Iris Murdoch and Angus Wilson. For the most part, however, the British writer, like the French writer and theorist, tries to look at his world clearly and to demonstrate personal and meaningful contemporary value within the chaos of that world. The good writer is seldom irresponsible.

Responsibility does not, however, necessarily involve defending the Establishment or the reigning society (the confusion between the two often seems to pervade the later work of C. P. Snow). Most existentialists, like most contemporary writers, constantly point out the folly, the lack of honest observation, and the adherence to vast and fallacious essences that permeate the reigning society. The fidelity to a principle in the face of concrete evidence to the contrary is the mark of the fool or the vicious man in the work of Amis, Angus Wilson, and Camus alike. Such fidelity is the identifying sign of all who unquestioningly accept the dominant values of the society or the Establishment. This fidelity, in its very intensity, is also the sign of presumption, of the faithful assuming more knowledge, clarity, and insight than the contemporary human being has. It may seem, from one point of view, that writers like Amis, Wain, John Osborne, or Arnold Wesker exaggerate the ridiculous or malicious side of such faithful presumption, that they simply vent ill-natured spleen against the Establishment. But, then, the kind of statement originating from within the Establishment is sometimes almost incredible. In the November, 1961, issue, *Horizon* magazine published a series of photographs of contemporary British life. Alan Pryce-Jones, the former editor of the *Times Literary Supplement,* introduced the photographs by pointing out that they depict the world of *Saturday Night and Sunday Morning,* even though the series included one photograph of ladies, all dressed in white, lawn-bowling at Brighton, and another of top-hatted gentlemen walking past the Throckmorton Street corner of the Stock Exchange. Mr. Pryce-Jones, after making the point that the photographer presented a grimy, slum-ridden England, continued:

> There are other Englands, however, and I should not wish all of them to be forgotten. . . . Landscapes are small and flat, villages still feel the double tug of the parsonage and the manor house. The country gentry are not very exciting, but they are utterly unmoved by such passing phenomena as Mr. K, the cobalt bomb, and massacres in the Congo. Here and there, at the end of avenues, stand the palaces, which lead a peculiar life of their own. Only two kinds of public gain easy access to them: blood relations of the owner, and trippers from the industrial cities with a half crown to spend. For neighbors are not encouraged, except at the annual Conservative fete in the park, at a Hunt Ball, or a coming-of-age. Such palaces may be out-of-date; yet even at the royal palace of Whitehall, in the days of absolute monarchy, the public was encouraged to stare at its betters, so that there is no break with the past in a great house which prefers to welcome its visitors by the busload rather than in social couples.   [P. 16.]

Sillitoe's sullen indifference to the Establishment, Amis' satire of presumption and gentility, and John Osborne's forceful presentation of the Establishment's lack of perception still seem welcome antidotes. And because, both for existentialists and for most contemporary British writers, value must be derived by the individual from the facts of his own experience, the Establishment, that abstraction of public value, maintained by faith, must be vulnerable to satire and criticism.

The intelligent man, clear, honest, and perceptive, must refuse to follow the pattern of the majority of society. He must, in Sartre's terms, react negatively to the easy formulations and abstractions he sees around him. But it is a great deal easier for the man of intelligence and sensitivity to know what he is against than it is to know what he is for. Amis' lucky Jim, Osborne's Jimmy Porter, and Wain's Joe Shaw can all define their antipathies more clearly than they can explain their affirmations. For them, as for Sartre and Camus, freedom is, in a way, dreadful and absurd. The individual has the freedom to act, but he must act in a highly complex and difficult world with little assurance about the value or consequence of his action. That he must act when he knows so little is dreadful; that he must act when the effects of his action are so trivial, yet the action itself so meaningful, is absurd. The heroism of a freely acting individual is severely limited once the dread and the absurdity of the situation are clear. Similarly, most contemporary British writers diminish the heroism of their central characters. Though heroes, in the work of Iris Murdoch, John Bowen, and Amis, are both free and responsible, they are not heroic in the sense of being admirable and effective leaders of society or champions of new causes. Man's situation and his problems, in addition to his own fallible humanity, make heroic action unlikely. In addition, when, as in the work of Angus Wilson, heroic action is barely possible, no one else is able to recognize or acknowledge it. The contemporary world not only makes heroism dubious and unlikely, but completely fails to notice its rare emergence.

The diminished hero, the vast and complex world, and the presence of numerous variations of abstracted folly all provide material for unexpected and incongruous clashes. Almost all the contemporary British writers develop their themes through comic methods; all sense, in one way or another, the ludicrous position of a man free to act in a world in which action is difficult and insignificant. Man's position is itself comic, vulnerable, incongruous. The existentialists have always viewed man in a similar way. Kierkegaard talked of the contradiction implicit in man's position in the universe, and believed that only the constantly ironic individual, the man aware of all sides of the contradiction, could deal with the anomaly. Sartre's dread in the midst of significant action and Camus's absurdity also acknowledge the comic ambivalence of man's position. Were man ever to forget the comic, ever to see his position as clear, single, other than incongruous, he would immediately fall into the simple definition, the abstraction beyond all concrete fact which would lead him to presumption, faith, and folly. The comic and unheroic hero can make choices, always qualified, but he has no stirring message with which to lead his people out of the wilderness. He has only a limited, comically qualified, control in the midst of twentieth-century chaos.

All the parallels between the existentialists and contemporary British writers are not intended to suggest that writers such as Amis and Keith Waterhouse have worked out a systematic and logical theory of human nature as a basis for their writings. But they do, like most other writers of their age, demonstrate an existential attitude toward experience. This attitude seems particularly relevant for the western European since 1945. It offers him the possibilities of freedom and responsible choice, possibilities valuable to the man both bored and frightened by the implications of Marxist determinism. At the same time the existential attitude prevents man from regarding his truths as sacrosanct, his government as the fount of all wisdom and virtue, and his own nature as a pattern for universal emulation, for the intelligent man can recognize the obvious existence of other fountains and other patterns. Yet, within the plethora of patterns, the responsible man can make distinctions and choices, can prefer quasi-rational muddles to Nazi bestiality simply because the muddles (and what the responsible man prefers is always less clear than what he hates) allow for more free choices than do the zealous brutalities. In addition, the existential attitude, with all its qualifications and its comic incongruities, seems appropriate for the civilized man caught in a civilization that, as he well realizes, may not last very much longer. His sense of humor will not entirely see him through (a belief in both the imperial virtue of the British lion and a benevolent deity is required for that), but the sense of incongruity and absurdity can defend him, with compassion or responsibility or observant understanding, from the folly of looking like the last absolute ramrod on a sinking island. It is one of the few choices he has left.

Contemporary British writers, using a meaningful perspective with which to examine the events and attitudes of their time, have, in the past decade, created fiction and drama of energy and forceful meaning. Dramatists such as John Osborne, Arnold Wesker, and Harold Pinter have captured contemporary attitudes on the stage with striking accuracy and perception; Kingsley Amis, John Wain, Keith Waterhouse, David Storey, John Bowen, and others have made the novel a fresh, energetic, and responsible statement of the 'fifties and the early 'sixties. But the existential attitude itself cannot rest on any such approbative generalizations. Considering all the artistic facts, the existential attitude requires separate, evaluative, and subjective choices among separate and individual artists. Among these writers, Alan Sillitoe, Iris Murdoch, and Angus Wilson stand out. Alan Sillitoe has provided, in rich and vital detail, a coherent account of the lower-class perspective so seldom handled with such complexity, force, and lack of sentimentality. In addition, he has already attempted a more abstract statement of his position, not content to let the fascination of colorful detail express his entire literary career. Iris Murdoch has created a series of intricate and imagistic statements about the nature of man and his illusions, never repeating herself and constantly attempting to shade the formless and chaotic into significant form. Angus Wilson, the most comprehensive of the three, has used a number of entirely different devices, all highly effective and unusual, to probe the personal, social, professional, and political nature of the contemporary human creature. All three are able to examine the multiplicity of current experience and derive some original, controlled, and comprehensive statement about that experience. This, itself a kind of existential process, is the method of the artist.

Notes on the Authors

1. KINGSLEY AMIS

One of the most widely read of contemporary British writers, Kingsley Amis was born in London in 1922. Educated at St. John's College, Oxford, Amis began to write hard, precise, clever poetry. He has published four novels: *Lucky Jim* (1954), *That Uncertain Feeling* (1955), *I Like It Here* (1958), *Take a Girl Like You* (1960). Amis' best poetry has been published in *A Case of Samples*, and he has written a survey of contemporary science fiction called *New Maps of Hell*. His literary journalism is straightforward, lucid, and highly intelligent. Until 1961, Amis lectured in English at University College, Swansea. He now lectures at Cambridge.

2. JOHN BOWEN

Born in Calcutta in 1924, John Bowen was sent to school in England and graduated from Pembroke College, Oxford. After a postgraduate year in the United States he became assistant editor on *Sketch*, but he soon moved into advertising. He was, until recently, the copy chief of a large London agency, but he resigned to devote all his time to writing. In addition to children's books and frequent critical essays, Bowen has also written four novels: *The Truth Will Not Help Us* (1956), *After the Rain* (1958), *The Centre of the Green* (1959), and *Storyboard* (1960).

3. SHELAGH DELANEY

Shelagh Delaney was born in 1939 and left school at the age of sixteen. She held various jobs, including one in an engineering factory, until her first play, *A Taste of Honey*, was produced in 1957 by Joan Littlewood at the Theatre Workshop at Stratford in the east end of London. Miss Delaney has also written stories and another play, *The Lion in Love* (produced in 1960). She lives in Salford, Lancashire.

4. NIGEL DENNIS

Nigel Dennis was born in 1912 in England, but grew up in Rhodesia. After receiving part of his education in Austria (his uncle was a British consular official there), Dennis came to the United States in 1934 and joined the staff of *Time* magazine. In 1949 he was transferred to *Time*'s London office and has lived there since. He has published two novels: *Boys and Girls Come Out To Play* (1949) and the well-known *Cards of Identity* (1955). The latter was dramatized for production at the Royal Court in 1956, and another play, *The Making of Moo*, was presented at the Royal Court in 1957.

5. LAWRENCE DURRELL

Lawrence Durrell was born in 1912. He went to school first in India and later at Canterbury. For many years he was connected with the British Foreign Office, serving in Athens, Cairo, Alexandria, Belgrade, and Cyprus, among other places. He had already published six novels and travel books, poetry (including a verse play and translations from Greek poetry), and a children's book before he became famous with the Alexandria Quartet. The Alexandria Quartet consists of four novels: *Justine* (1957), *Balthazar* (1958), *Mountolive* (1958), and *Clea* (1960). A volume of his collected poems was published in 1960. Durrell now lives in France.

6. WILLIAM GOLDING

Born in 1911, William Golding was educated at Brasenose College, Oxford. He has written a play (*Brass Butterfly*, 1958) and four novels: *Lord of the Flies* (1954), *The Inheritors* (1955), *Pincher Martin* (1956), and *Free Fall* (1959). A schoolteacher in Wiltshire for many years, Golding has given occasional talks and broadcasts about his work. He was a visiting professor at Hollins College, Virginia, for the academic year 1961–62.

7. MARGOT HEINEMANN

Margot Heinemann, a young social research worker, has written books describing conditions in the mining industry. One was called *Coal*, another *Wages*. Her first novel, *The Adventurers*, was published in 1960.

8. THOMAS HINDE

Sir Thomas Chitty, who uses the pseudonym of Thomas Hinde, was born in 1926 and graduated from Winchester and University College, Oxford. At various times he has been a tutor, a schoolmaster, a worker at the Battersea Fun Fair, an inland revenue rating assessor, and a public relations officer for Shell Oil Company. He has written three novels: *Mr. Nicholas* (1952), *Happy as Larry* (1957), and *For the Good of the Company* (1961).

9. BILL HOPKINS

Bill Hopkins, who was born in 1928, was hailed by his close friend, Colin Wilson, as an extraordinary talent before the publication of his first novel, *The Divine and the Decay*, in 1957. He had met and worked with Colin Wilson in Paris some years before. Hopkins also contributed an essay, "Ways without a Precedent," to *Declaration*.

10. BERNARD KOPS

Born in Stepney in 1926, Bernard Kops left school at the age of thirteen. He worked at various jobs in London, writing poems that he published in little magazines. His first play, *The Hamlet of Stepney Green*, was produced at the Oxford Playhouse in 1958. *The Dream of Peter Mann*, his next play, was produced at the Edinburgh Festival in 1960.

11. PHILIP LARKIN

Philip Larkin, principally distinguished as a contemporary poet, was born in 1922 and educated at St. John's College, Oxford. He is now a librarian at the University of Hull. His best-known poetry is contained in *The Less Deceived* (1955). He has also written two novels: *Jill* (1946) and *A Girl in Winter* (1947).

12. DORIS LESSING

Born in 1919, Doris Lessing spent most of her first thirty years in Southern Rhodesia. She moved to England in 1949 and published her first novel, *The Grass Is Singing*, in 1950. A prolific writer, she has since published three volumes of short stories, four novels, two plays, and two book-length autobiographical and sociological essays. Her best-known novels are those in the Martha Quest series: *Martha Quest* (1952), *A Proper Marriage* (1954), and *A Ripple from the Storm* (1958). She is active in publicly supporting racial equality and the suspension of nuclear testing.

13. ROGER LONGRIGG

Roger Longrigg, educated at Bryanston and Magdalen College, Oxford, was born in 1929. He works in advertising, making television commercials. He has written four novels: *A High-pitched Buzz* (1956), *Switchboard* (1957), *Wrong Number* (1959), and *Daughters of Mulberry* (1961).

14. IRIS MURDOCH

Iris Murdoch was born in Dublin in 1919. She was educated at Somerville College, Oxford, and during the war worked at the Treasury. After the war, she worked for UNRRA in London, Belgium, and Austria. In 1948 she returned to Oxford where she is now a fellow and a tutor in philosophy at St. Anne's College. She has written a critical book on Jean Paul Sartre. Miss Murdoch is married to John Bayley, novelist, poet, and critic. She has published five novels: *Under the Net* (1954), *The Flight from the Enchanter* (1956), *The Sandcastle* (1957), *The Bell* (1958), and *A Severed Head* (1961). A sixth novel, *An Unofficial Rose*, was published in the spring of 1962.

15. JOHN OSBORNE

John Osborne was born in Fulham, London, in 1930, and was expelled from school at the age of sixteen. He spent about eight years as an actor in provincial repertory. When his first produced play, *Look Back in Anger*, appeared at the Royal Court Theatre in Sloane Square, in May, 1956, Osborne immediately became noteworthy as the representative of a new generation of dramatists. *The Entertainer* was produced, also at the Royal Court, in 1957 and *Epitaph for George Dillon* in 1958. Since that time Osborne has written two additional plays, *The World of Paul Slickey* and *Luther*, as well as numerous articles and autobiographical essays.

16. HAROLD PINTER

A young actor before he began to write plays, Harold Pinter wrote his first play, *The Room*, in 1957, although it was not produced until 1960 at the Hampstead Theatre Club and then at the Royal Court. *The Dumb Waiter* was also produced on the same program. *The Caretaker*, his most widely known play, was written in 1959 and produced in 1960. He has also written another play, *The Birthday Party* (produced in 1958), in addition to several television dramas.

17. ALAN SILLITOE

Alan Sillitoe was born in Nottingham in 1928. He left school at the age of fourteen to work in a bicycle factory. He later worked at a plywood mill and as a capstan lathe operator in another factory. He began to write while in the RAF, stationed in Malaya, and he lived six years in Majorca on his RAF pension before returning to England. He has published three novels, *Saturday Night and Sunday Morning* (1958), *The General* (1960), and *Key to the Door* (1962), as well as a volume of short stories, *The Loneliness of the Long-Distance Runner* (1959). He has also written poetry and a number of essays.

18. ANDREW SINCLAIR

Younger than any of the other writers represented, Andrew Sinclair received his degree from Cambridge only three or four years ago. His first novel, *The Breaking of Bumbo* (1959), was widely praised, and Sinclair soon followed with another novel, *My Friend Judas* (1959). He has written another novel, *The Project,* and a history of prohibition in America.

19. C. P. SNOW

Sir Charles Snow was born in 1905 in Leicester. As a young scientist, he won a scholarship to Cambridge and became a fellow of his college in 1930. At the beginning of the war he left Cambridge to work administering scientific programs and personnel for the government. He was knighted in 1957 for his government work. He published his first novel, *The Search*, in 1934. Since 1940 he has published eight novels in sequence, known by the title of the first novel *Strangers and Brothers,* narrated by the character, Lewis Eliot. Sir Charles has also written numerous essays, the most famous of which is called "The Two Cultures." He is married to the novelist, Pamela Hansford Johnson.

20. DAVID STOREY

David Storey, the son of a miner, was born in Yorkshire in 1933. He earned his studies in art at the Slade School, University College, London, by playing Rugby for Leeds for four seasons. His painting has won several prizes and been represented at group exhibitions. He has written two novels: *This Sporting Life* (1960) and *Flight into Camden* (1960).

21. HUGH THOMAS

Born in 1931, Hugh Thomas was educated at Sherborne and at Cambridge. He went directly into the Foreign Office and spent two years as a secretary to the British delegation at a United Nations disarmament conference. He resigned from the Foreign Office in 1956 and has since been a Labour candidate for Parliament. He published one novel, *The World's Game*, in 1957, and has since written another novel, a history of the Spanish Civil War, and a history of Sandhurst.

22. HONOR TRACY

Honor Tracy, a resident of Dublin, has traveled over Europe and the Far East as a newspaper correspondent. She began publishing books in 1950 with a travel book on Japan, and she has also written on her travels in Ireland and in Spain. In more recent years she has written five novels, all of them satirical, the best known of which is *The Straight and Narrow Path* (1956).

23. JOHN WAIN

John Wain was born in Stoke-on-Trent, Staffordshire, in 1925 and was educated at St. John's College, Oxford. Until 1955 he was a lecturer in English at the University of Reading. He then left the university to devote all his time to writing. An extremely active man, Wain writes reviews and criticism regularly for the *Observer* and broadcasts frequently. In addition to this, he has edited critical anthologies, published poetry, written a highly perceptive collection of critical essays, and brought out five novels: *Hurry On Down* (1953), *Living in the Present* (1955), *The Contenders* (1958), *A Travelling Woman* (1959), and *Strike the Father Dead* (1962). He has also published a volume of short stories, *Nuncle* (1960).

24. KEITH WATERHOUSE

Keith Waterhouse was born in 1929 and went to local schools in Leeds. He worked as an undertaker's assistant and a rent collector, then, after military service, as a reporter on a local paper. He wrote his first novel, *There Was a Happy Land*, during a newspaper strike late in 1956. His second novel, *Billy Liar*, was published in 1959 and later made into a play. In addition, Waterhouse has written film, radio, and television scripts. He has reviewed fiction and art for the *New Statesman*.

25. ARNOLD WESKER

Born in 1932 in the east end of London, Arnold Wesker worked as a plumber's mate and a pastry cook (the latter in Paris, London, and Norwich) before he entered the London School of Film Technique. He then wrote *Chicken Soup with Barley*, presented at Coventry and then at the Royal Court in 1958. This play is the first part of a trilogy, also including *Roots* (1959) and *I'm Talking about Jerusalem* (1960). In addition, Wesker has written another play called *The Kitchen*.

26. ANGUS WILSON

Born in 1913, Angus Wilson spent most of his childhood in South Africa. He was educated at Westminster and Oxford, and then, in 1937, became a librarian at the British Museum. Returning to the British Museum, after spending the war with the Foreign Office, Wilson was given the job of replacing all the books that had been destroyed during the war. In 1955 he left the museum and has since been a full-time writer. He has published three volumes of short stories, a play, a sketchbook of reminiscences of the 1920's, and four novels: *Hemlock and After* (1952), *Anglo-Saxon Attitudes* (1956), *The Middle Age of Mrs. Eliot* (1958), and *The Old Men at the Zoo* (1961). He also contributes frequent reviews and critical articles to periodicals.

27. COLIN WILSON

Colin Wilson was born in Leicester in 1931. After leaving school at the age of sixteen and the RAF after six months, Wilson held a succession of factory, office, hospital, and dishwashing jobs in both London and Paris. His first book, *The Outsider* (1956), was hailed as a brilliant essay representative of the new generation, but, with the publication of his second public confession, *Religion and the Rebel* (1957), Wilson's reputation subsided. He has, more recently, published two novels: *Ritual in the Dark* (1960), and *Adrift in Soho* (1961).